Thi

Cl

Public works

Engineering in local government

R. H. Clarke

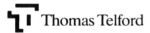 Thomas Telford

Published by Thomas Telford Publishing, Thomas Telford Services Ltd, 1 Heron Quay,
London E14 4JD

First published 1996

Distributors for Thomas Telford books are
USA: American Society of Civil Engineers, Publications Sales Department, 345 East 47th Street,
New York, NY 10017-2398
Japan: Maruzen Co. Ltd, Book Department, 3–10 Nihonbashi 2-chome, Chuo-ku, Tokyo 103
Australia: DA Books and Journals, 648 Whitehorse Road, Mitcham 3132, Victoria

A catalogue record for this book is available from the British Library

ISBN: 0 7277 2093 7

Typeset by MHL Typesetting Ltd, Coventry
Printed and bound in Great Britain by Redwood Books, Trowbridge, Wiltshire

Those who would carry out Great Public Schemes must be proof against the most fatiguing Delays, the most mortifying Disappointments, the most shocking Insults and — worst of all — the presumptuous Judgement of the Ignorant upon their Designs.

Edmund Burke MP, House of Commons, 1788

Foreword

The phrase 'local government is big business' was coined in the 1960s to emphasize the new image of public authorities as major employers, spenders and investors. It is still well-used, albeit a little more defensively and with a little less emphasis on the spending, and appears frequently in discussions on the management aspects of local government. Like any good slogan, it is memorable and direct, and it helps make an important point about the size and influence of local authority activity. However, it is also misleading: local government is certainly big, but it is not a business.

That deserves a bit of explanation. After all, local authorities control substantial budgets and employ — directly or indirectly — large numbers of people. A large, but not untypical, council will run an annual budget of £300 million and provide work for over 1500 local people.

The most obvious answer would be the lack of the profit motive. But it is not that simple. There are the restraints imposed on a local authority's area of operation in terms of both geography and function; the duties which it is required by law to discharge; the degree of political control over its activities; and the continuous, comprehensive public scrutiny of all that is said and done in its name. If that were not enough to define a distinct environment for local government, then the mixture of energetic locally-based opinion with powerful centrally-imposed controls is surely the final element necessary to produce a unique climate.

Once this special world had its own specialists e.g. the large in-house technical departments, supplemented by a distinct club of consultants who had long-established working relationships with local government, often with particular authorities on particular types of project. It is a world that is disappearing fast and with it are going — for better or worse — methods and attitudes which could once be taken for granted. Fee competition, a more erratic flow of work and the growing involvement of the private sector in what was once seen as the public infrastructure have combined to fragment the consultancy market in public works. Similar pressures have begun to affect local government departments: at first, by internal division into client and consultant units and by the introduction of market testing; but in the longer run formal contracts for professional and technical services will become the norm whether by choice or regulation. The reform and restructuring of local government, which all political parties advocate in one form or another, is accelerating this process of separating the providers of professional and technical services from the political management of a local authority and its associated administrative tasks.

The concept of contracting out is, of course, deeply embedded in the whole range of public works activity. Its sharper application to the professional services element has been evolutionary, and not revolutionary as it was for many other parts of what was the public sector. Perhaps that is why many of the younger generation of professionals and technicians who work in, or for, local government are contentedly ignorant of its methods, practices and participants. They have no experience of how council and committee meetings are organized and only vague stereotyped notions of the role and motivation of elected representatives; they are unaware of how programmes are funded and of the influence of the system of local government finance on them; they have little knowledge of the processes by which corporate policies are set and even less of such activities as policy development and performance review. As a result, the system in which the project is born, grows and lives (and can perhaps die) is seen as much less important than the management of the project itself.

Contractors, developers and consultants need to know how local government works if they are to cooperate with it effectively. Professionals working for local authorities need to understand the system both to explain it to others and to make it work for themselves. Outsiders and insiders all have their own ideas of what goes on and what is important, sometimes their perceptions are startlingly inaccurate and they are invariably incomplete or one-sided. Better knowledge means better results: not necessarily 100% success, for it would be naive to pretend that the size, content and pace of public works programmes are determined by expertise at playing the system alone, but better and more consistent results would be achieved by this approach than from ignorance or guesswork.

This is a guide book and not a text book. It provides a description of the system, its strengths and weaknesses, how it operates, and offers some advice on how to work within it and get the best from it. There cannot be a set of instructions or a step-by-step beginners guide to the promotion and execution of public works projects: there are too many people and organizations each with their own personality, too much change taking place and too much detail involved in any individual scheme for a precise guide of that sort to be a practical proposition. Of course, the specifics are important — no public works project will succeed if its promoters are careless of detail — but attention to detail is wasted if the broad principles, the general techniques and the setting in which they operate are ignored. The value to the community of effective, good quality public works is real, lasting and substantial. That makes them worth doing, and worth doing well.

Contents

Introduction

Any guide through a subject of such range, scale and diversity as public works in local government has to start somewhere. Because there is so much change in the public sector, it is tempting to take a 'snapshot' which stops the action and then base the whole exercise on the system as it appears at one point in time. This not only disguises the variety that would exist even if such a standstill were possible, but also invites the rapid obsolescence of any guidance because there is no context in which to place and follow the future developments which will inevitably come along.

For these reasons, to see the historical perspectives and recent political developments as a digression for those with the interest and spare time, but hardly relevant to the promotion and execution of public works projects, would be a narrow and mistaken view. The relationship between central and local government, the distribution of functions at local level, and the concept of 'public service' are all matters which shape policies and decisions made today, and which have themselves been shaped by the historical development of public administration in the UK. Understanding this background is essential to getting a feel for those traditions, assumptions and unwritten codes which make up the 'culture' of public authorities, the intangible yet pervasive atmosphere that conditions the way they operate and relate to the world at large, and to change in particular.

Historical perspectives

In spite of George Bernard Shaw's typically provocative remark,

> What experience and history teaches is this — that people and governments never learned anything from history, or acted on principles deduced from it.
> *The Revolutionist's Handbook*

the past does have an influence on the present and the future, even though it may be true that it is not always a positive one. Local government in particular has a long and occasionally tangled history, which is closely linked with the history of British civil engineering. Much reformed and reorganized, the administration of local affairs in Britain has evolved over centuries and exhibits many important features that represent the consequences of its past, the results of historical accident and, in some cases, the deep-rooted grip of tradition.

The origins of local government in England and Wales can be traced back to the 15th century, when feudal traditions gave way to a system of royal justice working through local units: the shires, boroughs and parishes. The parishes soon became more than agencies of law and order, for an Act of 1555 allowed them to appoint highway surveyors to maintain roads and bridges in their areas and to extract from local landowners the means — money or labour — to do so. Many undertook their duties conscientiously, but apathy and corruption were rife and the growth in goods and passengers that accompanied the agricultural revolution of the 18th century soon overwhelmed the ancient network of roads and tracks.

The answer to this unprecedented demand for mobility (and proof that there is nothing new under the sun) came not from new works funded through the parishes, but in the shape of private sector investment, the Turnpike Trusts, which were authorized by Act of Parliament to build and operate toll roads. The first trust was set up in 1706, to be followed over the next 100 years by 1100 others, controlling 22 000 miles of roads. Scotland had its own massive road building programme in the middle of the 18th century; not however, as public works nor yet private speculation, but as a military operation to subjugate the highlands after the failure of the '45 rebellion.

Out of all this activity came the two early giants of civil engineering: Thomas Telford and John McAdam. Telford, surveyor of public works in Shropshire, took major government commissions in Scotland and then went on to build the London to Holyhead road — including the suspension bridges at Conwy and Menai straits — for the postmaster general to speed the passage of the Irish mails.

In 1828 he became the first president of the Institution of Civil Engineers. McAdam, appointed surveyor to the Bristol Turnpike Trust in 1816, became surveyor-general of metropolitan roads in 1827 and a national expert on construction techniques, giving his name to the material which (although highway engineers know better) is recognized by the public at large as the basic 'black stuff' of road building.

Telford and McAdam died in the mid-1830s. Both had made their reputations in public works and were figures of great renown, but already a new, and from this distance of time strikingly glamorous, era of engineering had begun, funded by private capital and fuelled by Victorian self-confidence: the Railway Age. The 'great triumvirate' of Isambard Kingdom Brunel, Robert Stephenson and Joseph Locke dominate our perspective of 19th century engineering so completely and eclipse the memory of the earlier road and canal building pioneers so comprehensively, it is easy to forget that their working lives at the top of the profession spanned little more than 25 years overall, and all three were dead and buried (Stephenson alongside Telford in Westminster Abbey) between September 1859 and March 1860. Incidentally, it is worth noting that in a profession much concerned with protecting its role in project management from the inroads of accountants and quantity surveyors it is not Locke, the conservative organizer of detailed specifications and bills of quantities, who is the most acclaimed figure but rather the brilliant innovator Brunel, who overspent his budgets and broke his contractors in his restless pursuit of innovation and excellence.

While railway mania — and the engineers who made their names and fortunes from it — caught the public imagination, other events and personalities were reshaping the system of government in profound and enduring ways. The social change which marked the Victorian era was generated not only by revolutions in manufacturing and communications, but also by a political reformation — controlled and relatively slow but no less fundamental for all that — which produced a genuine participative democracy at national and local level.

The Reform Act of 1832 set up properly representative parliamentary constituencies. It was closely followed by the Municipal Corporations Act of 1835 that created in the boroughs a kind of local authority which is recognizably 'modern': elected by local tax payers, holding its meetings in public and submitting its accounts to independent audit. Over the following 60 years a succession of Local Government, Public Health and Highways Acts produced a framework of local administration that provided a comprehensive — if not always consistent — system in both town and country which acted through legally constituted bodies bearing statutory powers and duties. A public service was evolving, where there had once been a patchwork of royal and aristocratic patronage, charities, religious foundations and neighbourhood 'self help' associations.

In the shires of England and Wales, there were two levels of local democracy: the relatively new county councils, established in 1888, and the smaller units of urban and rural district councils and the boroughs, all of which could trace their ancestry back to the 15th century or beyond. The cities maintained a separate status, won by the ancient right or modern commercial clout, and were governed by single tier county boroughs; except Metropolitan London which had its own county council and 28 constituent boroughs.

This steady but somewhat haphazard evolution of local administration was accompanied by a rapid and purposeful expansion of public works activity. In London, the Metropolitan Board of Works was set up in 1855. In its 34 years of existence the board, with Sir Joseph Bazalgette as its chief engineer, constructed the city's main drainage and sewage treatment system, laid out the great thoroughfares of the West End, built a series of Thames bridges and raised the proud embankments which line the river from Chelsea to the Tower of London. In the great industrial cities of the north, huge schemes for water supply and sewerage, for central streets and squares, and for new roads and bridges were carried through with a style and confidence difficult to imagine now.

This great period of public works activity, driven by the civic pride of the new commercial centres, owed much to the economic development brought about by the railways. But the close of the century was bringing major change: by coincidence, 1895 saw both the winding-up of the last Turnpike Trust (ironically the Anglesey section of Telford's London to Holyhead road) and the repeal of the 'Red Flag' Act. Britain was moving out of the Railway Age into the Motor Age.

In a striking parallel with modern problems, roads began to suffer badly from traffic loadings far beyond those which they had been designed to take, and pressure mounted for national action to fund the growing burden of improvement and maintenance. The government's solution was straightforward: in 1909 the Road Board was established, financed by the revenue raised from motor vehicle licences and a three pence per gallon petrol tax. The money was specifically directed into improvement work — widening, levelling and dust abatement — and could not be used for routine maintenance, which continued to be funded from local rates. The board was replaced in 1919 by the Ministry of Transport, which drew up an ambitious programme of works aimed at coping with the growth in traffic and providing employment for workers released from war service. However, financial restrictions and recession meant that neither objective was achieved, but an important principle had been established: construction could perform a national role as an economic regulator. Successive governments have demonstrated that neither ideological nor practical difficulties are a bar to the frequent and rapid use of this regulator to operate policies of *stop* or *go* and, it sometimes seems, *stop and go*.

Some rationalization of local highway functions took place in 1929 under yet another Local Government Act, but the most decisive step came in 1936 when 4505 miles of main roads in England, Scotland and Wales were trunked and handed over to the central control of the Ministry of Transport. A national network — it now totals over 10 000 miles — meant not only unified direction and standardization for the country's major routes, but also a more precise and immediate means of applying the regulator.

In the same year's budget, the connection between finance for roads and the proceeds of vehicle and fuel taxes was severed. Instead, the money — then about £30 million per annum — was assigned to the Treasury general fund from which grants could be voted, depending upon needs and circumstances. By breaking the direct linkage between income from traffic and expenditure on roads, the government was freeing itself legally and politically to use the regulator to its fullest extent, unfettered by any obligation to balance the accounts. Today, the overall tax revenue — including VAT on cars and fuel — paid by road users amounts to £20 billion a year. This is about four times the government's expenditure on road construction and maintenance.

The 1930s saw a significant increase in public works. Keynesian economics, stressing the government's role in priming the pump in times of recession, provided the justification for a series of large projects such as the Kingston and Winchester bypasses and the coast protection works on the Mersey estuary. The aim was both to stimulate economic activity generally, and to provide jobs in construction for the workers rendered idle by the stagnation of manufacturing industry. This new and purposeful activity was, however, soon overtaken by events: by the middle of the decade the aims of the public works programmes were being achieved more quickly by another means — rearmament.

The end of the war and the subsequent period of austerity and shortages were followed by a gradual return to high levels of activity. The late 1940s and the 1950s were years of reconstruction. In the centres of the bombed cities ambitious redevelopment projects began to take shape, and on greenfield sites beyond the fringes of London the first generation of new towns was established. Extensive plans for national road networks — some of them originally conceived before the war — were considered and debated. The Preston bypass, designed by Lancashire County Council, was the first motorway standard road to be built. Opened in 1959, it was soon followed by the four contracts for the M1 and within a few years the motorway programme was in full swing. Joint civil service/local government road construction units, consultants and local authorities were all involved in the promotion and execution of a massive work load, shaping the new motorway system and also improving the trunk road network. Not since the 1850s and the most hectic period of railway mania had such a major civil engineering effort been seen in the United Kingdom and its effects on transport economics, living conditions and social patterns have been every bit as profound.

For all that, these great public works remain largely unsung. Perhaps because this century has been so filled with drama, fully and instantly reported from the furthest corners of the world, that such a parochial event as a transport revolution at home has been ignored; or perhaps engineers have lost the power of their Victorian predecessors to grasp the nation's attention and excite its imagination.

In 1972, at the height of a long and sustained period of growth in the public sector in general and public works in particular, legislation to reorganize local government was enacted. In October of the following year the Organisation of Petroleum Exporting Countries began a series of sharp price rises which took the cost of crude oil from US$3 to nearly US$12 a barrel in less than three months. Nothing could ever be the same again.

Reorganization and reform

The reorganization of local government began in the late 1960s. It was supposed to have been completed in 1974 (1975 in Scotland) but it continues by different methods and in fits and starts to the present day. Too often, it has been marked by confusion, inconsistency and gross underestimation of its costs and consequences. Small wonder, therefore, that in the world of local government there has been a widespread reluctance to accept whatever may be the current structural, financial and organizational arrangements as anything other than temporary and unstable.

Reorganization did not begin under favourable circumstances. Although the 1960s had been a time of growth in the national economy and local government services had expanded correspondingly, it had become widely believed that the whole system of public administration was inefficient and obsolete. Its failings were felt to be extensive and basic: an out-of-date structure incapable of recognizing the new developments needed in local services; an inflexible organization unable to react to change even if it did recognize it; a lack-lustre workforce unfit to make the adjustments necessary for any reaction to be effective.

Reform had long been in the air. The second half of the 1960s saw a succession of committees of the great and good investigating local government: the Maud committee on management in 1967; Mallaby (staffing) also 1967 and Skeffington (public participation) 1969. These committees — and the commentators who analysed and discussed their findings — were in no doubt that change was essential and ought to be far-reaching. Implicit in the setting-up of such enquiries was a deep-rooted national concern about local government's image and performance. The Maud committee's comment is typical

Parliament, Ministers and Whitehall departments have come increasingly to lose faith in the responsibility of locally elected bodies . . . there is often too wide a gulf in local government between the governors and the governed.

In 1969, the Redcliffe–Maud report was published. For the major conurbations centred on Birmingham, Liverpool and Manchester, it proposed a two-tier system closely modelled on the arrangements introduced in London six years before; elsewhere, there would be 58 unitary authorities responsible for the full range of local government services in their areas. To draw their boundaries, the Commission adopted the concept of the city region in most cases and defined the unit of local administration as the area surrounding a large town or city, which relied substantially upon it for services, employment and social life. The new authorities were, to a great extent, the old county boroughs writ large — too large, some felt. Although accepted by the Labour government, the proposals had not been implemented when the 1970 election returned a Conservative administration which drew up its own plans for reorganization, based on a two-tier system for the whole country with special arrangements in six metropolitan areas. There were to be no city regions, but the idea would remain at the centre of every subsequent debate on local government structure.

At the same time as the new structure and boundaries were being established, the government took the opportunity to take mains drainage, sewage disposal and the municipal water supply undertakings out of local authority control and place them in the hands of regional water authorities. These new units were organized to manage the entire water cycle on a river basin basis, and have now become the ten water and sewerage companies of England and Wales (in Scotland water remains under public control) with the regulatory functions vested at first in the National Rivers Authority, later the Environment Agency.

The proposals of the Royal Commission for Scotland, being based on a two-tier system of large regions subdivided into districts, went ahead unchanged. In Wales, a two-tier system accompanied by drastic boundary changes was drawn up by the Welsh Office without the benefit of independent review; some observers considered this to be a cost-effective short cut, arriving at the same unsatisfactory arrangement as the rest of the country but in one step instead of two.

Between 1974 and 1975 (reorganization in Scotland followed a year behind England and Wales) the map of local government changed beyond recognition. Ninety one counties, 284 cities, county boroughs and Scottish burghs, and 1446 non-county boroughs, urban and rural districts had vanished to give way to 65 top tier authorities (shire counties, metropolitan counties and Scottish regions and island councils) and 422 second tier districts. The city region concept had been abandoned because it was felt to be too big and remote, and possibly, too town-biased. Consequently, the idea of unitary authorities had also been set aside; and not just as a concept, for the county boroughs were all abolished, leaving many large towns and cities — some with ancient traditions of autonomy — relegated to the status of district councils.

The result was proclaimed to be a workable compromise between the achievement of the economies of scale and the maintenance of grass roots accountability. It soon became apparent, however, that the grass roots were often confused and thus poorly served, and that the two-tier system thus introduced had an inbuilt tendency to friction and duplication which has proved difficult to suppress. These concerns led first to the 1974–79 Labour government's abortive plans for organic change to devolve most functions to the district level, to be followed by the Conservative government's bitterly contested abolition of the top tier in London and the metropolitan areas in 1983–86, which ironically reintroduced unitary authorities.

The mechanics and historic details of the 1974–75 reorganization remained important throughout the 1980s and beyond because of the general feeling of missed opportunity that was left behind. While the introduction of the community charge in 1990 was planned as a reform of local government *finance* and not structure, it nevertheless had as an integral aim and intended benefit the heightening of public awareness and accountability in local politics. On that occasion and for a variety of reasons — this is not a volume of political history — the government lost the argument but succeeded beyond its wildest dreams in generating a very high level of awareness which led inevitably to an expectation that both financial and structural reform must take place. The introduction of the council tax and the latest round of reorganization, attended by the inevitable controversy, is the result.

What all this means is that every manager involved in public works must take account of an underlying theme of change and conflict: to promote projects and gauge the reaction to them of the public and their representatives as if an atmosphere of stability prevails is — at a managerial level — faulty risk assessment; at a quality of service level, it is gross ignorance of the market.

Into the unknown

The party's over.
Antony Crossland, Secretary of State for the Environment, May 1975

There is no more money.
Michael Heseltine, Secretary of State for the Environment, October 1980

Inside every fat and bloated local authority there is a slim one trying to get out.
Nicholas Ridley, Secretary of State for the Environment, February 1988

... the Left has learnt that a public bureaucracy can be a vested interest just like any other
Tony Blair, Leader of the Labour Party, June 1995

There has been a great pressure for change in local government over the last 20 years. Up to the 1974 reorganization, and even through that period of major structural upheaval, some things had always remained constant: deep-rooted assumptions about the nature of local administration, the methods employed to secure and deliver services, and the intrinsic value of their locally-based provision.

Three things changed: the availability of funds, public opinion and government policy. Each change has had a profound and irreversible effect.

At a time of growth, or at least continuing access to historic levels of funding with automatic inflation allowances, the resources available to local government posed no problem. Indeed, if there was any difficulty it was in finding the staff to carry out the projects and programmes. From the late 1970s, however, the situation changed and a combination of cash limiting, deliberate under-provision for inflation and real expenditure cuts began to bite (albeit inconsistently) into the public sector's resources. Programme slippage, reductions in maintenance standards and the scaling-down or even cancellation of projects were the results. As far as the people in local government were concerned, recruitment drag (the deliberate delay in replacing departures), managed vacancies (the conscious decision not to fill vacant posts) and early retirement schemes became the order of the day. Nevertheless, the idea of an *establishment* as a level of personnel to be maintained wherever possible, remained very much alive and staff cuts, i.e. compulsory redundancies, were virtually unheard of.

The tight squeeze on public expenditure at the end of the 1970s, followed by the winter of discontent of 1978–79 and the recession of the early 1980s transformed public opinion. For better or worse, the bottom line became part of everyday life and the public sector was seen as being in the red. Received wisdom in government and outside was that public sector organizations were overstaffed and underproductive. Opinion moved decisively in favour of exposing most public employees, the few exceptions being generally confined to the caring services, to the real world of market forces, competition and consumer power.

Government policy reflected, and to a considerable degree moulded, this view. Compulsory competitive tendering (CCT) was introduced for direct labour organizations in highway and building maintenance. Other blue collar services followed and the regulations covering both the processes of tendering and selection and the financial limitations on in-house organizations were progressively tightened. At the same time, the ability of local government units to trade or even sell-on spare capacity (always, it should be noted, an area of dubious legality) was specifically restricted by legislation and strong audit guidance. By the early 1990s it had become increasingly likely that white collar CCT would be the next policy step, and so it was.

The impact, consequences and mechanisms of CCT and its alternatives would fill a book in themselves. Suffice it to say here that while this policy direction by itself would be enough to stretch most institutions, it is accompanied by another very significant and interrelated change. The concept of citizens' charters or service guarantees offers the public some means of measurement and redress to apply to their public services. In particular, it makes professional/technical services more outward looking and performance oriented than traditionally they have been, and thus introduces a major element of culture shock for all concerned.

These upheavals have come at the same time as yet another review and reorganization of structure. While Scotland and Wales (once again) had their new arrangements drawn up by their respective government offices, England was the subject of a controversial review which generated a variety of structures, praised by its supporters as a reflection of diversity and denounced by its detractors as confusion. Whatever the merits of individual cases, the consequences of reorganizing local government to reflect modern communities and patterns of living goes beyond changes in the priorities and mechanisms of service delivery, and means a fresh start for many organizational and political structures. The unitary authorities that emerge will be different in shape and functional coverage from their predecessors, and those which are unchanged will nevertheless operate in a different environment: both will be looking for new ways of representing and serving the people.

The management of change is the single greatest challenge for everyone involved with the public services. The successful pioneers in this new territory will be those professionals (in-house or external) who know the basic skills best, have the most cost-effective facilities and, above all, are prepared to use them in new combinations.

1. The framework

Local authorities have, as we have seen, a long and somewhat chequered history. They have existed in many different forms with a variety of functions, as they still do today. This inconsistency, often a source of confusion and irritation, masks certain underlying principles which apply to local government in general and will continue to do so, reform and reorganization notwithstanding.

Structure

The structure is based on geographical units. Whether defined by history or generated by the latest round of reorganization, they are supposed to reflect communities with some form of local identity. This is not a particularly objective criterion. Large conurbations such as West Midlands, Merseyside or Humberside, whatever their coherence in terms of economics or transportation, are not seen as sufficiently local to form single authorities. Moreover, individual market towns, once the basis of the old urban and rural district councils which disappeared in the 1970s, are now considered too small to provide cost-effective services. The key to structure, therefore, is a balance between the added value of scale and the benefits of local identity. All project managers will do well to recognize, and avoid, the other side of this coin: extravagance and remoteness.

The 1992–1995 round of reorganization has given Scotland and Wales unitary authorities as the basis of local government. In England, outside the metropolitan areas, the traditional (ever since 1974, that is) structure of two tiers has survived reorganization in most shire counties. Nevertheless, unitary authorities will predominate in the country as a whole. This means that within one administrative area, one authority will be responsible for all local government services: schools, social welfare, highways and transportation, planning, housing, environmental health, waste management, libraries, recreation, consumer protection, etc. Parish and town councils can operate (their energy and effectiveness is highly dependent on local community spirit) as a separate tier at grass roots level, but their role in delivering services and projects is strictly limited by their fund-raising capability. It is as focal points of local opinion that they come into their own.

Where two tiers remain, their separate functions are shown in Table 1. Planning and waste management are exceptions, with significant elements of each service divided. Highway functions are also found shared between the top and second tiers through the voluntary granting of an agency by the former to the latter.

10

Table 1. Local government structure (1995)

England (part, from 1995 on) London and Metropolitan areas Scotland (from 1996) Wales (from 1996)	England (part)
Unitary Authorities	**Top Tier**
• Strategic planning[†] • local planning • highways • traffic • refuse collection • waste disposal[†] • building control • social services • education • housing • libraries • fire and emergency[†] • consumer protection • environmental health • leisure and parks • markets and fairs • cemeteries and crematoria	• English Counties (35) • Strategic planning • highways • traffic • waste disposal • social services • education • libraries • fire and emergency • consumer protection
• English councils (14*) • London Boroughs (32) • Corporation of London • Metropolitan districts (36) • Scottish councils (32) • Welsh councils (22) * Subject to review by Local Government Commission. † Joint arrangements often apply.	
Northern Ireland	**Second tier**
In Northern Ireland, district councils (26) have responsibility for environmental health, refuse collection and disposal, consumer protection, markets and fairs, leisure and parks, cemeteries and crematoria. Other functions, including planning, roads, water and sewerage, are carried out by government departments working through local offices	• English district councils (283)[‡] ‡ Subject to review by Local Government Commission. • local planning • building control • refuse collection • environmental health • leisure services and parks • markets and fairs • cemeteries and crematoria

Agency arrangements also exist between the Department of Transport (and the Welsh and Scottish Offices) and most local highway authorities under which the routine maintenance, and some of the reconstruction and improvement work, on motorways and trunk roads is managed by local councils. Such agencies — more and more an area of private sector involvement — are strictly contractual and council staff act as agents of the government, dealing directly with their civil service counterparts. Councils do not have any say in the process and there is no devolution of power or decision-making involved. While theoretically, and legally, in the same class, almost all county/district agencies are operated less as a contract for staff resources and more as delegation of control. This does not mean they cannot work effectively — many do — but the approach has been criticized for blurring accountability, weakening management and encouraging professional friction. It is probably endemic in any two-tier system.

For some activities or particular projects there will be good reasons — size, wide geographical spread, strategic impact — for joint arrangements and thus single units of local government will be found operating in formal or informal combinations. Joint boards, through which two or more local authorities formally act together as a single unit, require complex legal arrangements to cover terms of reference, membership and financial matters and are not common. Agreements to cooperate, while requiring proper votes of approval by the authorities concerned, are more flexible, easier to terminate and more frequent. Both will have to be used more often in the reorganized local government framework.

Structure does not tell the whole story. History matters too. Many local authorities are proud of their civic traditions even though change and reorganization may have curtailed their functions. Thus, some district councils will carry the courtesy title *city* or *borough* and may retain the ceremonial of mayoralty and other municipal dignities dating back to their charters. These authorities are not, however, legally different from other districts. Similarly, at parish council level the courtesy title *town council* will denote a long-established community, keen to keep its identity alive. In managing public works programmes it is important — especially at consultation stage and when key events are to be notified — to remember that public bodies, like people, can be very conscious of their status and will respond better if it is recognized.

Duties and powers

Notwithstanding the historic roots of some local authorities, it is from the reorganization of 1974–5 (and 1986 in the metropolitan areas) that the duties and functions of the different units are derived. Those existing at the time of these changes were redistributed by the legislation. Some were transferred out of local government; notably drainage, sewerage and sewage disposal, which went to what were then the newly-created water authorities. New ones, such as the role of coordinating openings in the highway which was created by the New Roads and Street Works Act 1992, are allocated as required by provisions enacted by Parliament. The new reorganization will, for unitary authorities, effect a consolidation of functions and also redraw boundaries. Duties in themselves will be unaltered.

Some duties have long pedigrees: the responsibility of the highway authority for a geographical area (county, Scottish region, metropolitan district or London borough) to keep the roads

in such repair as to be reasonably passable for the ordinary traffic of the neighbourhood at all seasons of the year

can be traced directly to a legal judgement about 150 years old, and indirectly to the parishes of Tudor times. Others are very modern in their origin and their nature: the top tier waste disposal authorities (English and Welsh counties) were given the duty to pay recycling credits to second tier waste collection authorities (districts) under a provision of the Environmental Protection Act 1989.

A fundamental principle of local government in the United Kingdom is that it rests on duties, funding and powers granted by statute. Certain tasks and responsibilities are imposed on councils, others are discretionary. Many duties, particularly those not introduced or revised by modern legislation, are set out only in very general terms.

There is, for instance, no legal definition of what a highway authority must do to satisfy its duty of care to road users. As with much of the criminal and civil law, the answer is found not in the precise wording of a statute but in the decisions of the courts over many years through which precedents are established, decisions reviewed and endorsed or overruled by higher authority, and particular cases distinguished by different facts from their predecessors to allow new rulings to emerge.

Case law tells us that a highway authority cannot be expected to know of every potential danger as soon as it develops, but that it must have an inspection system which ensures that a regular and reasonably frequent check is made to identify hazards and do something about them. Similarly, although the smallest damage or defect may be dangerous under particular circumstances, the courts have recognized that it is impossible to keep the highway always in perfect condition and acknowledged that reasonable levels of wear and tear must be expected.

The definition of what is *reasonable* leaves plenty of scope for interpretation, but the widespread development of national codes of practice, guidance notes, model specifications and other professional/technical standards has established a body of data on which local systems can be based. While these recommendations (on the frequency of highway inspections, for instance, or the size and depth at which a pothole becomes potentially hazardous) are not mandatory, they would have considerable significance and status and a highway authority would be presumed to have taken them into account in deciding how to discharge its obligations.

Legal judgements have established that it is no excuse for a local authority to say that it could not afford to carry out particular duties. It is, however, possible for a council to argue that limited resources mean that it must set priorities and adjust standards of service, within reason, and then do only those things that it can afford to do.

Thus, a highway authority which said that it did not have enough money to carry out any accident investigation and prevention work would find itself in great difficulties defending its position against a claim brought by the victim of a traffic accident at a known blackspot. However, if the authority allocated a limited sum of money to road safety measures and had a system of identifying and ranking the sites where that money should be spent, then it could defend itself if it had taken no action at a particular location on the grounds that an accident prevention scheme there had not achieved sufficient priority to warrant funding. The local authority's defence would depend on whether or not its budget allocation decisions were reasonable ones, and also on showing that its method of determining priorities was based on reasonable criteria.

The duties of local authorities, in the sense that they represent tasks which councils must carry out, are subject to a considerable degree of latitude as far as their scope, volume and quality are concerned. In the field of public works the range of tasks and the amount of latitude means that a minimum service in legal terms would be very restricted indeed and would certainly fall far short of what the public has come to expect as the norm, not to mention the levels set out in the various professional codes of practice and guidelines. In fact, the vast majority of public works activity is discretionary either in the sense that the legal minimum is topped up by additional provision or because the local authority is providing something which it does not have to make available at all. In these latter cases (for instance, a highway authority is not obliged to provide a bypass for a congested village or pedestrianize a historic town centre), a council is using powers that are provided by the law and are statutory, therefore, but it is exercising its own discretion as to whether and how they are employed.

Unlike private citizens, who have what is called *general competence* which is a power to do anything they choose so long as it is not prohibited by the law, local authorities can only do what is specifically permitted in an Act of Parliament. Furthermore, public bodies can only use these legal powers for the purposes for which they were provided. So if the law says a council has to do something (for instance collect domestic rubbish), then it must do just that, although the details of the method, such as frequency, are usually left open to reasonable choice (thus, once a fortnight would be acceptable, once a year would not). Where the law gives discretion (for example local authorities can charge for off-street parking), then anything reasonable may be done (a fruitful area of debate as far as parking charges are concerned), or nothing (so an authority could have free car parks or none at all). In all cases actions must be for legitimate purposes only: a highway authority can close a road without notice on safety grounds but not to allow a street party to take place (there is a different legal process for that) nor to divert a New Age convoy (that would be a police matter).

This is what underlies the *ultra vires* doctrine which is an effective, if rather negative, reminder that local government's powers to do anything are strictly limited by what is in the law. If something is *outside the powers* it cannot be done.

This is not merely the fine print of administrative law. It makes correct procedure essential because every project, straightforward or complex, must rest on secure legal foundations. Decisions have to be taken by the appropriate, properly constituted parts of the council; public notices must be displayed in accordance with the relevant regulations; due consideration has to be given to the responses to consultation and the views of objectors; land can only be acquired for defined public service purposes, and so on. One false step means the whole process can become *ultra vires* and the project loses its legal authority, becomes open to challenge, or impossible to progress to the next stage, and (at best) will require some complex and inevitably expensive work by the lawyers to restore the situation.

There are mechanisms to ease the practical problems of operating within this legal straightjacket, and they will be examined shortly. The fundamental point to recognize here is that public works projects and programmes rely entirely on careful and precise deployment of powers which are not particularly flexible, especially where timing is concerned, and often narrowly defined in terms of the uses to which they can be put. Project management demands clear knowledge of which powers are to be employed for what purpose, how and when.

2. The participants

The framework of local government is, as has been shown, somewhat complicated. This complexity, however, rises to new heights as the details of all the players who are involved, in many different ways, in public authorities and their services, are filled in. It is people, of course, who offer the most variety and the least opportunity for generalization. Whether people are serving in local government, working for it or participating in the role we all share — members of a local community — the only universally relevant guideline is: people matter.

Members

The most visible participants in local democracy are the elected representatives, i.e. the councillors or members. They stand for election, these days usually under party labels, to take on the dual and sometimes incompatible — but almost always thankless — tasks of pursuing political aims while representing local interests.

Councillors represent divisions or wards, the equivalent of an MP's constituency. Their geographical size and population vary considerably, particularly between urban, suburban and rural areas. Although some local authorities have as few as 20 members and the largest cities and counties more than 100, the general range is 40–80 with those authorities which are mainly urban or have significant urban concentrations tending, because of their population, to be nearer the upper end. The electoral arrangements also differ. In some councils all seats are contested at once to elect a completely new council for a four year term; others adopt a system in which one-third of the seats are contested in each of three successive years, followed by one year without elections, thus changing the council gradually through a four year cycle.

Elections and their approach obviously affect decision making and in particular the likelihood of controversial choices being taken. Although the turn-out in local government elections has remained consistently and disappointingly low in recent years — 40% is good, 30% more typical, for council elections, whereas 70% or even higher is a reasonable parliamentary average — they are often keenly fought and swings are likely to be more violent and sudden than at national level. Conversely, personal followings can be built up which, with more reliability than is usually seen in national politics, protect local members against voting trends. The arithmetic of council elections can be both interesting and relevant: project managers ought to research the decision makers and opinion formers they will be working with, and where politicians are concerned voting data has a special importance.

Surveys show that there are some typical characteristics of councillors as a group: more men than women (although women have a much better representation in local than in national government); older than the average for the population; academic professions significantly overrepresented, but businessmen — especially from large organizations — substantially underrepresented; unskilled and semi-skilled workers hardly represented at all, etc. These statistics are of limited value as the average councillor does not exist and each elected representative and his or her electorate deserve to be treated individually. This involves another bit of research for project managers, which will repay the investment of time handsomely. In particular, it is wise to avoid the short cuts of labelling, especially with the badges of party politics. The shades of opinion within parties at national level are well-known, but they exist to a far greater extent in local politics.

Nevertheless, politics do matter in today's local government and this makes it important to distinguish between the party political and representative roles of councillors. On issues of policy (such as the settling of priorities within the annual budget between, say, public transport support, and road capacity improvements), on controversial local topics (whether and how to proceed with the pedestrianization of a town centre, for instance) and on dealings with national government (for example, consultation on a motorway widening project) the members will work out their particular party line and, for the most part, follow it through in public as a united party group.

In these circumstances, influential members — the leader of the political group, other senior councillors with talent and/or experience, political activists — will make the running and shape the decisions. Professional advice will be part of that process, but many other non-professional inputs will be involved too. This activity, where the outcome is considered important enough to have a wide-ranging effect on the political future, image or long-term strategy of the council, is one where group dynamics predominate. The collective objectives of the party group — restraining expenditure, for instance, showing a capacity for action or just demonstrating unity — are what matter and will influence the behaviour of the individuals who belong to it. Project managers must seek to understand the broad issues which are important to the political groups, especially the one with the majority, and try to work with the grain and not against it. This does not mean compromising professional advice, but recognizing how it fits in to a larger picture.

A completely different set of priorities come into play when councillors fulfil their roles as local representatives. Here party politics matter less, although they are never completely absent. In many cases, this task takes the form of providing the link between local people or groups and the machinery of the council: passing on queries, proposals, requests for action and complaints. To large numbers of people, the local member is the human face of the council and the only point of contact they feel comfortable with; they believe that their councillor can get things done. Some councillors encourage this belief (something to do with getting re-elected), others labour under its burden, knowing that a large proportion of this demand will turn out to be unaffordable, impracticable or not even a local government function.

In any event, members will be constantly involved by letter, phone and personal visit, in the tasks generated by what is in theory their electorate — although in practice most of them did not vote — who expect a prompt and comprehensive response in all cases. Dealing with the points that involve public works projects or programmes is an integral part of project management and here it is personal service that counts. It is worth remembering when complaining about the volume of such work that a councillor will be covering everything from the shortage of books in the local library to the quality of dinners at the local infants' school. Quick replies, even if incomplete, can allow the member to demonstrate that something is happening; a piece of good news or a success, even a partial one, will always be a welcome boost to a member's local reputation and useful support to the project manager's credibility too. Grass roots politics may seem of minor importance, but it is the foundation on which local government rests and is not to be sneered at.

From time to time, a particular issue will generate local controversy and rise above the daily routine of the councillor's representative work: the lack of a bypass for a village, for example, or a plan to widen a radial route through a suburban area. Here, the individual councillor, or a small group of adjoining members, will act to promote or protect the interests of the local patch. Never, never underestimate the ability of an elected representative to mobilize action in the community and support in the council. Through petitions, action groups, the revival of long-defunct residents' associations or the creation of new ones, the generation of press publicity and support, political deals and a variety of other techniques, the status, urgency and technical details of a project can be changed and its perception as a political winner or loser shaped. This is when the grass roots can become a jungle in which projects, and their managers, can get hopelessly lost. Good understanding of local issues and the work and priorities of local members can help with communications, and — sometimes — find ways around or through the undergrowth.

All elected members have their local work to do and many take part in the broader political manoeuvrings and campaigns of the groups but only a few fill the key leadership roles. All political groups have their hierarchy: group leader; deputy; spokespersons on education, social welfare, the environment, etc. For the party in the majority, power means that their councillors become office holders, taking up the jobs of chairman, or chair, of each of the formally constituted committees of the council and supplying the deputies, and the corresponding posts in the many formal and informal subcommittees, panels and working parties which undertake the work of a modern local authority.

Chairmen/chairs may sometimes have the authority to take certain limited action on behalf of the council, and there is usually the benefit of the casting vote to be used to break deadlocks in the decision making process. Their real power, however, lies in their influence within the party group, their close working contact with the bureaucracy of the council and their opportunity to control the order and run of debate in the committees. This distinguishes them from the honorific posts of chairman of the council or mayor, which are most often bestowed on senior members who serve a term in a figurehead role acting as local ambassadors for the council and — in theory at least — impartially chairing some set-piece meetings. One title which brings together status and real power is leader of the council. Typically, combining leadership of the majority party group with chairing the most influential committee — invariably the one with overall control of the budget — this is the key role in the political management of the council.

Whatever their power, formal or informal, within the council, all members are bound by the National Code of Local Government Conduct 1990. The key expression is that an elected representative's *overriding duty as a councillor is to the whole local community*, and the detail of the code's 33 paragraphs covers the declaration of all significant private or personal interests, the security of confidential information, the acceptance of gifts and hospitality, and working relationships between officers and members. Although the code is supported by provisions in the Local Government Act 1972 regarding disclosures of interest, it is not itself statute law. Nevertheless, it carries considerable authority and weight and is not only widely respected but also — a tribute to our local government system — generally honoured in the spirit, as well as the letter.

As local government becomes more complex and more politicized, so the full-time councillor has developed into a frequent, if not yet a commonplace, feature of the council scene. The description is somewhat loose and it would be an oversimplification to apply it only to members who spend a full working week on council business, although some do. It can just as well be used as a general description for those councillors who commit a large amount of time to the work, particularly the strategic and party political elements, of the council, often operating through salaried assistants and office facilities on the premises. Members such as these are politically influential, usually expert at the procedures and administrative detail of local government business — and can be very well informed on technical matters in their area of interest.

Officers

The political leadership (majority and, to a lesser extent, opposition parties) and office holders have particularly close contact with the officers of the council. All the people employed by the council — managers, professionals, technical specialists, administrators and the many support staff — are local government officers, but the term *officer* is used principally as a label for the officials who carry specific and senior responsibility in professional, advisory or managerial roles.

Not so very long ago all councils were organized along similar and largely conventional lines with the staff deployed in two kinds of department, namely

- internal support — pre-eminently finance, with the lawyers and the committee secretariat (often combined) taking close second in the pecking order ahead of property and personnel
- service delivery — education and housing, the biggest spenders at top and second tier respectively, with social services, engineering, planning, leisure/recreation/libraries, environmental health and the direct service organizations (the in-house blue collar contracting units) taking their

positions in the hierarchy depending on the type of authority and its priorities.

As organizational structures have changed and diversified, so titles, once traditional and almost immutable, have become varied, sometimes impenetrable and often filled with management buzz-words. Translation, if it is to be accurate, must be done at local level, but a few samples follow, ranging across both the time-honoured and contemporary titles for some of the key chief officer posts.

- *Chief Executive/Corporate Manager*: the head of the paid service (all councils must have one); chief executives, if not extinct like their predecessors the town or county clerks, are looking very like an endangered species as members themselves seek to take more positive control over executive action and expect a more responsive, less pro-active, managerial style from their principal official.
- *Treasurer/Director of Finance*: another statutory post (section 151 of the Local Government Act 1972 requires every council to have an officer responsible for its financial affairs) and one now widely considered to be the most influential as members become more reliant on those who can solve, or at least mitigate, the problems of public finance, and forecast, or at least guess more plausibly than others, its future developments. This trend notwithstanding, holding the purse-strings has always been a powerful role and project managers will benefit from researching the director of finance's methods and procedures, studying his committee reports and building good working relationships with his staff.
- *Director of Social Services*: not a traditional title, for this is a relatively new statutory post (1971) with the responsibility for one of the few areas where, through Care in the Community, the work of local government has been extended; in this area there are large budgets, even larger demands and very emotive pressures — when home helps and highway maintenance compete for the support of politicians, there is no contest.
- *Director of Education/Chief Education Officer*: another post specified by statute (Education Act 1944) but with older roots, covering the delivery of the largest and most expensive of local government services (and the one most rapidly leaving the effective control of local authorities); the current trends in the administration of schools are producing a steady reduction in the power of this once highly independent post. Nevertheless, when it comes to reviewing budget priorities, this officer still holds some very high cards in the legal obligations of local education authorities and the people power of governors and parent-teacher associations.
- *Surveyor/Engineer/Director of Technical Services*: local government's oldest paid post has no legal status whatsoever, and the incorporation of disciplines outside engineering and service responsibilities other than highways has led to a range of peculiar — in the sense of unique — titles which tend to reflect departmental coverage rather than role (the author's former local government title was lengthy and, thus, often

inaccurately addressed by callers and correspondents; most memorably as 'Dictator of Hugeways and Planning', although this may have been a satirical thrust by an anti-roads group). The impressive, and now almost defunct, title of *Bridgemaster* implied a professional exercising personal command over the council's highways and structures — those days, like the title, have vanished.

- *Planning Officer/Director of Environmental Services*: a relatively new job (the Town and County Planning Act 1948 created the function although it did not make the post statutory) which tended to remain relatively unchanged until recently, when organizational mergers with engineering and/or property departments have generated variations similar to the director of technical services theme; responsibility for advice on planning strategy and applications brings a considerable potential for controversy with the public, members and other officers.
- *Librarian/Director of Arts, Archives, Culture, etc.*: nobody seems to want to own up to running public libraries any more, although they remain one of local government's most popular functions and the one that has most firmly retained its status as a traditional public service; libraries offer an effective, if not comprehensive, means of passing on information on proposals or projects to the local community.
- *Architect*: a post which flourished from the 1960s to the mid-80s but now, with a very few outstanding exceptions, is disappearing into property departments, contracted-out arrangements or (as building programmes diminish) oblivion.
- *Director of Housing/Housing Manager*: once a major job in all districts and boroughs that had very large stocks of council housing to build, maintain and run as landlord; the 'right to buy' legislation, the virtual demise of funding for municipal programmes and the transfer of large parts of the existing tenanted property to housing associations have dramatically reduced the strategic role to an estate-management task and in some cases almost eliminated it entirely.
- *Chief Parks Officer/Director of Leisure*: the recent growth of leisure infrastructure such as swimming pools, fitness centres, etc. has resulted in a much larger, more varied and market oriented operation in most districts and boroughs, more complex too, as the traditional ancillary responsibilities such as cemeteries are often supplemented by car parks, networks of private roads and paths and some very sophisticated mechanical/electrical installations: nowadays, the work is frequently contracted-out.
- *Personnel Officer/Director of Human Resources*: as employment law, equal opportunities and a whole range of workplace regulations from Whitehall or Brussels complicates life in labour-intensive organizations, so this role gets more important and, it seems, more tied up in management jargon.
- *Director of Property*: another recent addition to the cast of local government characters, whose status, long-term prospects and capacity for controversy (with the planning officer if no-one else) are much affected by the fact that for most local authorities management of the

property estate means minimizing maintenance costs and maximizing sales; usually the officer responsible for handling the land acquisition tasks involved in works projects although, understandably, this tends to be viewed as a bit of a sideline.

- *Secretary/Solicitor/Monitoring Officer/Head of Secretariat*: the days when the council's most senior official was always a lawyer have long gone, and the separation of chief executive and head of legal services and administration into two jobs did not last very long either; the county, borough or district secretary has often developed into a trio of posts providing
  - ○ the head of a legal practice delivering services for statutory processes, contract documents, acquisition and disposal of land, etc.
  - ○ the whistle blower who by law must monitor all council activity to ensure its legality and probity
  - ○ the manager of the administrative function that runs the committees and the entire paper-chase on which they are based.

Given the complexities of local government's legal processes these officials often play key roles and can exert considerable influence.

Although the local government code of conduct is written for members and not officers, it is generally expected (and often written into senior officials' contracts of employment) that they will follow its principles, just as consultants working for local authorities are assumed to be aware, as a matter of good professional practice, of the need to avoid or declare any conflict of interest. To reinforce this general guidance, the Local Government Act 1972 specifically requires local government officers to formally disclose any financial interest they may have in any contract which the authority may have or be considering. Officers in particular, because of their role in decisions which can involve substantial payments or long-term financial benefits, have to be careful about their working relationships with contractors, consultants, suppliers and developers. The code also stresses that officers and members are *indispensable to one another*, but emphasises the basis of mutual respect on which this cooperation must rest.

There is a particular difference between public servants in local government and their colleagues who work for the national government and it lies in the relationship of the officials with their political masters. Officers serve the whole council and must make their advice available, generally in public, to all political groups through the processes of committees etc., on which all parties are represented. Civil servants work for the government of the day and advise, usually in private, through the structure of the Ministries and Departments of State which are of course, under the control of the majority party in Parliament.

We will return to the delicate relationship between officers and members as we reach the end of this book: for the moment the key theoretical concept is that members make policy and strategic decisions, officers advise on options and choices and then carry out the council's wishes. Of course, the reality is not so clear cut, but more of that later.

Consultants

Local authorities have used consultants to supplement their in-house staff over many years. Indeed, up until the 1960s a large proportion of the design and supervision of public works projects was carried out by private practices. The growth of the public sector in the 1960s and 1970s changed this balance dramatically and saw a very significant expansion of in-house professional resources. The wheel has now turned almost full circle and consultants are returning in increasing numbers to this business area, but in a different way: now it is continuous service programmes like highway maintenance, bridge inspection, traffic management and development control that are being provided as well as the traditional, and now much scarcer, single projects such as a major bypass, a bridge or a transportation study.

In many ways, the council's relationship with a consultant is the same as with an in-house professional team. A piece of work — defined in a project brief or a service specification — is delivered to a required standard in accordance with a set timetable for an agreed price. There are two key differences. The price for an in-house organization is the salary bill and other running costs associated with the council employees doing the work; whereas for the consultant it is a fee settled as a lump sum or via a formula, in a commercial bargain. The in-house team delivers direct, with quality control in the hands of its own management or another in-house unit; but the consultant works externally and delivers through some form of client body which monitors the standard of the finished product and certifies the fee.

Many public authorities replicate the client/private consultant split by a division of organizational responsibilities — again, more of this later — but the fundamental issue in local government terms is that consultants work to a contract of service, in-house staff work to contracts of employment. Although consultants now provide services which involve dealing with the public and contact with members, the relationship is bound to be different because of the legal requirement that a local authority can only delegate its powers to its own employees, and must have advice leading to statutory decisions delivered via its own officials. This requirement, established in the Local Government Act 1972, may not survive in its present general form indefinitely as deregulation spreads ever wider, but it is in any case of relatively limited significance. Consultants can provide professional/technical advice up to and including a recommendation for action or the exercise of statutory powers provided it is checked for *due diligence*, i.e. reasonable professional standards, relevance, completeness and general clarity, by the council's own officers who then endorse the consultant's conclusions.

This process of giving advice includes the preparation of reports, their presentation at council committees and other formal or informal occasions, giving evidence at inquiries and tribunals as well as the many other procedural tasks associated with the promotion and progression of public works. Consultants can manage any and all aspects of service delivery once the council has made a decision on the extent and nature of the project or programme and authorized a start. Similarly, delegated decisions can be taken by council officers on the advice of consultants without the need for firsthand involvement in details, provided that systems exist and are used which allow checks —

random spot-checks will suffice — to demonstrate that the council is not merely rubber stamping each and every recommendation it receives.

Consultants are not bound by the letter of the local government code of conduct, for the simple reason that there cannot be the same exclusive relationship with the employing council which exists in the case of an officer in an in-house department. As far as the spirit of the code is concerned, however, there is no substantial difference, and once again the reason is a simple one: professional ethics require a consultant always to have regard for the client's best interests, respect his confidentiality and apply due diligence (not, incidentally, merely a quaint phrase but a term with a clear legal definition). The standards which the engineering profession has set for itself over the years have always been high and incompetence, carelessness and corruption are very rare. (about as rare as they are in the public service).

Nevertheless, the fundamental difference that a consultant can have more than one employer and a public servant but one, gives the issue of conflict of interest a significance which cannot be ignored. Consultants are used to the potential problem as it can arise between commercial clients and every firm can report cases where the presence of an existing commission, or a long-standing relationship with a particular client, has meant that some new business has had to be turned away. Similarly, there are many examples where clients have given permission, subject to the establishment of clear separation and the erection of 'Chinese walls', for work with elements of potential conflict to be dealt with in the same firm.

Of course, the vast majority of any consultant's workload involves no conflict of interest, but where public sector clients are concerned the question of perception is always just as important as substance. It is doubly important therefore, for consultants working in the public sector or taking on public sector commissions, to ensure that the potential for conflict is kept under continuous review and their local government clients advised of any possible difficulties so that an agreed course of action can be followed. (An unacceptable, situation would arise if, for instance, a consultant supervising a contractor on a council road scheme was simultaneously working with the same contractor on a joint venture locally.) For those cases where there is no actual conflict and no disadvantage to the local authority, but public sensitivity or controversy may be attached to some aspect, the early declaration of the consultant's involvement and the council's open acceptance that its interests will not be prejudiced will defuse what could otherwise be an explosive situation. (A typical example would be a consultant working on, say, a long-term programme of major road maintenance for a council being offered a commission by the Department of Transport to investigate the possible routes for a new bypass in its area, to which there is some localized, but fierce, opposition.) The important point is that the consultant recognizes the need to protect the position of the public sector client by keeping it fully informed — no surprises.

The public

At the most fundamental level, public works are done for people and local authorities are there to serve the public, or that's the theory. In practice, public interest and involvement are, to say the least, erratic, and it is all too easy for project managers to see the public as an obstacle to providing a good professional service, instead of the reason for it.

The right to be present at council meetings and to see the agenda and reports of committees in advance has existed for over a century and been reinforced by recent legislation, but the public now plays a stronger role in local democracy than ever before. Petitioners and action groups are part of the normal toing and froing of public affairs and many authorities encourage the dialogue between the council and its citizens by giving individuals or representative groups the opportunity to address committees, ask questions at meetings and contribute their views as a part of the decision making process rather than a response to it.

There was a time, still close enough for some people to reminisce about it, when the general public was prepared to accept the proposals of the council as likely to be correct, reasonable, workable and for the best. In effect, this meant that proposals would be seen as not subject to debate and therefore, and very importantly, not open to change. A new bypass or just a junction improvement, the introduction of a one-way system or the preparation of a whole land-use transportation strategy, would tend to go ahead — funds permitting and the formal approval of councillors forthcoming — with little non-professional discussion, hardly any attempt to obtain the views of the public and no serious expectation of a challenge. There might be some people or businesses directly affected by the project who would complain, but their concerns would either be dealt with by the statutory processes of compensation (if they were eligible) or be ignored (if they were not). The idea that public opinion could legitimately oppose the decisions of an elected local authority, let alone succeed, was considered unrealistic, not to say radical and smelling strongly of anarchy. 'And quite right, too' said the majority of professionals, who were confident that they knew what the public needed.

Attitudes have changed. Individuals and groups are recognized as having a voice and the right to challenge proposals and decisions, including those which do not affect them directly but in which they feel they have a broad interest. The obligation to consult and to invite participation is now entrenched in our way of life and a well-educated, articulate public will accept nothing less.

This involvement, it must be noted, is selective. The turn-out in local elections has not risen dramatically and the general activity of local government seems to remain, for most people, a matter of indifference unless some specific national issue grabs the attention of a wide cross-section of the populace. The poll tax retains the all-comers record in that contest: recent challengers such as league tables and opting-out for schools, the ineffectiveness (or over-enthusiasm) of social workers in dealing with child abuse, and even local government reorganization itself have turned out to be no more than also-rans. Nevertheless, people now feel able and *empowered* (a word we will meet again) to take an interest in local government activity in a way no politician or project manager can ignore.

The transformation came about in the 1970s when a number of projects — mainly roads, but also new commercial development and redevelopment — acted as a focal point for a generation which believed in protest, self-expression and the power of the people to overrule the faceless bureaucrats. In 1969

25

involvement of public opinion had achieved official recognition through the Skeffington report and a whole range of changes followed which widened the requirements for consultation and the scope for objection. This shift, complete and irreversible as it is, may not please professionals, who will never again have only to convince a small, familiar group of councillors to get the go-ahead for a scheme or programme, but it has encouraged people to see public works as an area in which they can exercise some influence.

Public involvement in works projects has been institutionalized, therefore, in procedures for notification of proposals, consultation, objections and public inquiries, and project managers must build them into their programmes and commit significant resources to the task of getting them right. That is, however, by no means the whole picture. Nowadays, people expect to play a more active role in the wider public works scene: identifying problems, advancing solutions, considering options, expressing preferences, opposing or supporting alternative plans, evaluating detailed proposals and monitoring the speed and quality of the execution of the project. The public is not prepared to be inserted into selected compartments, labelled *advertise route, consider objections*, etc., in a long chain of events and the requirement is for involvement in the complete process. This is not, of course, just true of public works but of local government as a whole.

Although both the procedural and general involvement are real and ever-present, the concentrated power of the public — and sometimes individuals or very small groups who have influence, or can command attention — is most effectively mobilized over specific localized issues, and often quite late in the process. It is part of the modern project manager's job to take a view which is broader than the narrow professional one, and to understand the legitimate concerns of people affected by his plans and appreciate that their subjective, emotional and, at time, selfish reactions are as much a part of the input to a project as the site investigation and the latest design guides.

Not all public contact is about policy or protest. Individual citizens look for service, information and action, and therefore are ever-present in the whole range of local government activity as customers, users and recipients. Citizens' charters have established standards and by stressing the status of the citizen as a consumer, given a market dimension to the relationship between public authorities and the public. They did not create that relationship, however, which rests on a more fundamental role and one which must recognize that not all citizens are willing, let alone satisfied, consumers of local government services. Behind every petition, action group, letter or telephone call lies the basic power in the ballot box to elect or dismiss politicians and parties. Members of the public participate, indeed form the essential element, in the most important part of the whole local government process — they are the voters.

3.   The mechanism

Local government involves the exercise of extensive legal powers, the discharge of major responsibilities and the undertaking of very significant obligations affecting the people, businesses and institutions in each council's area, or with which it comes into contact. Councils make long-term decisions and spend very large amounts of public money. The methods by which public bodies operate are circumscribed therefore by law to an extent far greater than its deceptive appearance as a traditional, but not excessively formal, bureaucracy implies. Beneath the surface impression that things just happen is a complex, and often quite rigid, machine.

Council and committees

Almost without exception, the duties of a local authority and its powers to discharge them, or act within its discretion, rest with the council, which is the full complement of elected members acting as a body in a properly convened meeting.

The council, which may have anything between 25 and over 100 members, has a legal personality. This means that, like a company, it is considered to behave as if it were an individual. The purpose of such an arrangement is for the machinery of the law, which is primarily based on concepts of personal rights and obligations, to be used by (and if necessary against) a collective body. In particular, it allows the council of individual members to decide by majority vote how to tax, spend and deliver specific services, regardless of the inevitable differences that would exist between those individuals.

Obviously, there are limits to this legal fiction. While it is possible for a council to be charged with a criminal offence, to be found innocent or guilty, to sue or be sued and so on, it cannot commit personal crimes like murder or manslaughter (although its negligence can be judged to be the cause of death), and it cannot be imprisoned (but it can be fined and even have its powers of action, if not its liberty, taken away).

However, individual councillors can be held to account for their own actions, especially if they ignore or subvert the process within which they are supposed to work. Well-publicized cases in the 1980s led to financial penalties and disqualification from public office for certain councillors in Lambeth and Liverpool who were found guilty of failing to set a budget as part of a deliberate programme of opposition to government policy, which they were organizing and controlling. Similarly, if one or more elected members use their positions to carry out any improper or illegal acts (fraud, embezzlement, sexual harassment, etc.) then they are personally liable and not the whole council.

The full council must meet at least once a year, must set a budget and can reserve to itself any decision within the powers of the local authority. Generally, it acts as the forum for set piece debates on matters of great local controversy, broad party-political dispute or long-term strategic importance for a number or all of the authority's services. As most of these issues are either pure politics without any significant technical input, or have already been discussed with professional reports in the service-based committees, the debates are invariably conducted solely by the elected members and officers take no part, providing, at the most, briefing papers.

There is another side to the council meeting, which often turns the spotlight on to very local topics. Petitions are presented by individual councillors on behalf of residents' associations, protest committees and other community groups, frequently supported by some of the petitioners. These items are not debated, and after what the usual rules (although not the custom!) of council business requires to be a brief introduction, they are referred to the appropriate committee for consideration. By far the largest proportion are about road safety and traffic-related problems. In addition, a session is provided when questions can be put to the chairmen/chairs of the committees by back bench councillors on any matter connected with the local authority's services (and, increasingly, this facility is being offered to members of the public). Notice is required, so information and responses on professional and technical aspects can be prepared in advance by officers. However, in true parliamentary style the questioner is normally allowed one supplementary question and this gives the opportunity for members of the opposition to catch out the ruling group or score a few points in the competition for publicity. It is not a one-sided contest, however, and a well prepared or quick witted respondent can turn the tables. On the one hand

> *Councillor:* Is the chairman aware of the great local concern about the appalling state of the roads and footways in the North Hill area?
> *Chairman of Transportation Committee (reading from prepared officer brief):* The condition of the highways in North Hill has been assessed but, as they are not considered in any way to be dangerous, they have not achieved sufficient priority to form part of the current year's maintenance programme. They will be reassessed in due course for incorporation in future programmes.
> *Councillor:* Doesn't the chairman agree that his statement is a complete whitewash which shows his party has no regard whatsoever for the people of North Hill?
> *Chairman (on the defensive):* That is not true. We are concentrating our efforts on road safety, we do not intend to ignore North Hill, but we have to look at our other priorities.

and on the other

> *Councillor:* Is the chairman aware of the great local concern about the appalling state of the roads and footways in the North Hill area?
> *Chairman:* Yes.
> *Councillor (frustrated and wrong footed):* So what are you going to do about it?
> *Chairman (on the offensive):* What we are doing is concentrating our efforts with great success on the most important issue for the people of the whole county: saving lives through our road safety programme.

(He then launches into a barnstorming political speech, ending up with a quick recital of the officer brief.)

The rough and tumble of political debate, and the imaginative (and sometimes aggressive) use of the debating rules to secure advantage may have an affect on the progress of projects, but there is no role for the professionals apart from ensuring that full briefings — in layman's language — have been prepared for all the participants. As far as project management is concerned, the process of debate and decision making takes place elsewhere.

The full council is not the most effective forum for making decisions on the majority of the varied and detailed issues that come before a local authority, and these tasks are delegated to a range of subsidiary bodies, smaller in size and generally charged with looking after a particular service area. These are the committees, subcommittees, sections and panels with memberships ranging from 25 or more to less than half a dozen, which handle the bulk of the work of the authority. A typical arrangement is shown in Fig. 1, but there are few rules about the committee structure of a council and the detail, particularly of subcommittees and smaller groups, will vary from one authority to another and will probably change over time within the same authority.

Next to the council itself, the key body in Fig. 1 is the strategy and resources committee, sometimes called the policy committee, strategic management committee and other similar titles. This body has overall control over the

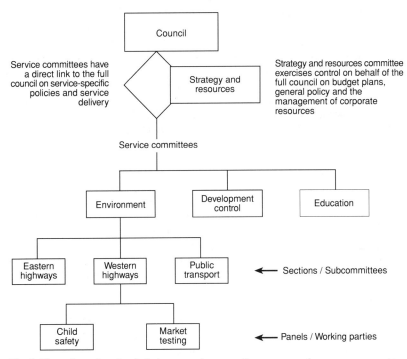

Fig. 1. Flow chart showing links between the council, strategy and resources committee, and various service committees.

29

fundamental resources of money, property and people as well as a coordinating role on political and managerial policy across the whole authority. Thus the strategy and resources committee would

- decide on the broad approach to the preparation of budgets (e.g. setting cash limits, fixing the allowance for inflation, selecting the services to benefit from the sale of assets, etc.)
- direct the overall management of the council's property stock (endorse a programme of sales, determine the criteria for priority for maintenance funds, etc.)
- oversee the authority's personnel policies (e.g. annual pay review, ethnic monitoring, provision for people with disabilities)
- determine the council's stance on major political issues (the privatization of British Rail, for instance, or the relationship between local authorities and the police)
- set the key management policies on which the authority would operate (contracting-out, for example, or the reorganization of the in-house departmental structure).

Not everything would be dealt with by the full committee, and, as with the council itself and the service-based committees, the principle of delegation would allow the setting-up of subsidiary bodies such as a personnel subcommittee, or a property sales working party.

The other major subdivisions of the full council, which because of their importance and permanence are given the status of independent committees, are normally organized around its main services. Where two-tier local government operates there will be distinct differences between the committee arrangements reflecting the distribution of services: thus, only the upper tier would have an education committee, while the lower tier would be where the housing committee would be found. Some committees — development control or planning — would be present at both levels. Unitary authorities cover all the services, with a corresponding full house of committees.

The environment committee, as it is titled in Fig. 1 exemplifies the change from the roads and bridges committee typically found in the highway authorities of yesteryear. It deals with a dauntingly wide range of issues from highway maintenance, through traffic calming, to the development of long-term plans integrating transportation policies and infrastructure with land use strategies and the requirements of a sustainable local and global environment. New roads and, even more so, bridges are a welcome novelty in its deliberations as far as the professionals are concerned.

In most cases the main committee will have a number of subsidiaries, some in permanent operation and others set up for specific time-limited tasks: the basis of the former, commonly called subcommittees or sections, may be either functional (e.g. public transport subcommittee) or geographical (e.g. western area highway section); the latter, normally named panels or Working Parties, will be organized around their particular roles (e.g. competitive tendering strategy panel, child safety working party) which may be investigative or action-oriented.

Whatever the arrangement of committees and their particular areas of operation, they will all have certain key features in common. Some are requirements of legislation: there are rules governing the representation of political parties on committees so that the numbers broadly reflect the balance of the whole council; the meetings must be held in public, after due notice of the time, place and topics for discussion has been given; and only items relating to defined areas where confidentiality is permitted can be discussed in private session; the reports prepared for the meeting (confidential items excepted) must be accessible to any interested person at least three full weekdays in advance; and the minutes recording the proceedings of the committee must similarly be available for inspection, and even the confidential items have to be covered by a general note.

Under these universal legal requirements, committees (and the full council itself) operate within local frameworks, known as *standing orders*. Every local authority will have its own set, duly approved by the council, which is the only body with the power to amend or suspend them. Each will have differences of detail, but all will share a similar coverage and will often contain identical passages or provisions, tried and tested over long years of local government usage.

Standing orders will include the terms of reference of the various committees and other permanent subsidiary parts of the council, and the details of the normal cycle of meetings. They will also cover the process for calling specials, not scheduled in the calendar of meetings and usually put forward to deal with extra business or some major event (such as the response to a motorway widening proposal); and for urgency action, where an item or a meeting is brought forward without the usual period of notice because action has to be taken more quickly than normal timetables would allow (authorization for the disposal of highway land as part of a fast-moving property deal, for instance).

There will be a large section devoted to the rules of procedures: defining the circumstances and means for bringing matters forward for debate; the rights of council members to speak, interrupt and respond; the voting process; the powers of the chairman/chair to control the meeting; and so on. Points of order — sometimes highly imaginative, and based on the assumption that nobody knows the standing orders from memory — tend to arise at full council with its more parliamentary style of debate and are less common in committees and (usually) are frowned on in the subcommittees and panels which tend to concentrate on the detail. This does not mean that points of procedure are all irrelevant to professionals. The treatment of petitions, items brought forward at short notice, and the general time tabling and organization of decision making meetings and decision influencing debates are important factors in project management. Professionals cannot control them, but they should know how the system works and make the best of it.

The nuts and bolts of practical committee work are important and complex enough to warrant special attention in a later chapter, where it will be shown how much more of an art they are than a science. Nevertheless, the overall mechanism and its theory of operation, while apparently dull and bureaucratic, set the framework for all the triumphs, disappointments, frustrations and amusements that emerge from the practicality of council business.

Thus, the ability to defer a decision to the next scheduled meeting of the committee, some three months away, and the difficulty of calling special or urgency meetings can be used to allow time to run out on a key element of a project so as' to cancel it indirectly and with the minimum of publicity. Conversely, the hierarchy of panels/subcommittees/committees can allow a potentially controversial issue to be exposed gradually and without sensation, to facilitate a decision which might otherwise be impossible.

Even the dry words and procedures of standing orders can conceal the human factor. An ill-timed call of nature, which allowed the opposition in a finely-balanced council to call and win a snap vote on a key topic, is the reason why one local authority now requires all votes in full council to be preceded by a warning whistle and a two minute wait for members to resume their places!

Delegation

Just as full council is not the right forum for detailed debate and decision making on service matters, so is it impractical for all the multitude of actions which make up the routine of local government to go through formal committee processes. The response to this is the exercise of delegated powers, sometimes by nominated office holders (e.g chairman and vice-chairman of the committee) or small groups of members representing the political balance of the committee, but more usually by senior officials.

The scheme of delegation in regular use by a council is generally found in its standing orders and defines the capacity of the specified delegates to commit the council. As most delegated decisions are non-political (in theory, at least) and based on the application of professional/technical judgement within clear legal or policy guidelines, the majority of them are taken by officials, usually under the authority of the chief officer of the department.

Typically, delegated powers are a mixture of major and minor issues, with some in constant use and others hardly ever employed at all. A scheme of delegation might have several pages devoted specifically to the powers of the chief technical officer or county engineer, including the following excerpts

24 To approve
a) the placing of structures within highway limits
b) the laying, maintenance and inspection of pipes, cables or other lines over or under the highway
c) the erection of stiles, gates or cattle grids
d) arrangements for motor vehicles and cycle trials.

25 To exercise the council's powers including the giving of formal notices
a) to prohibit horses, cattle or vehicles entering on ornamental gardens within the highway
b) to pipe or culvert and fill up roadside ditches
c) to require the execution of works to prevent soil or refuse from land from falling or being washed on to a street
d) to take action in relation to any obstruction of, or damage to, or nuisance to, the highway or users thereof

e) to exercise the council's powers and duties under Part III of the New Roads and Street Works Act 1991 (other than the institution of legal proceedings)

f) to require the removal of obstructions to sight lines at corners and to remove unauthorized signs on any part of the highway.

26 To carry out

a) minor temporary repairs in private streets required to remove danger to persons or vehicles

b) emergency works of any kind whether or not provision has been made in the estimates where justified in his/her opinion and that of the solicitor, by the scale of the potential legal liability.

27 To grant permission for the erection of banners over highways subject to appropriate conditions including conditions necessary for public safety.

49 To respond to petitions where a clear committee policy exists or where a similar petition has been considered by the committee in the previous six months.

56 To expend the budget of the area highway sections to deal with small-scale traffic management issues, subject to such expenditure being in consultation with the local council members and the chairman of the relevant area highway section and up to a limit of £1000 per item.

C8 Where a tender does not exceed the value or amount indicated below for the contract category by a chief officer concerned, namely

a) Disposal of estates and interests in land — £300 000

b) Building and engineering works. The sum provided in the approved capital or revenue estimates, subject to variations allowed by regulation C9 and subject to consultation with the county property officer in the case of building contracts

c) Supply and disposal of goods and materials — £100 000

d) Supply and disposal of vehicles and plant. The sum provided in the approved capital estimate

e) Supply and disposal of services — £100 000

f) Repair and maintenance — £300 000 subject to a report to the next appropriate meeting of the appropriate committee or section and subject to consultation with the property officer in the case of building repairs and maintenance

g) Engagement of consultants or agents — £50 000.

C9 Where a tender for the execution of any building or engineering works exceeds the written estimate required under paragraph 12 above by an amount not exceeding the greater of five per cent or £10 000 then, subject to these regulations, such tenders may nevertheless be accepted by the chief officer concerned or the appropriate committee or section. Any action taken by chief officers under this section, shall be reported to the committee concerned. A tender which exceeds the estimate by more than the greater of five per cent or £10 000 shall not be accepted without the approval of the committee or section concerned.

Less frequently, and for specific purposes, power may be delegated to members to take a decision or select an option. This freedom to operate outside the formal process of the committee can only be granted by the committee itself and is not something an office holder, still less members, can have as a right or as part of the job. So, while it is in order for a committee to agree to give the chairman and vice-chairman authority to approve the layout of a particular consultation leaflet, or to delegate to a group of four members the selection of a short list for a consultancy bid, it is not possible for this kind of delegated authority to be exercised as a matter of course without a committee decision, nor for it to be maintained indefinitely on a general basis.

British local government restricts the capacity of individual elected representatives to exercise the powers of their councils. There is nothing comparable to the position of American and European mayors and while we have seen over the last 30 years the appearance of some high profile civic bosses they have deployed their authority and influence through political machinery and adept publicity rather than the exercise of any personal legal powers.

So professionals must realise that, while members may be influential and carry some weight because of their status as office holders, they have no general power to issue instructions, make decisions or commit the council. Listening to their advice, taking note of their comments and paying attention to their local knowledge, is especially important because of their status, and they may well be able to make promises and political commitments they can be relied upon to deliver. In official and legal terms, however, their powers must be exercised through the appropriate committee process.

As a consequence of these legal and political constraints on elected representatives as individual decision takers, and the practicalities of making frequent routine decisions in which the justification for the exercise of the authority's powers is primarily technical, the widest range and largest volume of delegation is to officers. This is frustrating to many members, particularly when they find a decision, taken by an official without their knowledge, is referred to them by an aggrieved constituent or, worse still, a whole group of constituents. Such circumstances tend to raise arguments (in the academic sense) around the meaning of local democracy, and more pressing arguments (in the raised voices sense) about the local credibility of individual councillors.

More and more, the emphasis on local accountability and customer care is limiting the application of delegation and, where it does operate, requiring much better communications about the exercise of these powers. Mechanisms are needed to ensure that councillors fully understand the scheme of delegation, setting-out

- who can take decisions about what
- whether and to what extent local consultation takes place
- how the procedure for handling and recording each case works
- which council policies and professional best-practice guidelines are relevant and what they say
- how rigid the framework is within which decisions are made and what discretion (if any) exists.

Channels of communication are required to enable members to know about the operation of the scheme in their wards or divisions. This is the difficult part because not every councillor will want to know about delegated decisions; and it is unlikely that even the most involved patch politician will want to know about every single delegated action. The essence of all effective communication is relevance and officers have to cooperate with individual members to find the right need-to-know criteria for each individual. For some, sensitivity is by topic (anything to do with on-street parking); for others it is location (every issue affecting the North Hill estate); and for yet others a combination of the two (all decisions to do with the Western park and ride project). Hard-and-fast definitions will not work every time, of course, and there will always be occasions when instinct or common sense will identify a case which should be treated as need-to-know in spite of being outside the usual parameters.

Each and every case should be recorded so that a member can have access to the process on request.

The purpose of all this effort — and a great deal of effort is involved — must be to keep local members informed of the use of delegated powers and to avoid their being caught unprepared, with consequent embarrassment for the council and confusion in the decision making process. The aim is communication when required, not participation as of right. So, it is not a means of transferring delegated powers to individual councillors who have no authority to use them, nor should it become an unofficial and secret way of influencing the exercise of professional judgement. There may be rare occasions when officials have to resist these kinds of pressure, and it is a key part of the local government officer's role to recognize the difference between the helpful local knowledge which a politician can offer and the unacceptable diversion of council powers to purely political ends. Delegation to officers must mean what it says: the passing down to the council's non-political officials of the authority to make decisions by exercising their professional or technical skills without — subject of course to their exercise of reasonable competence — further involvement of elected members.

Consultants and contractors cannot exercise delegated powers. The Local Government Act 1981 confirms the long-standing restriction that only the directly employed officials of the council can be given its powers and authority. Notwithstanding the growing trend to deregulate many local government activities (i.e. to allow formerly exclusive powers such as building regulations approval to be made available to a wider range of authorized providers), this is not as sweeping or drastic a constraint as it appears. While the specific action itself — the issue of an exemption certificate from a local heavy goods vehicle ban, the award of a contract for the supply of coated chippings, or the decision to close a road for essential repairs — may only be taken by a duly authorized officer, all the preparatory work leading to it and the activity flowing from it can be carried out by the consultant or contractor in their capacities as the council's agent.

The acquisition of land for a major parking facility has been identified by the consultant working on the park and ride project, and all the necessary survey, design and environmental impact work has been done leading to a recommendation on the detailed scheme with land-take, access and accommodation works requirements. The consultant's report is accepted by the officials and put to the transportation committee which, exercising its delegated powers, approves the report and the use of the council's powers of compulsory purchase to progress the scheme.

The consultant prepares all the necessary plans and schedules and the council's solicitor drafts and publishes the order. The objections are received by the council and the consultant advises on how they might be overcome and at what cost in terms of accommodation works etc. This advice, together with that from the council's property experts (who may be in-house or contracted out), is coordinated by the client officers who exercise their delegated powers to agree various works, purchase or compensation payments which are within the approved budget for the project. If a public inquiry has been avoided the tender list is drawn up by the consultant, choosing appropriate contractors from the council's select list, and documents are issued. The consultant makes a recommendation to award a contract, which if it is for the lowest bid and within the approved budget can be accepted and actioned by the client officer, if not then a report and a decision by the transportation committee will be required. The contract is signed with the council as Employer and the consultant as Engineer for the works.

4. The money

Local government finance has always attracted a lot of attention and some degree of criticism. This is understandable as it has consistently occupied a substantial corner of the public purse: out of today's £300 billion of public spending, local government at something over £40 billion comes, along with health, second only to social security (a clear leader at £90 billion) and well ahead of defence.

About 20 years ago, local government finance would have been a subject which could have been described in relatively simple terms and with a fair degree of confidence in its stability. There were four basic elements: locally-raised tax (then the domestic and commercial rates); other income and receipts at local level; grants from national government; and borrowing. Today, the same four elements are still there (although the rates have been replaced — via the infamous community charge — by the council tax on residential property, and the national non-domestic rate on commercial premises) but you would need second sight to forecast more than a few years ahead the shape of local government finance, the relative proportions of the four sources of funding and the mechanisms that will exist to control expenditure.

Change may be the norm, but some things are certain. The money, wherever it comes from and in whatever quantity, will become the raw material in the processes of public finance: processes which are far more than book-keeping and play a key role in the promotion and management of projects. Because they are public works, paid for with public money, the allocation of funds and the means by which they are spent have to be subject to controls and scrutiny, which can appear very complicated. Indeed, cynics have sometimes suggested that public finance experts have deliberately created the system's complexities in order to make themselves powerful and indispensable actors on the local government stage. Even if there were a grain of truth in this — and it would be a rash person who even suggested such a thing — there is no doubt that plenty of outside assistance has been available to turn local government finance into a puzzle.

When Lord Palmerston was British Foreign Secretary in the 1860s, he became deeply involved in intractable negotiations over the sovereignty of one of the Baltic provinces. He said of the issue

> There are only three men who have ever understood it — one was Prince Albert, who is dead; the second was a German professor, who became mad; I am the third ... and I have forgotten all about it.

There are some who would say that local government finance has surpassed even the complexities of the Schleswig–Holstein question. Nevertheless, although project managers do not need to know the fine details of the system and all its variations — that challenge can be left to the public finance accountants — they should be aware of the broad principles under which it operates and be able to recognize the effects which can be felt on the funding, timing and control of public works projects. What follows, and the glossary of terms listed in Table 2, may help unravel some of the mystery.

Where it comes from . . .

As the four main components of local government finance are likely to continue as the basis of the system for the medium term at least, it is useful to examine each in turn, starting with a broad definition, reviewing the present trends and complications, and moving on to the practical effects on project management. However, it is indicative of the changing detail of public finance that it is necessary to point out that the information which follows reflects the position at the beginning of 1996.

The council tax is fundamentally a property tax and perpetuates the long history — interrupted for three years by the community charge or poll tax — of raising funds locally by making a charge on householders to reflect a notional valuation of their property, determined in this case by placing it in one of eight standard bands. An assumption is made that each house is occupied by two adults and a system of discounts, extras and exemptions allows adjustment to be made where occupancy differs from the standard. These, relatively minor, variations allow some recognition to be given to the different demands on local services made by different kinds of households, which are not properly reflected by the type of dwelling in which they may live. Householders in a particular local authority area with property in the top band pay two-thirds more than those in the band D (which is near the middle and acts as a kind of benchmark) and two and a half times as much as those in the lowest band. The relative proportions for each of the eight bands are specified by the government and cannot be altered by the authority.

The total amount raised through the council tax in each area, and the tax level for each band, is determined by the council's budget process, which will be examined later in this chapter. Whatever decisions are made, the proportion of the authority's funds coming from the council tax will be relatively small. On average, about 20% of local government spending is funded locally, the vast majority of the remainder being provided, and controlled, by central government. This average figure disguises local variations that arise because some authorities have relatively high property values and in others values fall well below the average. Thus the proportion of local government spending funded locally can range from nearly 25% to around 15%.

Nevertheless, the locally-raised figure is always small compared to the grant-aided sum, which leads to a phenomenon known as *gearing*. If an authority chooses to spend over the target assessed for it by the government, then all this extra, and not just around one fifth or 20 pence in the pound, has to come out of the council tax thus causing a very rapid increase in local tax bills. This gearing effect is not only a stark demonstration of the power that central government

Table 2. Finance glossary

Accounts: local authorities are required by law to produce annually a balance sheet showing income and expenditure, with the spending analysed in detail; all being subject to independent *audit* and available to the public.

Aggregate external finance (AEF): the total amount of money contributed by the government to an authority.

Annual capital guideline (ACG): the amount the government considers a particular authority will need to spend on *capital* projects.

Assets; items of value owned by the authority which may be fixed (e.g. buildings, land, roads) or current (e.g. stock in hand, loans to other public authorities, debts owed to the council).

Audit: inspection of a set of *accounts* or any financial transactions by a person other than the one who prepared them, followed by a report; now generally extended to cover the independent review of any function or activity.

Balances: the accumulated surplus of income over expenditure; also known as *reserves*.

Basic credit approval (BCA): permission from the government to use credit arrangements, including borrowing, *leasing* and *deferred purchase*, to finance spending on *capital* projects.

Budget: the authority's annual financial plan, usually known internally by some familiar and unimaginative title such as *The Red Book*, and comprising the corporate summation of the budgets of the various committees.

Capital expenditure: spending which produces a fixed *asset* intended to last a long time; e.g. building a new bridge or school; reconstructing an existing road; major refurbishment of a swimming pool; reclaiming derelict land, etc.

Capital receipts: money raised from the sale of fixed *assets* such as land; its use, to repay debt or finance new capital projects, is specified by government regulations and it cannot be used for *revenue* expenditure.

Capping: the government's power to set a ceiling on the expenditure of a local authority.

Cash limits: a device to restrict growth within a budget, whether caused by cost overruns or inflation, by fixing the sum of money available in advance and requiring any subsequent extras to be funded by corresponding cuts.

CIPFA: Chartered Institute of Public Finance and Accountancy, the professional body for local authority treasurers and finance officers; it produces guidelines and codes of practice for financial activities, and publishes a range of comparative statistics which are much used to cross-check councils' spending levels and performance (in spite of strenuous efforts, the input is not always compatible and the data must be used with care).

Consolidated loan fund: a fund set up in the authority to pool external and internal borrowing so as to finance spending on *capital* projects and the repayment of loans through *debt charges*.

Contingencies: an amount included in the corporate or committee budget for unavoidable expenditure which could not reasonably have been foreseen (e.g. clearing storm damage).

Debt charges: payments made from the *consolidated loan fund* or the authority's revenue account to repay the original loan and interest on borrowing for *capital* schemes.

Deferred purchase: a method of funding *capital* projects by getting another party, for instance a developer who has an interest in seeing a new bridge being completed when planned (or a year or two early), to meet the cost with the authority paying at a later, and financially more convenient, date.

Diversion: the authorized transfer of money from one project or programme to another; also known as *virement*.

Financial year: all local authorites must work on the period 1 April–31 March.

General fund: the main fund in a local authority from which payments are made to meet the *revenue* costs of providing services.

Inflation allowance: provision for price increases over a year which may be by a flat-rate figure arbitrarily applied to everything, a series of estimated percentages for different items (e.g. electricity supplies, construction materials, etc.) or links to published indices.

Leasing: property — land, buildings and major items of equipment — can be rented from the owner to avoid the full cost of purchase; local authorities can (within regulatory limits) sell assets and lease them back for further use, thus generating a *capital receipt*.

National non-domestic rate (NNDR): also known as the *uniform business rate*, this is the equivalent of the council tax for commercial premises and is pooled centrally for redistribution by the government.

Objective accounts: analysis of expenditure by purpose in which all costs of a particular service, e.g. highways, waste management, etc. are grouped together (see also *subjective accounts*).

Out-turn: the actual income and expenditure as determined when the accounts for the *financial year* are closed, thus allowing for the true final cost, including inflation, of projects and services.

Precept: the amount which a public authority raises under its local taxation powers.

Price base: all the estimates for a council's *budget* are prepared on the basis of price levels in the previous November, in order to avoid inconsistent variations due to inflation.

Recharges: provision in one committee's *budget* for costs incurred by another committee or part of the council.

Reserves: the accumulated surplus of income over expenditure, also known as *balances*.

Revenue expenditure: the day-to-day spending which does not produce a long-term physical *asset*, e.g. salaries, rents, running repairs to the highway, grass cutting, etc.

Revenue support grant (RSG): government grant paid to local authorities to support their running costs.

Standard spending assessment (SSA): the amount calculated by the government to be sufficient for a local authority to provide services at a standard level.

Subjective accounts: analysis of expenditure by type in which the same kind of spending from different services is grouped together, e.g. salaries, *debt charges*, etc. (see also *objective accounts*).

Supplementary credit approval (SCA): extra borrowing allowed by the government for specific projects.

Top slicing: money held back from existing funding provisions to finance specific schemes; can be applied by central government to local government funds, or by a council to its own budget.

Transport supplementary grant (TSG): a specific grant, distributed by the Department of Transport to highway authorities in response to bids for funds for transport infrastructure, maintenance, road safety and public transport projects; can include *supplementary credit approval*.

Uniform business rate (UBR): also known as *the national non-domestic rate*, this is the equivalent of the council tax for commercial premises and is pooled centrally for redistribution by the government.

Virement: the authorized transfer of money from one project or programme to another; also known as *diversion*.

exerts over local government spending, but also a very real, and usually insurmountable, obstacle to projects which, because of their size or priority, cannot be found a place in a budget based on the target spending level.

Although every type of local authority, including parish councils, can levy a local charge through the council tax, the collection is simplified by bringing the individual elements, or precepts, into a single bill. The local police authority also makes a precept and the Environment Agency raises a charge for its land drainage function, although neither are prominently featured on the bill. Water supply and sewerage charges are dealt with separately, by the private water companies in England and Wales and the independent public authorities in Scotland.

The unitary authority, or where the two-tier structure operates the district council, distributes the tax demand which must be in a form specified by Government regulations, although additional explanatory leaflets are usually published to explain in layman's language the spending plans and savings efforts of the local authority.

The council tax is relatively simple to administer and predictable in its yield, as it does not depend on complex variables such as the income of the authority's inhabitants or the profits of local businesses. It is difficult to avoid: property is the most fixed of assets. While it attracts nothing like the degree of unpopularity and active resistance generated by the community charge, it shares the general low level of esteem under which the old domestic rates laboured for many years. This is partly because, although it can be paid in instalments, the unfortunate taxpayer sees the full extent of his liability on a single bill delivered (to add insult to injury) in advance. It is entertaining to speculate on the results if this method were to be used for the collection of income tax, but it is essential for those managing projects and programmes to remember the basic dislike which the public harbours for local authority expenditure and for which the council tax bill is largely responsible.

Local authorities have access to other income and receipts, which come in a variety of forms to provide a second source of locally-raised funding.

Councils can charge for some of their services (council house rents, disposal of trade waste, car parking, use of leisure facilities, etc.) and are free to spend this income as they wish. For some district councils these sums are quite significant and can have a substantial effect on the budget or the level of the rate, but there are not many that enjoy such a benefit. More typical as a source of income are the capital receipts generated by the sale of property, mainly housing or developable land. Local authorities are substantial property owners and not just as landlords of council houses. Large holdings are accumulated, both as the sites of existing buildings and other facilities, or for future proposals: roads; old people's homes; schools; playing fields; waste disposal sites and so on. As existing property becomes surplus to requirements, and acquisitions are left over from completed or cancelled projects, so the land and buildings can be brought forward for disposal on the open market, often yielding very large sums. This income can be used to clear existing debts and to finance new capital projects.

Capital receipts have always been subject to the vagaries of the property market. It is never possible to forecast accurately what the income will be or when it will be received, and property deals can collapse without warning. A project that relies to any great extent on a contribution from capital receipts is bound to bear this sort of risk. In recent years added complications have arisen due to the policy of central government to limit public expenditure. In accordance with a philosophy — by no means undisputed — that all local government spending, even that financed by what is effectively the recycling of its own capital assets, requires to be controlled, restrictions have been applied to the way in which capital receipts are spent. Thus the current regulations allow 50% of receipts to be used in any one year for capital projects or purchases, with *capital* being defined in specific terms (presently, items over £5000 in value with a life greater than one year). As a consequence the timing of projects funded by capital receipts requires not only flexibility, but also some very careful programming.

A second source of finance for infrastructure is the contributions obtained from agreements with developers, designed to overcome planning or highway objections to specific applications. These developers' contributions may go beyond the bare minimum necessary to eliminate the unwanted effects of the development and include some element of improvement once known as *planning gain*, a title now largely superseded by the more positive *community benefit*. Government guidelines cover the typical circumstances and acceptable objectives of negotiations between local authorities and potential developers. Clearly, there can be no question of community benefit being sought as some kind of compulsory but unofficial tax on local development, nor can an attractive offer of contributions be used as a good reason to permit development which is contrary to planning polices. Indeed, their availability depends on the relative buoyancy of the development market over time and from place to place, and the political priority given to new development: when it is desirable, say to encourage employment, it may be welcomed without any other community benefit except the jobs themselves and infrastructure may be provided with public funds; when development is unpopular, no amount of contributions may make it acceptable.

If successfully negotiated, the contributions can be used to finance major public works projects of general benefit to the community which, while associated with the development, are not confined to the site itself nor its immediate surroundings and approaches.

Thus a new industrial estate might finance a road link that not only gives access to the site and carries the traffic it will generate, but also relieves existing congestion and unsafe rat-running in a nearby residential area, which the new development would otherwise have aggravated. Similarly, a major residential development would be expected to include public open space, community buildings and perhaps a contribution towards a primary school as well as its essential highway, drainage and sewerage infrastructure.

As developers' contributions arise out of private agreements between property companies and planning or highway authorities, they are not subject to government restrictions. Once negotiations are concluded, planning permission granted and the various appeal procedures avoided or successfully completed — and none of these obstacles is necessarily easy to surmount — developer's contributions are generally a secure source of funding provided the development goes ahead.

Government grants are provided to local authorities for three reasons: to assist local authorities in carrying out services which are in the broad national interest or duties imposed by national legislation; to even out the differences in resources between rich and poor authorities; to compensate local authorities for their varying needs. Some local government commentators might add a fourth reason: to keep local spending under central control.

Sixty years ago, government grant was less than 20% of local government income. In the 1960s and through most of the 1970s, however, the growth of local government activity and the many new functions which were placed in the hands of local authorities meant that grants of one kind or another came to represent an ever-larger proportion of total income, and by the mid-1970s they accounted for almost 65%. This was all very well in times of expansion and when central government chose to make little or no use of the great influence over local government which this role of paymaster offered. Things changed as the troubled economic climate of the late 1970s brought a more restrictive attitude, not only to the amount of grant available but also to the way in which it could be spent. By 1977/78 the Labour government had begun to scale down the size of its payments to local authorities, and after 1979 the Conservatives set out to continue and accelerate the trend. While central government's proportion remains very high, both the total amount and the specific purposes for which money is made available, are now much more tightly controlled. The primary aim of this policy has been financial, and the benefits claimed range from those of simple good housekeeping to more sophisticated counter-inflationary effects.

The Government assists — and controls — local authority spending through three main sources of funds

- revenue support grant (RSG) which is for general day-to-day service provision
- the national non-domestic rate (NNDR) — sometimes known as the uniform business rate (UBR) — which comes from the rates paid for commercial premises, pooled centrally and redistributed to councils on the basis of population
- a series of specific grants paid out for defined purposes.

The total amount of local authority funding to be provided, how it is distributed via the various sources of supply and the size of each council's share are all decisions made by the Government in a complex process which stretches across the financial year.

In May and June the local authority associations send their representatives to a series of meetings with government officials to discuss next year's spending needs. The outcome of these discussions is a submission which is presented for consideration in July, and leads to a response in the shape of an announcement of the Government's view of the national total for local authority spending. This figure is, unsurprisingly, rather less than the local authorities' submission.

Next the Government makes its assessment of what the standard level of council tax for a band D property should be, and also determines the figure it will charge as the NNDR on commercial property. The difference between what the Government calculates these two sources of funds will realize and the overall total is made up by RSG and specific grants.

The specific revenue grants are primarily directed straight into police and other law and order functions. There is some money for housing and urban programme activities but most specific aid for public works comes in capital grants which will be looked at shortly.

Having done the national sum along the lines of

$$\text{Assessment of total standard spending} = \text{Standard council tax} + \text{NNDR} + \text{specific grant} + \text{RSG}$$

the Government moves on to consider how much each authority should spend and, as a consequence, to decide how much RSG each will get.

The basis for this exercise is the concept of assessing what a local authority needs to spend to provide a standard level of service, leaving aside any expenditure covered by special grants and taking account of the social, demographic and geographical characteristics of its area. This is the standard spending assessment (SSA). The assessment is made using seven service blocks: education (the largest), social services, police, fire and civil defence, highway maintenance, capital financing, all other services. Each is determined separately on the basis of some relevant indicators (for example, highway maintenance: basis is road length, split between primary route network and other routes, with supplementary allowances where traffic and/or population per kilometre exceed given thresholds, etc.) but for individual authorities the overall total is treated as an aggregate within which councils have discretion to spend above or below particular service assessments, and often do, usually to the disadvantage of highway maintenance and capital financing.

The figures — control totals — are published after the Chancellor's Budget Statement, in November, and confirmed in February. They are not derived in a vacuum, of course, and take account of overall Government policy on public spending. If the trend is reduction, or redistribution away from local government, then this will affect the national total directly, and work through into the share which individual authorities will get. The SSA announcement is crucial as it completes the equation and determines the funding coming from central government to each council, thus

$$\text{RSG} = \text{SSA} - \text{NNDR} - \text{standard council tax}$$

In theory, an authority can spend above its total SSA, but two factors work against this. Firstly, the gearing effect described earlier makes it an expensive luxury; secondly, the capping limit set by the Government on each council's budget has tended to get closer to the SSA. There is little room for manoeuvre.

For those who have stayed the course as far as this, there is only a little more to come. The grants described are all revenue funds, to be spent on the costs of day-to-day services. The Government also makes certain capital grants available for investment in the building, improvement or refurbishment of fixed assets such as roads, schools, etc., of which transport supplementary grant

(TSG) is by far the most significant in public works terms, although there are other schemes, such as urban regeneration grants aimed at specific areas or kinds of projects.

The TSG process is typical of the operation of most capital grant schemes: specified authorities (highway authorities in this case) prepare bids in accordance with a standard procedure (the transport policy and programmes submission presented to the Department of Transport in July), and after a total sum invariably smaller than the total of the bids has been divided up centrally, councils are notified (in December) of the financial support they will receive in the following financial year and, where projects taking longer than a year to complete have been approved, beyond. The support is in the form of a partial cash grant (50% in the case of named TSG projects) with the rest coming from the authority's own resources, although permissions to borrow will be given and the capital financing block of the SSA will be adjusted to take account of the expenditure needed to repay the loan.

Indeed, borrowing provides a much larger proportion of funding for capital projects than grants and, except where capital receipts or developers' contributions are available, is the most likely source.

Councils, because of their special status as established public corporations, have favoured access to credit. The Public Works Loan Board is a government agency which provides long- and short-term loans to local authorities at interest rates generally lower than the private sector and only slightly above those at which the Government itself can borrow. Any lender will offer a council favourable terms.

That is the good news. The other side of the picture is the tight control which the Government exercises over the public sector borrowing requirement (PSBR) and the local government component of it.

Each year, after the Government announces its broad public expenditure plans, local authorities are told what their annual capital guidelines (ACGs) are going to be. This is the amount which it is considered appropriate for each authority to spend on capital projects. As part of this assessment, the Government makes an assumption that councils will pay for some of their capital spending with receipts from the sale of assets such as land. These receipts taken into account (RTIA) are counted as part of the authority's capital resources (even though, as it is an assumed figure, they may not be available in the particular year), and the rest of its needs are then covered by permissions to borrow known as basic credit approval (BCA). Thus

$$BCA = ACG - RTIA$$

An authority must use up its basic credit approvals in the year they are issued, as they cannot be carried over. However, it is possible, where the level of BCAs and the requirements of the capital programme do not fit together, to arrange swaps with other authorities. This facility can be extremely useful in smoothing out peaks and troughs in both capital project requirements and BCA availability and is a very good reason for keeping on the right side of the director of finance, without whose cooperation nothing can be done.

In addition to BCAs, extra borrowing may be permitted via supplementary credit approvals (SCAs) given in respect of particular projects, for instance named schemes in the transport policy and programme (TPP). This reflects a trend towards directing investment into particular types of project. In general, however, government policy is to restrain borrowing and every local authority is required to repay a proportion (currently at least 4%) of its outstanding debt every year.

Apart from these four main, and in one form or another long-established, sources of funding, two alternatives are emerging to take on a significant role. European funds are distributed under a number of programmes, for which authorities can submit proposals for new or improved infrastructure if they satisfy the criteria for eligibility, which typically depend on economic or geographic factors. Another range of schemes involves the application of new technology, particularly in relation to improved communications. In some cases the grants are direct, in others distribution is at a national or regional level; funding is sometimes complete but more usually involves a proportion or equal share coming from local sources; frequently, and especially with technological developments, there is a requirement for collaboration between regions or municipalities from different member states. The programmes and the areas which may be eligible are under constant review, and the procedures for submission are often complex. Operating effectively in this system requires a real investment of time and effort, which many authorities recognize through the establishment of regular contact with the European Commission.

Newer, and a much greater departure from the norms of funding by government agencies, is the introduction of private finance. The key difference from the contributions made by private developers is not in the source of the funds — typically merchant banks or other commercial lending institutions — but the reason for the investment and the direction from which the expected return comes. Developers will pay for a new road or bridge because it will help generate a profitable property transaction: access increases the value of the site, which is realized by sales or rent. An infrastructure operator will build a new river crossing or road link to provide a source of income: access itself is the product and tolls, whether collected directly or transferred indirectly (as shadow tolls) by the public authority which benefits from the new infrastructure, are the price paid by users for a quicker or more convenient transportation service.

The Government's rules aim to ensure that the risk accepted by the private investor is sufficient to take the funding outside the PSBR; the policy justification for financing public infrastructure through borrowing, which is bound to be at a higher interest rate than would be charged to national or local government, is that the management expertise and innovation that would be brought to bear will themselves add value. The concept has had relatively limited exposure so far on a small number of high profile, major projects to close gaps in the transport infrastructure. The role it will play on the broader scene of public works programmes, while still developing, is clearly important.

What happens to it . . .

The funds of a local authority, whether real money in the form of council tax payments or the more sophisticated varieties such as credit approvals, represent substantial quantities of public money and are rightly subject to complex controls to ensure their proper management and use.

The Local Government Act 1972 focuses responsibility for the financial activity of a council on the section 151 officer, commonly titled the treasurer or director of finance. His key functions are

- implementing sound financial systems and procedures
- providing authoritative advice and guidelines on financial management
- ensuring internal control over spending activities.

On the face of it, these are significant and onerous responsibilities of an administrative and regulatory nature, but very much in the background except in cases of misuse of funds or similar, infrequent departures from the norm. Once, a long time ago, this was a fair description of a job that combined bureaucracy with the duller aspects of accountancy. No more, the treasurer/director of finance is now a very influential and, therefore, very powerful figure indeed.

Two interrelated factors, at work over the last 20 years have caused this transformation. Firstly, the steady downward pressure on public spending made it essential to exercise control of funds and expenditure in order to stretch limited resources as far as possible. Secondly, and simultaneously, the increasingly complex government regulations for assessing, grant-aiding, controlling and restricting council finances put a premium on knowledge of the system and how to make the best of it. In combination, these factors have placed the public finance experts in vital roles at both the strategic level, where budget policy is set and decisions on corporate resources made, and the service delivery level, where money and projects have to be matched. The height of central government's efforts to restrain local government spending in the late 1980s gave birth to the science of creative accountancy and made its jargon the essential, albeit untranslatable, language of progress. The days of clawback and close-ending and all the other terms which one commentator called 'the verbal sludge of municipal-speak' are past, but the status of, and reliance on, financial expertise as the key to decision making remains.

It would be a cynical (and unwise) manager in any service delivery role who implies that the accountants have consciously kept public finance as an impenetrable black box. It would be inexcusable to go further and suggest that some have used this to expand a support role into one commanding influence and control which should properly rest only with politicians. Nevertheless, the lesson is clear: understanding the system and working with it, and the experts who operate it, is the most effective way to the successful promotion and management of projects. It is never quite as difficult as it sometimes appears.

The principal vehicle for setting the council's financial strategy is the budget process. Every local authority must set its budget by the beginning of March, which in practice means a meeting of the full council in February. This set piece is really the culmination of a programme begun well over six months before: starting slowly and without much sense of urgency in the summer; picking up speed through the autumn as pay awards and government announcements on overall support and specific grant take place; and ending in what is often a rather tetchy rush as last-minute political deals are made to decide which services are to be winners and which losers.

The first stage begins with a forecast based on initial indications from the Department of the Environment of its policy on local government spending: a cash freeze perhaps, or a tight limit on inflation provision, or maybe some small and specifically targetted growth. Local factors such as expected levels of income or receipts, and any significant changes in the number of households paying council tax, are included and a broad brush estimate is made of the authority's income.

The next step is to predict expenditure. Basic year-on-year commitments, and new ones resulting from decisions made in the latest budget, are factored up by an allowance for inflation; an estimate of increases due to pay awards is added; and then any special adjustments — for instance, an expected increase in the level of debt charges — made to produce an overall total. At this point, the finance officers can usually be found spreading gloomy messages of the 'if you thought last year was bad ...' variety, and forecasting the need for cuts.

This sensible and prudent caution (somewhat countered by 'We've heard it all before' reminiscences from other officers) is designed to restrain the growth of wish lists in the service-delivery committees and departments. These will have begun to grow almost straight after the previous annual budget meeting, invariable based on the maintenance of current spending programmes, plus any commitments, plus the items which failed to get budget approval last time, plus new pressures for more — or higher quality, or different — services.

As the summer goes by, so the first stages of assessing these expenditure requirements and ranking them in some kind of priority order are carried out. We will look at this in more detail in chapter 7, so suffice to say now that the downward pressure exerted by the treasurer's grim warnings will have produced a rough idea of what are the real unavoidable spending commitments in the coming year, and what are the optional extras. The latter will begin to attract political support to varying degrees.

As autumn turns into the festive season, so government announcements on the general level of support grant and specific grants such as TSG (usually distributed during Parliament's Christmas recess) give the finance officers firmer data for their calculations. Major items such as the local government pay awards are also known by now, and so the estimates of income and expenditure become progressively more accurate. So, too, do the forecasts of political priorities: the sacrifices which would be acceptable if necessary, the promises which must be fulfilled if possible ...

This is the point when the treasurer often begins to revise some of the earlier warnings and reveals some previously undiscovered sources of funds, or unexpected loopholes in the regulations, which by skilful financial management can be utilized to help the council achieve, if not everything it wants, then at least some of its key objectives. The cynic who occasionally appears in these pages would probably find the timely extraction of this rabbit from a hat so conclusively and recently demonstrated to be empty as an example of stage management, rather than financial management. Nevertheless, the process will have served its purpose of keeping professional, financial and political objectives under some sort of control.

The final shape of the budget will now begin to emerge as service committees put their draft proposals together in January, working to guidelines issued formally by the policy/strategy and resources committee, and informally, and perhaps more importantly, by the council's political leadership.

Now the crucial financial decisions are made: the level of balances and reserves which will be retained, and the contribution which they can make to supplement income from council tax and government funding; the use of revenue to fund capital projects or the capitalization of revenue expenditure so that it is met from capital resources; the availability of capital receipts; the identification of unspecified efficiency savings to offset increased running costs such as pay awards. The use to which such devices are put will reflect the priorities given to the discretionary spending areas. Those which do not achieve sufficient political support will, at best, be put on a reserve list to await possible unforeseen receipts, or the diversion of funds from programmes which fail to meet their expected timetable, or cost less than the estimated budget provision. More likely, they will be struck out of the draft budget, to be carefully explained as postponements, or loudly denounced as cancellations, depending on the political slant.

The last act in this drama is the formal budget meeting of the full council, which by law must vote through the authority's spending plans by 10 March at the latest. This can be a piece of municipal theatre, with last-minute deals, amendments, close votes, emotional speeches and finance officers checking the running totals and computing the band D council tax level as the debate unfolds.

Table 3. Summary revenue expenditure 1995–96

	1994–95 £000	1995–96 £000
Spending controlled by services		
Community services	13 770	13 053
Corporate support	10 691	6 303
Education	267 771	261 231
Environment	37 228	38 107
Public protection	21 088	21 536
Social services	83 049	93 404
	433 597	433 634
Spending not allocated to services		
Capital financing costs	26 888	27 256
Interest on balances	−3 726	−4 594
Total spending (excluding precepts)	456 759	456 296
Provisions and financing items		
Provision for future inflation etc.	−167	1 403
Contribution from balances	−4 418	−5 933
Funding from special reserve (revenue)	−6 700	−8 000
Funding from special reserve (capital)	−5 700	−1 600
Total budget within the council's control	439 774	442 166
Precepts on the county council		
Police authority	36 664	N/A
National Rivers Authority	1 100	2 256
Total county council budget	477 538	444 422

Table 4. Environment committee: budget summary 1995–96

	1994–95 £000	1995–96 £000	Change £000	Change %
Road safety	1 063	927	−136	−13
Highways maintenance programme	564	524	−40	−7
Highways maintenance services				
centrally managed	13 234	13 709	475	3
managed by districts	3 643	3 961	318	9
Electrical engineering	2 715	2 725	10	—
Bridge maintenance	534	555	21	4
Project and highways management	729	795	66	9
Traffic management	1 687	1 759	72	4
Transportation planning	536	526	−10	−2
Public transport	1 479	1 421	−58	−4
Environment	1 120	1 142	22	2
Waste regulation	1 094	879	−215	−20
Waste disposal	5 253	5 487	234	4
Development control	530	548	18	3
Strategic planning	982	835	−147	−15
Client side costs	1 950	2 197	247	13
Property management	115	117	2	2
Revenue budget	37 228	38 107	879	2
Core capital programme	3 054	1 345	−1709	−56
Total budget	40 282	39 452	−830	−2

The council will know the Government's proposals for the capping criteria — provisionally issued in the autumn — and will almost certainly be aiming to avoid having its expenditure reduced by central regulation. (The final criteria cannot be set until all councils' budgets have been notified to the Department of the Environment, so, in theory at least, it could be some months before capped authorities know for sure what they must do to bring their budgets into line.) Once the council tax figure is decided, it becomes the precept for that authority and feeds into the billing process.

The budget itself will be published, looking something like Table 3 overall, and Table 4 as a summary of the environment committee's section.

The spending figures are compared with the previous financial year's, on a common price base, so that the ups and downs can be clarified (the example has been a rather tough budget). Capital and revenue expenditure is separated, and the resource effects (mainly repayment of loans) of capital spending are identified, together with any permissible exchanges between revenue and capital items. These distinctions are important as capital spending usually involves borrowing over a 40 year period, with significant implications for the authority's level of debt and its commitment to loan repayments well into the future.

The overall figures for both types of expenditure are settled in the budget, but there will often be detailed adjustments to programmes and projects within these fixed expenditure headings which are left for service committees to decide, at their next meetings.

For instance, the environment committee may not have endorsed its programme of new footway and cycleway schemes until it was aware of the extent to which this work would suffer or benefit from the final horse trading in the council's budget meeting. Similarly, its proposals for school safety projects may have been kept private, so as not to raise expectations, until it was clear that there would be any money at all for this new initiative. Thus, this environment committee's budget will be the subject of further consideration and decision making within limits of discretion laid down by the council, which may be very tight (e.g. choice of individual projects within only one or two specific programmes, but keeping the distribution of funds unchanged) or relatively loose (e.g. staying within the overall committee total, but freedom to divert between any and all programmes).

As well as budget headings relating to service delivery, there are some major blocks which are not service-specific. One may be a contingency fund, set aside for unforeseen expenses and emergencies, and usually kept under the control of the strategy and resources committee. Councils are not obliged to have such a fund and many do not, working on the principle that unexpected expenditure will have to come from diversions within the service budgets.

The item likely to raise most comment (among service departments anyway) is the central recharges. These are the running costs of the corporate, centralized units — legal, financial, committee secretariat, etc — which are charged to the service budgets as a kind of overhead. The spread of service level agreements, specifying what standard of delivery is expected from central support, and the application of stricter rules governing the trading accounts of units operating under competition regulations have exposed the recharges to critical scrutiny. Like any head office overhead they will always be seen as overpriced and overprotected, a view all too often reinforced by what appears to be relatively gentle treatment when budgets are being cut.

Where it all goes . . .

Setting the budget is the key step in the spending process. It provides the basic authority from the council for its committees, sections and officers to take the subsequent actions of committing money and passing sums for payment. There may be delegation and discretion as set out in standing orders and defined in the powers of specific officers, but they can only operate in respect of funds identified in the budget.

Apart from the direct running costs of the in-house departments — chiefly payroll, accommodation, subsistence and travelling, office sundries and the inevitable central recharges — the majority of expenditure on public works programmes and projects goes on payments made under contracts for construction, maintenance and the supply of goods and services (this last item including consultants' fees). The process for tendering and awarding contracts is covered in chapter 11, so it is sufficient for our present purposes to note that a combination of the council's standing orders, its detailed procedures for contracts and, where appropriate, the European regulations on procurement will provide a rigid framework within which valid commitments to spend can be made.

The other component is measurement and certification. For the major, recurring direct costs such as payroll and rent and rates on premises, the use of central databases normally held in the finance department allow payments to go through as a matter of routine. Payment is supported by control systems such as timesheets and adjustments are by exception reporting as, for instance, when overtime is authorized or an individual is promoted to a higher salary. A long-term contract for services, such as providing an emergency call-out arrangement for traffic signal faults, or a professional consultancy team to manage all bridge inspection and repairs, could be dealt with on a similar basis.

Construction and maintenance works require more hands on supervision and control of expenditure. There are many practical texts on the management of contracts and sites, and any attempt at a summary would not do justice to this wide and quite distinct subject. Nevertheless, the fundamental requirement of effective financial management can be simply stated: good record-keeping. With a clear and complete set of contract documents to start off with (not a situation which should be taken for granted), the records of progress, materials, working conditions, instructions and approvals will allow the specified items, or properly authorized variations, to be measured and paid for. Thus, a system of supervision aimed at ensuring the safe production of the works, to the contract standard and with a full set of contemporary records will satisfy all the requirements for proper control over public money.

This is, of course, much easier said (or written) than done: not all contract documents are as comprehensive as they should be; not every potential risk is adequately covered and allocated; and complete agreement may not be reached on each variation during the life of the project. These practical problems, real as they are for a construction contract, can become particularly difficult when the product is the delivery of professional services. All the more reason for spending time and effort on the preparation of briefs, specifications, bills of quantities and legal agreements, and being absolutely clear on what is to be the acceptable standard of quality. The recording system which concentrates on quantitative measures — typically deadlines and response times and perhaps adherence to the more mechanical elements of codes of good practice and similar sources — may give inadequate weight to the qualitative aspects which are written into the specification and on which ultimate acceptance of the study, plan or design will depend.

Take the case of a pedestrian footbridge. In simple terms, the strength and finished appearance of the component materials, and their line and level as erected, would be the basis for certifying payment to the contractor for the completed bridge. However, the consultant commissioned to prepare the design might meet all the requirements for delivering a complete set of drawings and calculations, on time and with all the appropriate check certificates and quality assurance (QA) procedures, but if its appearance was so insensitive to the surroundings as to fail to get planning consent, then payment of the full fee would not be certified by the client.

———————

This simplistic example is intended to convey the message that records, measurements and certification must focus on the relevant outputs, and must be tailored to suit the specific product or outcome which is to be supplied and paid for.

The process of payment will follow the council's standard financial procedures, with certified invoices being passed to the finance department or perhaps a devolved accounting function in the service department itself. Management accounts operating on a monthly basis will record expenditure under each approved budget, keeping finance officers and project managers informed through detailed breakdowns and cumulative totals. Increasingly, the monthly cycle of financial reporting involves more data such as a spending profile and forecasts of percentage completion and future payments, all designed to tighten control and sharpen accountability. Likely overspends or savings, and the possibility of slippage in a scheme's progress affecting the pattern of payments, are the objects of this exercise, and the tendency nowadays to adopt a detailed, rather than generalized, approach to budgets makes it a complex undertaking. The resources which need to be devoted to the process, and the strictness of its timetables, should not be underestimated.

Reporting will follow a standard format governed by the procedures in use across the authority. These tend to be similar, partly as a result of professional guidelines and partly due to the widespread introduction of computerized management accounts. A typical report, owing a lot to the layout of the computer screens generally in use in public authorities, is shown in Fig. 2.

The purpose of regular reporting should not be just to keep records of expenditure in today's local government environment, which would be close to fiddling while Rome burns. The benefit lies in obtaining management information, and using it to make decisions on the progress of projects within a particular financial regime; invariably, these days, a tightly constrained one. Overspending has to be identified so that it can be stopped or — if unavoidable — assessed and controlled within strict limits. Similarly, any underspending needs to be evaluated at an early stage, and its causes pinpointed just as rigorously as for overspending. If there are genuine savings, and the project is going to be delivered as planned for less cost, then the money may be released to fund inescapable additional expenditure elsewhere; if, however, the shortfall is because of a late start or slow progress — what is euphemistically described as slippage — then there is no overall saving as the costs will have to be met later, although perhaps not in the same financial year. The objective is to match total available funding against the requirements of all the projects in the programme: this may mean managing the progress, content or even the start of schemes to get as much as possible done within the financial limits authorized by the council.

The end of the municipal financial year is particularly important in this regard as it can have a significant effect on the availability of funds. As far as financial regulations are concerned, the year-end brings an important distinction to the fore

GACC

***** MONTHLY EXPENDITURE ACCOUNT *****

Account No. K271B	Description Routine Highway Maintenance		Status A

Month	Last year	Current year	Budget profile	Variance
01	20,299	59,669	80,000	-20,331
02	180,549	151,180	200,000	-48,820
03	419,073	521,778	400,000	+121,778
04	739,618	412,975	600,000	-187,025
05	491,525	765,230	600,000	+165,230
06	354,298	0	500,000	-
07	418,180	0	500,000	-
08	545,745	0	500,000	-
09	366,842	0	300,000	-
10	329,699	0	300,000	-
11	280,024	0	300,000	-
12	672,032	0	500,000	-
13	326,536	(0)	(200,000)	(-)
Total	5,144,420	1,910,832	4,980,000	+30,832

This screen is a specifically designed layout providing one of a series of standard financial information records. Its particular reference—GACC—allows authorized managers to call up a particular set of data about account number K271B: the actual expenditure on routine highway maintenance, compared with the profile of spending predicted at the beginning of the financial year and the historical record of the previous year. The status of the screen is A, which means it is active and automatically brought up to date each month with the inclusion of every item charged to the particular account.

All spending is to a common price base (conventionally the November of the previous year) and the months run through the municipal year, so month 1 is April. Month 13 is the facility for carrying over any under or over-spends into the next financial year. The profile is input by the project manager; in default of any specific distribution the system will assume a uniform spread (i.e. one twelfth in every month and nothing carried over).

The variance column provides a check on the difference between the profile and the actual spend. Last year's figures help in explaining the variations, pointing towards corrective action should any be needed, and getting the profiling more accurate next time.

Running totals are provided in the current year and variance columns. At present the project manager is looking at a well-controlled budget; the overspend is relatively small and well within the carry over allowance, so the programme might be completed within budget at month 12, alternatively, this may be the start of an overspending trend.

Routine highway maintenance covers all the general housekeeping activities: pothole repairs, grass cutting, repair and renewal of signs and white lines, accidental damage to street furniture, etc., and the uncertainty of winter salting, gritting and snow clearance.

Fig. 2. Computer screen showing a typical management account.

- revenue funds not spent *can* generally be carried forward into the following year, although usually subject to some upper limit such as 1% of a committee's overall revenue budget
- capital funds not firmly committed *cannot* normally be carried over.

This gives special prominence to the close down procedure which begins in March and runs through into May. This is where revenue spending carry-overs are formally notified for identification in the council's accounts. The process also picks up revenue commitments made but not yet paid (perhaps because the supplier has been slow submitting a final invoice), and money due to the authority but not yet received (delayed payments for services provided by the council, perhaps, or outstanding insurance claims for repairs to damaged property); but its prime purpose is to reserve funds where the out-turn has not reached the authorized budget. Traditionally, as long as the financial records clearly confirmed an underspend, whether slippage or savings, the money was carried forward to complete the programme or pay for extra works. This is no longer necessarily the case, and hard-pressed councils may divert the money into other spending areas, or balances. The risk of losing funds which are authorized but unspent encourages tighter control throughout the year so that potential underspendings are picked up well before close down. Justified cases can then be advanced for reallocation with the programme area, i.e. to highway maintenance projects which just failed to make the priority list when the original budget was approved, or diversion to associated services, e.g. from traffic management schemes to road safety publicity. These are legitimate and professional responses, much to be preferred to a last-minute scramble to spend the full allocation on trivial items or unimportant projects: in such circumstances, the right response is to declare the spare funds, and let the council determine the best overall use for them.

Capital schemes, with their long-term consequences in loan repayments and their frequent linkage with government grants, are subject to a more rigid regime. The end of the financial year on 31 March is a very sharp cut-off and nothing will be carried forward. Thus, if the requirement is to ensure that allocated funds are fully spent, there will need to be a major effort to certify payment for works carried out, including materials delivered but not yet incorporated in the works, and to clear other expenditure such as payments to utility companies and land acquisition.

Therefore, this will also require monitoring through the year so that any delays and their consequences can be discovered as early as possible and appropriate corrective action taken. Certification for March must be set up carefully, particularly where it relates to the valuation of partly completed work and unused materials: the temptation to certify generously must be resisted, as it may lead to disputes later if the work turns out to be unsatisfactory or the materials are unacceptable.

Alternatively, when a capital scheme is heading for a possible overspend, the monitoring process should be used to control and minimize additional costs in the project and, on a wider front, pick out possible savings elsewhere to offset them. There should be no attempt to delay or depress payments in the last month of one financial year to slip an overspend into the next in the hope that something will turn up. These and other tricks to blur the precise line drawn across the end-of-year accounts are no substitute for effective project management, nor will they survive the scrutiny of the auditor.

Audit is the process of independent examination to which, almost without exception, every company, organization and public body must submit its financial affairs. Where public money is concerned, this process is more extensive and continuous and will go far beyond the minimum requirement of examining the accounts to see if they can be certified as a true and fair record, into the realms of value for money reviews with associated policy recommendations as typified by the high profile national reports of the Audit Commission. At a local level these activities are carried out by a combination of internal audit (which may be internal to the local authority, but will be conducted by staff from the finance department and so is external to the service department itself) and external auditors (either the district audit service, an offshoot of the Audit Commission, or an approved accountancy practice).

The job of the auditor has been described as 'coming on to the battlefield after the fighting is over to bayonet the wounded'. This rather unkind comparison stems from the basic task of checking the accuracy and completeness of financial transactions, which frequently leads to the discovery of mistakes and gaps. That the check is carried out calmly in a warm office, while the errors it exposes may have been made under pressure on a wet and windy site, does not help. Nevertheless, the process is not only essential, but also a very useful discipline that encourages the establishment of clear procedures — audit trails — which track the financial history of each project and are designed to build in public accountability and value for money at every key step.

A good audit performance, particularly on the wider issues of value for money as well as the details of management accounting, does more than save time and trouble, it reinforces the credibility which is vital to securing support for new or continuing projects in a climate of tight financial controls.

5. Aims and objectives

Government, local and national, is about achieving aims and objectives set in a political context. It is not necessarily about change: the aim may be to maintain or preserve a position; nor about making decisions: the objective can be to avoid or delay action. Delivery of services, while an essential component of this machinery, is part of the means and not the end in itself.

The essence of effective government is in its policies, i.e. what it is setting out to achieve. The implication is that action will be proactive rather than reactive. Indeed, a policy of reacting to events could be described as no policy at all. To achieve the aim of the policy, some form of strategic plan is needed to set the objectives which will define progress, or the ultimate success of the policy. The services that will deliver the policy aim, or which represent the success of the policy need to be defined too, if they are to be consistent with it.

These three elements — policy, strategic plans and definition of services — can be illustrated in an example from transport planning. Here, the policy may be to reduce the environmentally damaging effects (air pollution, noise, visual intrusion, accidents) of private car use in an urban area to benefit its residents; the strategic plan could identify the establishment of park and ride facilities on key routes, increased passenger loads on commuter bus services, reduction in car trips with corresponding falls in key measures such as personal injury accidents; the service delivery components would include details on, for instance, increased frequency of services on key routes, traffic management deterrent measures to cut down rat running and speeds, bus lanes, etc.

Set out like that, the whole thing can appear very neat, simple and no more than common sense. Getting there tends to be a bit more complicated.

Policy
Some policies are always necessary: for instance, minimizing road casualties or reducing river pollution can both be taken as givens, regardless of political background. However, these tend to be of the *motherhood* variety which, while no-one would disagree with them, tend to generate little political excitement or

motivation (this does not mean, of course, that they can be planned or defined easily, nor that their detailed implementation is uncontroversial). Other policies, for example the restriction of car access to a town centre, may well generate keen support and also active opposition. Developing such a policy, let alone setting it down as a plan and then working out the definition of how it is to be delivered, not only requires a careful combination of political drive and professional support but it also needs some identifiable purpose.

The essential first step is to understand the current problems and/or future advantages which generate the policy. Obvious problems might be

- congestion for commuter traffic
- accidents to pedestrians
- pollution from noise and fumes.

Potential advantages could be

- road safety
- more attractive environment for town centre residents and visitors
- resistance to unwanted edge-of-town development.

Disadvantages will be perceived by many, for instance

- difficult or expensive access to town centre shops and services
- reduced trade
- environmental impact of edge-of-town car parking facilities.

Some of these issues stand alone, some are complementary and a few are mutually exclusive. The task of politicians and professionals is to make a 'saleable' and workable policy that maximizes the benefits and, if possible, eliminates or mitigates the disadvantages. If that is not achievable, then the policy must be developed to show the balance of advantage falling clearly in its favour, so that its difficulties are seen as an acceptable price for the positive results which it will deliver.

Owning the problem, or focusing the demand, is critical. If most people believe congestion and pollution around the town centre are inevitable, or that the benefits of attractive, lively city streets are unimportant, then the policy is going to generate no enthusiasm and little support. Objections, or apathy, will predominate.

Technical data (delays due to congestion, accident statistics, levels of pollutants, etc.) play an important part in this process, but will only work effectively if presented in a relevant and persuasive way. So the congestion information might best be expressed as the time lost by the employees of local businesses; the accident data categorized to identify pedestrian injuries; and the pollution levels illustrated by comparison with standards set by health organizations.

However, persuasion should not become propaganda and professional advice in policy making must be just that, professional. The technical data cannot be bent or massaged, and the counter arguments cannot be ignored or suppressed.

Thus, if the most effective way of restraining private car trips into the town centre is to cut back dramatically the availability of on-street parking spaces, then this must be stated and the consequences — lost revenue from parking meters, perhaps, or the loss of potential 'passing trade' for some businesses — reported. Similarly the alternative policy options such as park and ride should not be described exclusively or simplistically in ·wholly positive terms without mentioning the possible disadvantages of, for instance, long term subsidies or the environmental impact of the parking area.

Professionals will, of course, speak their minds more freely in confidence. Policy formulation is, therefore, a particular example of the office–member process which will be considered in some detail towards the end of this book. It is usually — and definitely most effectively — carried out in private meetings where debate, discussion and sometimes what is politely called 'a full and frank exchange of views' can go on free from the constraints and inhibitions that inevitably accompany the public proceedings of a political body. Closed meetings are perfectly proper provided the participants do not make those decisions — and that amounts to most of them — that legally have to be taken in public. Right up to the point of decision, therefore, formal policy consideration can be undertaken in closed session, as long as the meetings are authorized by the council and have a membership which reflects the political balance of the parties.

Provided these safeguards are observed, the process can be conducted in reasonable privacy to allow the pros and cons of the policy to be explored thoroughly. Naturally, the ruling group will control and direct this exercise politically, and to do this effectively it will want its own separate briefings at the outset and at any other appropriate stages as the process develops. This is quite legitimate, as the same facility is available to the other political groups. Once again, the aim is to ensure that the professional options, with arguments for and against, are put clearly to the politicians so that the consequences of pursuing a policy or (indeed, of ending or opposing one) are explained.

The process may seem long-winded and over-complex, but the point to remember is that an effective policy must set the framework for many detailed decisions (or provide the loopholes for special cases) over a long period. It has to be thought through: at least, that's the theory.

The development of a policy — unless it is of the pure conviction politics variety — cannot be done without taking account of how it would be done, what it would cost and the results expected from it. So policy making does involve studying — although in outline form only — the effect on strategic plans and the service definitions that different options and approaches might produce. By

59

looking ahead in this way the options can be narrowed down and the chosen policy framed for public exposure.

Thus, the initial policy aim of restricting car access to the town centre would be discussed in terms of its political and practical advantages: generally 'green'; favouring public transport; positive support for an attractive town centre; specific benefits to residents of inner suburbs affected by congestion and rat running, etc. In each case, these advantages will need cross checking with existing strategic plans — for instance, the council's environmental audit, the TPP, the structure plan and local plans, etc. — to ensure that there is consistency and, if not, that the required changes are made or gaps plugged as soon as practicable. Taking things a step further, the service implications — changes in the regime for town centre car park operations; a new pattern of public transport routes and capacities; major traffic management initiatives — will require assessment to provide a broad evaluation of the short and long-term impact of the policy on budgets as well as current services.

Similarly, the perceived disadvantages of the policy — environmental impact of big car parks; extended commuter journeys; unattractive buses — need to be reconciled with strategic plans and assessed in service terms. Thus, the conflict between large urban-fringe development in the shape of car parks and a structure plan dedicated to protecting green spaces around towns has to be faced and justified through the special widespread benefits that will accrue to the town as a whole, and the specific measures to be taken in the design and operation of the car parks to minimize their local effects.

Strategic plans

The process of checking new or changed policies against current strategic plans demonstrates an important aspect of the process of government: in today's complex world, policies can rarely work in isolation and are more likely to be effective and accepted when grouped and coordinated in some kind of recognizable plan.

Strategic planning has been well established in the public sector, and particularly in local government where the 'best practice' authorities have been operating it in a number of forms for 20 years. There are two main influences responsible for this. The first is in the nature of local government which places a legal obligation on each council to set and put on public record a budget that covers all its services; and so is forced, at least once in the year, to reconcile its competing priorities within its available means. The second is inherent in the services and projects in which local government is involved: some can be switched on and off with relative ease, such as car parking charges or book purchases for the public libraries; others like rising school intakes, for instance, or waste disposal volumes, have to be accommodated without discretion over long periods; many have long lead-times, particularly infrastructure projects;

and for a few the consequences of changes in resources or policy will take some time to work through, whether for good or ill (highway and building maintenance are classic examples, so is economic development). Making some sense of all this requires a strategic plan that takes account of current circumstances and longer-term trends and commitments, thus giving a framework for making promises and implementing change.

The preparation of such a plan revolves around a combination of tasks, resources and results that are intended to deliver the policy aim within realistic constraints of time, money and sheer practicality. So strategic planning for services means assessing priorities.

- What has to be done as part of the council's legal obligations? (For instance, the level of maintenance necessary for safe passage; the basic funding for the national curriculum)
- What has to be done because of contract commitments? (Works projects already underway, long-term contracts for services such as street light repairs and refuse collection.)
- What is being done because of firm political commitments? (Nursery education, for instance, or bus passes for pensioners)
- What are the new political promises which must be delivered? (Traffic calming outside schools, perhaps, or a new day-care centre for the elderly)
- Then, for each particular service area, what are the tasks or projects which are professionally and/or politically desirable, but are discretionary and capable of reduction, postponement or cancellation without major consequence? (This is the question most likely to be answered with silence, because it involves the 'nice to do' projects of professionals — building conservation, state-of-the-art traffic control, etc. — and the investments in local popularity of politicians, e.g. a resident's parking scheme or a refurbished children's playground.)

It is the last category that is the most difficult to identify, as there will always be a reluctance to offer candidates for what may be the axe. After all, if they are cut *someone* will miss them, though it may only be the people involved in their delivery.

Except in times of continuous growth, strategic planning has to be based on change by substitution, not expansion. Engineers, of all professionals, should be able to undertake the clear cost-benefit analyses that underpin the hard part of strategic planning. Assessing the residual life of carriageways allows costs and consequences to be put against different maintenance strategies; accident records can pinpoint the most effective areas for accident prevention. Regrettably, partly because rigorous assessment procedures may be less applicable and partly because of the more direct personal and emotive impact of decisions, other services find strategic planning, or the substitution part of it, more difficult. This tends to make the slippage of major projects or the reduction of major programmes, such as highway maintenance, soft targets.

To some extent this is because engineers are inclined to take strategic planning at its face value, putting little thought into presentation and preferring to 'let the figures speak for themselves'. They have to be very telling to do that, and no strategy can be expressed solely in quantitative terms, any more than an effective plan can exist without any measurement to judge its progress and success.

So the congestion-reduction policy which has been our example would appear in a strategic plan as a series of proposals

- park and ride projects on key commuter routes, phased over a number of years to allow for the time needed to organize and implement the land acquisition, construction and commissioning and to spread out the cost
- projected targets for the new bus services in terms of passengers attracted from private cars
- target savings in pollution, environmental impact and accidents
- linked proposals for improving the town centre environment: pedestrianization schemes, for instance, or landscaping
- coordinated and phased changes to parking policy and capacity to minimize on-street parking and encourage long-term stays to go into park and ride rather than town centre car parks
- traffic management measures to give buses priority and avoid rat running on parallel routes.

Comprehensively expressed as an interrelated set of proposals with targets and timetable, the policy can be given a clear status and priority both in terms of funding and as a political commitment. As the strategy is taken forward (and a major policy may take some years to implement) it is better placed to withstand the inevitable budget pressures, local controversy and opposition when it is based on an approved plan and agreed long-term benefits.

The build up of a strategic plan for a service has to be coordinated with the wider range of plans in which a local authority is concerned. The transport policy and programme, prepared each year for the Department of Transport by every highway authority as both a forward plan and a bid for grant, is an obvious cross-reference. The structure plan, unitary development plan and local plan will all have transportation elements, which should fit with the strategy to ensure that decisions on development take it fully into account. This is not just for consistency in presentation, but for the very practical reason that today's plan-led system means that applications (and major items of infrastructure such as a park and ride facility will need planning permission) that do not conform with the broad policies and detailed allocations set out in these statutory plans are very unlikely to succeed.

Defining services

Policy preparation and strategic planning are essential tasks, but to the public (and, although with less justification, to the engineer also) they appear as just words and paper — they do not do anything.

The doing part (which engineers always consider the real work, although in reality it all depends on effective policy and planning work) is found in the definition of services. Individual projects, large and small, and long-term programmes, subdivided into constituent parts or continuous operations, are the components of these definitions. They form not just the action plan which politicians use to demonstrate the delivery of their policies and which professionals use to organize their resources; increasingly, they are becoming a key part of the indicators employed to assess the cost-effectiveness and performance of service providers (whether in-house departments or external consultants). This trend, and a growing demand from the public for full information about how local services are delivered, has made definition essential and details of cost, timetable and outcome ever more important ingredients.

Thus, where the highway maintenance service may once have been swept up in a single line in an authority's annual budget, it is now broken down into distinct sections complete with programmes of work (for the larger scale reconstruction work, or surface dressing); frequencies of delivery (for grass cutting, for instance, and road sweeping); and response times (pothole repairs, defective street lights, etc.). Similarly, road safety will be covered by specified projects at specific sites, planned campaigns and publicity events, and a set of approved criteria to assist in responding to the inevitably long list of requests for action, petitions and unforeseeable problems which will build up in any year.

As for the congestion-reduction policy, the components which have been given such prominence in the strategic plan will now be defined and specified in concrete terms (no pun intended). The park and ride projects are set out with a timetabled programme from initial public consultation on site options though the necessary statutory procedures to land acquisition and construction, with a matching expenditure profile. The traffic management schemes on the commuter routes and in the corridors alongside are similarly detailed, specifying where bus priority measures will go and which sensitive areas will benefit from traffic calming or other protective treatment. The introduction of environmental improvements in the central area, critically timed to interlock with the reduction of on-street parking and a new pricing structure for off-street car parks, represents the part of the action plan where the political stakes are the highest and the policy will come under the greatest pressure. These activities would be carefully scheduled with time built in for consultation, publicity, trial periods and other means of providing room for manoeuvre.

Service definitions are likely to be developed in the form of briefs as shown in Fig. 3, particularly for projects which will be handled by a consultant, whether in-house or external.

This level of clarity and firmness in definition is not only applicable to projects: it can be — and is — adopted for programmes of routine work such as local highway maintenance, and even the reactive services provided in the politically-sensitive areas of traffic management and road safety. In these cases,

ELMWOOD AREA CONTROLLED PARKING ZONE

Background
Following a petition from residents in the area around Elmwood Station concerning difficulties relating to parking, the transport committee instructed the director of technical services to investigate the problem and possible solutions. One possible solution is to introduce controlled parking which is the subject of this brief.

Objective
The objective of the study is in two parts. Firstly, to identify the extent of parking generated from residents and other sources. Secondly, to design a controlled parking zone (CPZ) for the area to restrict commuter parking associated with the station. The CPZ should be designed to avoid producing an unacceptable shift of the parking problems to adjacent areas.

The study area
The study area is shown on the attached plan but if the consultant considers that this area should be amended as a result of his work this will be drawn to the client's attention.

Considerations
St George's Hospital, which is located in the area, is known to produce extensive on-street parking although in recent years the amount of on-site parking has been increased. The main car park for the hospital is accessed from Victoria Road. Elmwood High Street and Forest Road represent a significant local shopping area and there are two public car parks, one in Church Road and the other in Orchard Street.

Requirements
The location and capacity of legal on-street parking is required to be identified together with the amount of parking associated with residents. The extent of existing problems are to be clearly identified together with an estimate of the extent of parking associated with the station by commuters and other sources. All surveys are to be carried out in accordance with the council's standard specification for traffic counts and surveys. All the streets are to be continuously surveyed between 08.30 hours and 18.30 hours on a weekday and a Saturday. The survey must gather data on parking durations, occupancy and turnover. The consultant shall supply all drawings necessary for the surveys and design of the CPZ.

Three copies of the draft report with appropriate drawings of the study shall be submitted to the client within 25 working days of the instruction to proceed. When approved by the client a further three copies of the final report shall be submitted within 10 working days of approval. The report shall include the results of all surveys and details of the CPZ design with all the implications outlined in detail.

Fee regime
The consultant is to indicate fees for the following :

● a fixed fee for the survey work to be undertaken, together with details of the resources to be used for the surveys
● the number of man hours and rates for each of the staff to be employed on the design of the CPZ.

Fig. 3. Part of a typical well-designed brief.

the development of the brief must reflect the local requirements and levels of service and so will concentrate more on the quantity and quality of the resources needed to sustain an acceptable and continuous standard, rather than a definition of a specific task and its final output.

Indeed, the service charters or customer guarantees now offered for most routine, locally-delivered services are themselves definitions set out from the point of view of the recipient rather than the provider, and in straightforward layman's terms

We guarantee to make all dangerous potholes safe within 12 hours of a report.

We will repair faulty street lights in no more than three working days.

Every new pedestrian crossing will include facilities to help blind and visually-impaired people.

In many ways, these are the best definitions, free from professional jargon and bureaucratic fudge, such as the following

Highway lighting outtage will be minimized by, wherever practicable, identifying faults and instructing the term maintenance contractor in sufficient time to permit a repair or other appropriate treatment to be effected within three working days, etc.

They concentrate on outcomes rather than process. That is not to say, they are trouble-free, as anyone who has tried to explain the difference between a dangerous pothole and the other kind (safe?) to a local resident can testify. The importance of building customer care into service definitions and then monitoring its delivery will — in this book and in the real world — remain a continuing theme.

6. Standards

Consultants and in-house organizations alike often bemoan the ill-effects of price-based competition, quoting in aid the great philosopher of 19th century art and architecture, John Ruskin. Although he may never have said that

> There is hardly anything in the world that some man cannot make a little worse and sell a little cheaper, and the people who consider price only are this man's lawful prey

the sentiments fill well his documented lack of enthusiasm for competition

> Nothing is ever done beautifully which is done in rivalry
>
> *Ethics of the Dust*

and generally dismissive view of the price-mechanism

> The distinguishing sign of slavery is to have a price, and be bought for it
>
> *Crown of Wild Olive*

and, of course, he and his modern advocates are right, up to a point.

A potential flaw in Ruskin's argument is that without the spur of price there is a probability — in the days when everyone charged Association of Consulting Engineers' scale fees it was often a reality — that clients find themselves paying for a level of quality they may not want or might not get. In other words, uncoupling price completely from quality — effectively saying 'money no object', may have been acceptable for Ruskin's audience of rich Victorian patrons of the arts and crafts movement, commissioning the design, building and furnishing of their houses, but it is inapplicable to public services and works. The public cannot exercise personal choice about the quality and cost of collective services: where one person might be willing to pay a high price for top quality, others may be content with a minimum standard; a service valued highly by some may be seen as unnecessary by others. Making the money go as far as possible to satisfy as many demands as possible has been a long-established principle in public sector procurement and has strengthened the practice of lowest price wins.

This does not mean that Ruskin's advice is ignored. It does mean that a careful balance must be struck between what standard of service provision or finished product is required and what money can be found or afforded to pay for it, thus ensuring that a quality framework is set within which price competition can take place. This approach allows value for money to be assessed and monitored in total, and not just as an over-simplified 'how much does it cost?' question.

Fitness for purpose

One apparently easy standard to adopt, which would have appealed to Ruskin and his contemporaries, would be *fitness for purpose*, i.e. simply asking that the product be capable of doing the job required of it, no more and no less. This approach can be made to work for an electric kettle, say, or a dry cleaning service where the use is clear cut and the user well defined. For professional services such as those supplied to the public sector neither is the case, and fitness for purpose has very serious implications.

To understand why the phrase is enough to make the blood of most private consultants, with their real commercial concerns about liability and professional indemnity, run cold, let us take an extreme but realistic example. When a brain surgeon sets out to operate on a patient, the purpose of the procedure is to counteract the effects of disease or injury; the surgeon would certainly accept that he must exercise *reasonable skill and care* in his delicate work and apply himself with *due diligence* to the task, but he would not expect the operations to be judged on a *fitness for purpose* basis as this means every patient, however desperately ill, would be expected to achieve a full recovery. The extent of the obligations attached to the legal meaning of the phrase is very considerable.

The design of a retaining wall should obviously be competent enough for it not to fall down in normal use and, on that basis, most engineers would be tempted to offer a fitness for purpose warranty rather than imply their structures were liable to collapse. The temptation has to be resisted as far as possible because the real world is not a simple place of blacks and whites, but shades of grey. The wall may be very carefully and safely designed, a thorough site investigation made to check ground conditions and the construction competently supervised and carried out, but if an isolated soft area escaped detection and subsequently caused major settlement in a section of the wall then it would not be fit for purpose and the cost of all remedial work and other loss would fall on the unfortunate designer.

An accident prevention scheme at a complex junction with a bad record for crashes caused by its confusing layout would have, unsurprisingly, an end to these casualties as its purpose. After all reasonable skill and care had been applied to the design and the execution of all the proposed measures diligently supervised, there may still be some injuries resulting from vehicles following the wrong route through the junction. Fitness for purpose would place the liability with the professional whose reasonable efforts had failed to achieve the ideal result.

These, and a multitude of other instances, demonstrate the reason why professional suppliers (and equally important, their insurers) will avoid accepting fitness for purpose as a service standard wherever possible. When they must, the level of risk rises dramatically with a consequent and inevitable effect on costs. Not only the fees, but also the works costs as fitness for purpose tends to produce overcautious designs in which saving the client money is hardly likely to figure as a priority. Similarly, the potential for disputes after the event about the measurement of *fitness* and the definition of *purpose*, even though everyone thought they were obvious before, should likewise encourage specifiers to avoid building such an expensive risk into the cost of the project. There are no short cuts to being clear about standards.

Quality

Quality is not an absolute but a moving scale. It can be set at the highest level of excellence that can be achieved, or it can signify a standard well within the practical capability of the average supplier. To say 'I want a quality product' is meaningless and although this is often used with the intended meaning 'I want a *high* quality product', sloppy phrasing such as this has no place in the procurement and delivery of public works and services. Quality must be specified. If you mean 'the very best', you must find a way of defining it; if you mean 'the best we can afford', or 'the best we can get in the time available', that is not just a different standard but also a different way of assessing options (or perhaps bids).

One standard of quality is that embodied in the term *professionalism*. The implication is of trained and skilled providers, regulated through a code of conduct administered by a body which is part learned society and part court of ethics, and dedicated to serving clients' interests to the best of their ability. This is a fine concept and deserves the prestige and respect which still clothes, if rather patchily, some of the professions. However, it suffers from the inevitable isolation of any exclusive group: it takes one professional to assess the quality of another. Neither is it an objective nor a consistent standard: each professional's view of what constitutes reasonable skill and care or due diligence, and the capacity to deliver it, will be slightly different. Nevertheless, for advice such as reports and studies and for design work both in concept and detail, it has been the standard traditionally used in public authorities. Chief officers and their senior managers exercise quality control over the work of their staff, and their consultants, by applying professional judgement as the criterion of what is acceptable.

There are, of course, many benefits in this approach, which puts the emphasis on achieving the highest level of quality, uncompromised by considerations of profit margins or competitive pressures. With an unfortunate degree of oversimplification this has become summarized in the phrase 'designing up to a standard, not down to a price'. It is the ultimate expression of trust: the professional will give full attention to producing the advice, solving the problems and delivering the project, and will self-regulate the quality of his work to ensure that it conforms with all professional standards; the client will accept the professional's word that the result is everything that is required — and will meet the cost of all the work.

The standing of the professional, like almost every other aspect of traditional authority, has been much questioned in recent years. The potential disadvantages of professionalism as a standard, particularly for public works, are inherent in its nature as a sophisticated variant of the closed shop: it is not readily open to external scrutiny; it tends to be based on judgement and opinion rather than objective measurement; and it does not necessarily share — indeed it may tend to disregard — the priorities of the wider world. It is this last charge of professional arrogance, which is the most telling and which is perceived as carrying the most weight. (Professional solutions to congestion, for instance, concentrated on increasing capacity by physical improvements long after environmental arguments for managing demand had won public acceptance.)

This does not mean that professional judgements are irrelevant (after all, taking congestion as our example, although demand management commands great public support as a general concept, limited personal commitment to any specific action still puts pressure on capacity); nor that the standards of professionalism do not serve the public interest. Indeed peer pressure is a very effective way of maintaining consistency and competence. What it does mean is that, in a world of public accountability, open communications and constant change, professionalism *by itself* cannot be used as a standard of quality. It is not enough to rely on the approval of professionals, regardless of whether a genuine client/consultant relationship exists or not, as the only check on acceptability in public service delivery.

An effective means of ensuring and demonstrating the independent review of quality is via certification for quality assurance (QA) to the former BS 5750, now the international ISO 9000 series. It not only provides the discipline of rigorous and repeated external assessment but also imposes standards which are set in the outside world and thus avoids the organizational stagnation of 'it's always been good enough for us in the past'.

QA has become widely accepted as an industry standard for the core areas of engineering design. Its application to services involving regulation and enforcement, such as waste licensing, and responsive delivery to the public, such as local highway maintenance, is growing. Even services involving policy interpretation and judgement, transport planning and development control, for instance, can be brought into the QA framework through the certification of the records, data collection and procedures which make up a large and essential part of the activity.

The great benefit of QA is its focus on the combination of activity and responsibility: every step or stage in a project has to be assigned to someone who is responsible for assuring its correct completion. The key element in QA's effectiveness is the audit, which tests the logic and relevance of each procedure and checks that their contributions to the quality of the finished product are being made in practice. The credibility of QA certification rests on the cycle of surveillance and its continuous pressure to maintain procedures in full working order. The important caution about the whole system is that while it does give assurances that processes which are directed at achieving a quality standard both exist and are consistently operated, QA does not specify the detail of the standard, nor can it guarantee that inputs or outputs will be at that standard, as these must remain subject to the human factor.

So QA is a useful — virtually essential — additional component of professional quality control. It provides robust external checks and monitoring, encourages rigorous internal control and review, and tends to avoid complacency and traditionalism. But it is still not enough for today's expectations of public service delivery.

Quality is no longer measured solely by technical evaluation, nor through compliance with procedures. By indicating performance levels through the definition of a range of factors that will be understood (or even experienced) by the recipients of the service, elected representatives and the public, too, can participate directly in the assessment of quality.

The kind of performance indicators most relevant to setting and measuring quality standards in public service projects are those which cover outcome as much as output. This balances the popular and political expectations of public works with professional evaluation, and gives elected representatives a clear and genuine say in what is required from the service and its providers.

One example of this concept might be the consultation process for a park and ride proposal. A professional standard would tend to concentrate on the clear explanation of the options, with coverage of the pros and cons (probably expressed in technical and cost-benefit terms), accurate location plans and other relevant visual aids; a comprehensive method statement for distribution of the information, requirements for identifying and contacting interested representative groups and holding appropriate local exhibitions and meetings. Quality of output would be assessed in terms of the content of the published material, the coverage of its distribution, and the organization and delivery of the exhibitions and meetings. All of this is valid, but quality of outcome would also bring in the reaction of the public and interest groups to the consultation

Did the form and character of the information leave the consultees satisfied that they knew enough to give a view?

Was the attitude of the staff likely to encourage responses?

How well did the exercise convey the council's willingness to consider options or did it give the impression of a *fait accompli*?

None of this is likely to fit in easily with professional measures of quality. But it is reasonable, indeed essential, to have a non-professional assessment of the standard of the consultation, and that is bound to be significantly influenced by the reaction of the laymen (and women) who are being consulted — what in marketing is called 'customer feedback'.

The key lies in ensuring that measures of quality are devised which allow for the involvement of the council, both as purchaser and as the representative of the public, in their setting and monitoring. Without such involvement, a credibility gap is inevitable, leading to uncertainty about the value of what is being done and lack of appreciation and support for the resources being applied. The ideal combination, therefore, comprises three elements

- external assessment via QA of inputs and processes
- traditional professional control over the standard of the output
- evaluation of the outcome by those for whom the service is being delivered.

   In practice, this still puts the coordination of standard setting and quality monitoring with the in-house professional, whether acting as manager for internal providers or client officer to a consultant. This task will not be done in isolation, however, as the requirement to measure up to external standards, and the need to consult with elected representatives about both what is expected and what is delivered, introduces new checks and balances on the old, inward-looking quality standards.

   Without diminishing the real effort that is needed to achieve, and then maintain through regular surveillance, the certification for quality assurance, it is the involvement of elected representatives that presents the most difficult challenge. Council requirements expressed as non-professional outcomes will inevitably be subjective, but they must not be parochial, personal or party-political. So it is reasonable to measure the quality of service delivery by asking questions such as

> Did frontagers on this road maintenance scheme generally feel their needs for access had been taken into account?
>
> Has the message that cycling is a practical alternative to car commuting in the city been delivered convincingly?

What the process must avoid is drawing broad conclusions about quality from single anecdotes such as

> Mr Jones couldn't get his car into his drive because of the road works,

which begs questions about the duration of the problem, how avoidable it was and whether advance warning had been given. Nor should it equate successful service delivery with political point-scoring along the lines of

> more emphasis should be given to the increase in cycle provision since the change in control at the county council.

(There is, of course, nothing wrong with public works being used to gain political objectives: it is simply that these are for politicians to deliver, not professional advisers.)

   Keeping this sensitive balance is difficult and requires not just strong management of the process, but a clear understanding of what outcomes are being looked for and what levels of achievement are expected. Leaving them open is an invitation for unreasonable and inappropriate personal or political standards to fill the vacuum. Thinking them up afterwards is not merely unfair, but a very ineffective way of getting the result that is required.

   A programme to encourage more cycling in an urban area has its quality standards set as follows

- review existing designated route and check against current design guidelines, etc.; draw up list of consequent improvements and get endorsement from the October environment committee
- identify local cycling and other relevant interest groups, arrange meetings; consult with them to produce an agreed schedule of informal recommended routes and a priority list for new officially

designated cycleways before Christmas
- prepare outline designs and estimates for priority schemes. Designs to be in accordance with latest guidelines etc., overall programme to be within budget guideline
- draft cycling leaflet showing existing cycleways and, recommended routes, identifying proposed new schemes and providing safety information, etc. Obtain endorsement from cycle groups etc. and present to the February environment committee together with a programme of priority schemes for approval
- launch leaflet with suitable event (e.g. refurbished signing and road markings on a prominent existing cycleway) during March. Achieve positive media coverage and arrange distribution via interest groups, libraries, schools, etc.
- monitor cycle traffic on town centre routes and feed information back into the environment committee to review success of programme and priority of cycleway expenditure in time for start of next budget drafting cycle in September.

Some of the standards of acceptance are professional and technical, others are more subjective and will rely to some extent on past measures of acceptability, common sense and the professional judgement of the client officers, who may be called upon to give a balanced view on the quality of a consultant's work (in-house or external) and the reasonableness of the expectations of the council.

While quality is not a fixed point, and must be selected from a scale when the task is being set, there has to be provision for reassessment and change when necessary. This should be the exception rather than the rule, but nevertheless it is in the nature of many public works projects and services that requirements will change during their lifetime. A particular scheme or service might become more critical to the council's aims and need to be delivered at a higher quality; alternatively, other pressures may reduce its importance and permit a reduction in standards. The ability to achieve these exceptional adjustments smoothly, and to record and recognize the consequential effects — not least on costs — is an essential part of public service delivery.

Value for money

The concept of balancing quality standards and cost became a major issue in the public sector in the late 1970s and was given particular emphasis by the Audit Commission when it was set up in 1981 to be, in tabloid press shorthand, the town hall watchdog. The Commission advocated an approach to the assessment of existing and proposed services based on the three principles of effectiveness, efficiency and economy.

As a label, these three short words (soon abbreviated further to *value for money* (VFM)) certainly measured up to the third of the Commission's principles; and in its widespread acceptance as the acid test for local government and other public services, it satisfied the other two as well.

The approach stresses a fundamental point lying at the heart of all evaluations of the value, quality or just plain usefulness of public services, and which is brought out by a stark summary of the *Three Es* and, particularly, the first

- Effectiveness — doing the right things
- Efficiency — doing things right
- Economy — doing things for the right price.

The hard questions — the ones which frequently go unasked and even more often are left unanswered — are not those which investigate the expenditure and the amount of output being produced, but the ones which set out to probe the key issue of whether that output provides what is really wanted or even whether it is needed at all.

While a professional manager might point to efficiency, demonstrated by a drawing office full of staff working busily and to high technical standards on a series of road improvements with the latest in urban traffic control systems, a politician might question its effectiveness by asking why there are insufficient resources to keep the council's programme of pedestrian priority and cycleway projects on schedule.

This is where professional complacency contrasts with political frustration.

Cost-effectiveness — another watchword of the 1980s — has often been measured and expressed in terms that are really standards of cost-efficiency. Staff may be working at high levels of utilization, producing work which meets technical standards with the minimum of correction or modification, and their costs and that of the works or services they deliver may be managed down to meet the toughest market comparisons, but if the output does not generate the required outcome then all that economy and efficiency is simply ineffective. The value for money process involves four steps, as the question about price has to be addressed twice, at the beginning and at the end. Thus

---

- *Economy:* the council wants to raise the standard of highway maintenance on rural roads in response to growing public complaint that the quality of service in urban and suburban areas is not matched in the villages and countryside; an assessment of the breakdown of the maintenance budget indicates that about £0.4 million could be diverted annually from the urban network, now in relatively good condition, without significant short or medium term ill-effects; similarly, a review of the existing rural programme indicates that economies of scale, different contract packages and market changes will generate £0.3 million savings in a typical year; the council has also committed itself to releasing new money from its reserves amounting to some £0.6 million in each of the next two years . . . Thus, the right price is £1.3 million a year for a two-year programme.

- *Effectiveness:* the present and proposed programmes are tested against the criterion of public satisfaction; their features are ranked in priority order based on some research into actual preferences (grass cutting may be much in demand not only on sight lines but also in village areas which otherwise look untidy, surface dressing may be unpopular because it is considered a messy operation and tolerated only when skid resistance is a clear problem); problems and solutions are assessed in service delivery terms as well as from an engineering or procedural standpoint. (Do people want fast repairs to potholes or just the certainty that they will definitely be treated within the promised period? Are the parish councils being consulted about the proposals for new road signs in their areas or just told? Would the rural communities prefer to see tidier surface dressing rather than more of it?). The programmes are revised to take account of these factors and coordinated as a package aimed at increasing public satisfaction, again with full costings.

- *Efficiency:* an assessment of all the present work programmes (e.g. patching, surface dressing, grass cutting, etc.) and supporting activities (e.g. response times for complaints, liaison with parish councils, etc.) identifies current unit rates and costs, and room for further improvement by increasing the use of existing resources to match published national best practice standards; the shortfalls below the service levels operating in the urban/suburban areas are identified to calculate the resources needed to close the gap in each case; the capability of the latest technology to make services quicker, more reliable and of better quality is investigated. A new programme aimed at bringing rural highway maintenance up to the standard of the urban/suburban network is the result, fully costed.

- *Economy:* the package (as a set of outcomes) and its cost is compared against the right price, not to see if it uses up all the budget but to consider its cost-effectiveness; if it costs less than £1.3 million that may be good news and leave money to be reassigned elsewhere, or it may mean that some lower priority but still desirable items which were left out can be brought in; if it comes out at the proposed budget figure, it is still critically examined to see whether there are any unnecessary luxuries included that do not contribute significantly to the overall effect; if it costs more than £1.3 million then there may have to be some trimming unless the whole package is seen as so important and attractive that the extra will be found by reallocating funds from other work programmes; the future beyond the two-year period will be examined to see how the possible scaling down of the package should be handled if funding cannot continue, with the items yielding the best long-term benefits (reliable pothole repairs and good communications with parish councils, for instance, as against extra grass cutting) being ranked highest for protection. The scene is now set for implementing the programme and managing its long-term consequences.

Value for money, whether applied to new proposals or as an audit on existing practices, has to create a tension between the professional/technical interests and the service delivery outcomes. If it fails to do that, or if it fails to do it constructively, then it will be no more than a catch phrase. The objective of all expenditure is to add value and so produce a better result than would otherwise be the case. VFM sets out to measure and evaluate that improvement and ensure that it is continuous. So it is a never-ending search, which recognizes that the big benefits usually come early and (if the task has been done rigorously) are unlikely to be repeated subsequently on the same scale. There is a point when the law of diminishing returns sets in and the effort and disturbance to achieve incremental improvements begins to balance out their advantages, but that is usually a long way off, particularly in a world where new technology provides a regular stimulus for beneficial change.

The gains to be made in the mechanics of winter maintenance operations from more efficient gritters, more flexible use of specialized plant, optimization of salting routes to save time and fuel, etc. may have been approaching exhaustion, but are now being taken forward on another level as the methods of control are tightened up to take advantage of the opportunities of thermal mapping, remote sensors and more precise weather forecasting. Similarly, the previous best practice levels for the inspection and maintenance of a highway authority's bridges stock are now being raised through the introduction of computerized management programs.

Nevertheless, the VFM approach must be based on realism and acknowledge the practical limitations of resources, cost and technical capability. Challenging traditional methods of working, established timetables and Rolls–Royce estimates of cost is right and proper, provided it is done realistically. Driving down costs and pushing up quality is an excellent discipline as long as it is aimed at a realistic target, such as matching, or marginally improving on, the best which is being achieved under similar circumstances elsewhere.

So, speeding up an organization's response times to letters is a legitimate goal provided reasonable allowances are made for postal deliveries and collecting information on non-standard enquiries; and provided also the unpredictable calls on staff time, generated by detailed research in the files, site visits, etc., are recognized as involving overtime costs, more staff, or delays to other work. Similarly, maintaining existing satisfactory standards for the repair of faulty street lights at a lower cost may well be possible through efficiency savings, but if the price is already set through genuine competition, then something else has to give.

———————

Value for money is a vital ingredient in the management and delivery of public services: it highlights the issue of 'you get what you pay for', which cannot be ignored. Long ago production engineering in the United States found a marvellously precise way of putting the fundamental choice to all specifiers, estimators, cost accountants and purchasers. We can do it three ways:

quickly
cheaply
high quality

Choose any two.

7. Programmes and priorities

The greatest change which has overtaken the public sector in the last 20 years is the end — gradual in some cases, sudden in others — of the old certainties of base budgets, carry-overs and annual programmes. In those far-off days when steady growth, or at least a steady level of resources, could be taken for granted, it was only the urgent or the unexpected that seemed to be important, as everything else was covered by the budgets for work programmes and staff establishments which rolled forward from one year to the next.

The ending of that golden age brought public service projects and programmes up against some hard realities, political as well as financial. Shrinking resources and rising expectations meant critical re-examination of almost every function, particularly those where the units of activity or production could be identified in tangible form, rather than in the emotional and highly sensitive images of personal services. Consequently, it became increasingly difficult to maintain large, annual budgets for services described broadly as, for instance, highway maintenance without more specific subdivision. The idea that there was a basic underlying requirement for service provision which had to be funded each year, to be supplemented by extra money for growth items which themselves tended thereafter to be absorbed into the base, began to be challenged; and the difficulty in raising finance for even these allegedly basic service requirements, let alone new projects, made setting priorities essential — at first within programmes and services, then between them.

These pressures are predictable and should be anticipated and planned for. If, in a wish to avoid the hard choices which they bring, decision making is delayed until far too late, then dire consequences for the quality of decisions and services will follow. Increasingly, the harsh realities of public finance have worked their way deep into the fabric of local government and it is now part of the routine of most authorities to draw up detailed programmes, set them and their components into some kind of priority order and juggle the whole system to try to accommodate the ever-changing urgencies of the political environment, the community, legislation and circumstance.

Identification

Identifying and labelling the components of a project or service may seem to be a straightforward task, but it is rarely as simple as it appears. The application of broad descriptions to complicated mixtures of different activities, with their cyclical, seasonal and random variations, is indeed a useful means of integrating resources; but it is also an effective way of protecting them from scrutiny, and so there are human as well as operational problems in moving towards narrower definitions.

Personal reactions to a changing, more questioning environment apart, there are some real practical difficulties in breaking down large, wide-ranging services and allocating staff and other costs to the components. The cost-effectiveness of many such services depends on the flexible deployment of resources to meet demands that are hard to predict in terms of frequency or scale, or both. Staff, fixed assets and operational costs are not always packaged in neat compartments; and even when they are, these do not necessarily coincide with the service delivery packages which would be recognizable to the public and their elected representatives. Nevertheless, the effort has to be made, both to justify the build up of major services and to demonstrate management control.

Local highway maintenance, the organization of day-to-day activity to maintain the network in working order and safe condition, is a framework for what is in effect a set of continuous projects that share some common features. It is not a single, indivisible function and some activities are significantly different from others in their nature, frequency, method of funding and purpose.

Local highway maintenance — £10 million (works and staff costs)

- *Inspection and reporting of faults*: daily, weekly and monthly routines of visual examination for defects etc., plus a system for recording information from other sources, to discharge the duty of care obligation of the highway authority; carried out by directly employed staff.   *Overall provision* — £650 000
- *Condition assessment*: annual programme of tests on selected lengths of the network to determine structural and surface characteristics as a means of identifying requirements for repair and best use of resources; carried out by directly employed staff and/or specialist contractors.   *Overall provision* — £320 000
- *Patching, haunching, etc*: limited repairs to surface defects identified by inspection etc. to discharge duty of care and to prevent minor faults becoming more damaging or hazardous; carried out by term contractors on unit rates, called-off and supervised by directly employed technical staff.
  Western area — £2 100 000
  Central area — £3 200 000
  Eastern area — £2 500 000
- *Winter maintenance management*: preparation and organization of system of salting routes, works contracts, weather forecasts, sensors and communications, including topping-up of salt stockpiles and rental/lease cost of specialist equipment; carried out by directly-employed staff (including standby payments) and annual contracts for supply of materials and plant.
  Overall provision — £520 000

- *Winter maintenance operations*: salting/gritting runs on specified network with additional emergency routes and snow clearing operations in exceptional circumstances; carried out by term contractors on unit rates, budget based on average winter conditions; no contingency for emergencies which must be met by diversion of funds.

  Western area — £330 000
  Central area — £150 000
  Eastern area — £230 000

This process of identifying specifically the elements of a major service has clear links with the value for money approach to setting and monitoring standards. By isolating each component, the good performance areas do not cross subsidize the bad; nor do small, low priority activities continue in operation because they are lost within a large and generally important service. While some activities such as street lighting maintenance are in effect continuous processes, involving many similar actions that all share a single identity, others can be broken down into separate units which in terms of their effect on local people and communities are individual projects.

Thus, for instance, an annual programme of footway reconstruction works, once left to professionals to prepare and implement within a block budget allocation on the basis of technical judgement, would in this climate of greater public involvement be presented as a draft list for scrutiny and approval.

Annual footway reconstruction programme — £1.4 million

- *Station Road, Newtown*: — 1050 pedestrians/day, school walking route, includes widening and cycle facilities £110 000
- *Wood Lane, Binford*: — 350 pedestrians/day, only partly surfaced at present, two vehicle/pedestrian accidents £45 000
- *West Street, Overhill*: — 490 pedestrians/day, schoolchildren and elderly people, includes dropped kerbs for crossing. £20 000 (plus £15 000 contribution from utilities)
  etc

Undoubtedly, subjective consideration will produce modifications to what is, in theory at least, an objective schedule based on engineering and safety criteria. This is difficult for professionals, aiming for economy and efficiency by packaging work together to get the best price and minimize long-term deterioration. However, it allows the public and their representatives to question and understand the justification for selecting the individual items and, by modifying the programme, improve what they see as its effectiveness.

While the separate identification of key functions or activities within the large service blocks such as highway maintenance is a relatively recent development, individual public works projects, such as a grade-separated interchange or a multi-storey car park, have always been identified as named capital schemes in local authority programmes. Even so, today's requirements for information and accountability are stimulating a more detailed exposure of the components of these projects, which are now unlikely to be accepted as single packages.

The Overhill High Street improvement has a place in the capital programme with £900 000 budgeted, £500 000 in the coming financial year and the rest in the next. The project is described as an environmental improvement and accident prevention scheme and the drawings show a realignment of kerbs at two junctions at each end of the village, wider footways, some speed reduction measures and two lay-bys to accommodate bus stops. A one line programme entry might conceal some interesting features that more detailed analysis would bring out, see Table 5.

This breakdown reveals that the largest single item is the utility diversions, necessitated by the realignment of one of the junctions and the construction of the lay-bys. The council may wish to balance the benefits of the full scheme — which in any case are not available for another twelve months because the utilities will not schedule their advance diversion works until the end of the first year — against some cheaper, quicker alternatives.

More information usually means more questions, some of which are not easy to answer. A simple, indeed perhaps simplistic, example such as the one above only serves to illustrate the extent of the decision making process which this approach opens up. Some professionals may groan at the prospect of applying it to a very large and complex project: the pedestrianization of a city centre, for instance, or a rural bypass. Yet there is no doubt that the combined pressures of

Table 5. Breakdown of the Overhill High Street improvement budget

Overhill High Street improvement	£000s Year 1	£000s Year 2
Land and accommodation works	50	—
Utilities diversions (estimate)	400	—
Carriageway works	40	300
Lighting and signs	—	50
Landscaping	—	30
Fees	10	20
Total	500	400

Current three-year accident record:	8 personal injuries
Estimated three-year accident reduction:	4 personal injuries

value for money and greater public involvement in the preparation of schemes from which the community is supposed to benefit are making it unacceptable to promote projects without this level of information.

Assessment

Identifying the content of services, programmes and projects means management control over their delivery can be exercised in a focused way and accountability for performance and value for money is clarified. However, these benefits are about the provision of activities and there are deeper issues to be tackled which come before the questions of 'how shall we do it?' or 'how are we doing?' and ask 'why are we doing it?'

The legal obligations and duties of local authorities are very wide, but they are not always particularly deep, and rarely set out in legislation with much operational detail. For instance, the duty to provide safe passage for the normal traffic of a neighbourhood is, as has been seen in an earlier chapter, wide ranging in its application to the whole network of public highways, but not applied in any depth (after all, a safe highway is not one which is in perfect condition but rather one free from obvious hazards). A large part of the activity carried out by highway authorities, and for that matter education authorities, housing authorities, etc., is above the minimum level for the discharge of their statutory responsibilities and represents the legitimate exercise of discretion to extend and enhance basic provision, and to introduce beneficial services only loosely related to their legal obligations.

While such activities are discretionary, they are not always seen as such and the passage of time frequently leads to the custom and practice of more expansive days being treated as unavoidable obligations long after the time when pressure on expenditure should have brought them under critical review. Yesterday's discretion may have to make room for today's new or additional obligations, or at least be reassessed to see whether it offers better value than competing alternatives.

There is no black-and-white division between statutory minimum requirements (which are, as has been seen, a matter of judgement in any case) and these discretionary extras. The shades of grey have to be acknowledged, but not too subtly. Most authorities have recognized the need to apply an assessment process that distinguishes between the things which must be done, those which ought to be done and those which, to one degree or another, it would be nice to do. This rather crude expression can, and should, be translated into a rigorous process that takes the identified components of each service and programme and assesses them against a set of criteria such as

---

- *category 1:* statutory minimum level of service below which the council would be open to successful legal challenge
- *category 2:* statutory services currently provided at a higher level than that defined in category 1
- *category 3:* discretionary services for which there is an existing and specific council commitment
- *category 4:* statutory services outside category 1, and dis-

cretionary services, for which there is no explicit council commitment.

———————

Applying this type of process involves considerable self-discipline: engineers as professionals want to see their work done to a high standard and are acutely aware of the long-term costs of short-term reductions in those standards. But this is not what the exercise is about.

———————

A local authority can, faced with hard decisions on its services, cut back on the traditionally high quality of its salting/gritting operations (it would, in fact, be under no obligation to provide any), or extend the response time to traffic signal failures from 24 to 72 hours (provided it has a system for putting up signs to warn of the potential hazard during the period between report of the failure and its correction), or adopt a policy of superficial repairs to worn-out carriageways.

———————

It is part of the professional's duty to make the authority's decision makers aware of the consequences which flow from such choices, but not to cloak with statutory obligations activities that, however technically justifiable, are within its discretion.

Human nature and the internal politics of public bodies being what they are, this exercise is commonly carried out in two or more stages. The service providers examine their functions, activities and programmes and produce an assessment of their components against the criteria. A separate scrutiny group, usually set up corporately and consisting of representatives from different service departments together with the (allegedly) disinterested central finance and policy advisory groups, then carries out an independent review, usually interviewing staff who have prepared the initial assessment to challenge and check the categorization and its justification. The cycle may need to be repeated, depending on the quality of the input and the depth of the scrutiny. The end product of what can be a tough probing investigation if taken seriously, or a smooth and self-serving charade if treated too cosily, is a full categorization along the lines of the example in Table 6.

This kind of schedule, repeated for all services, gives the council a full assessment of all its current obligations, commitments and discretionary choices. When carried out for the first time, and provided it is done rigorously, there will be quite a few surprises. Thereafter — for, like the value for money process, assessment must not be allowed to stagnate — changes in legislation, national and local policies, political objectives and financial pressures will have to be accommodated within this framework. The exercise is not supposed to be a comfortable one, either for the professionals justifying their services or for the council facing the difficult choices that come with detailed exposure of what is being done and why.

The assessment should not pull any punches. The tasks necessary to discharge

Table 6. Assessment schedule showing full categorization of highway services

Service Area Project	Categorization (£000s)					Duties/Commitments and Comment
	1	2	3	4	Total	
Highway Maintenance Basic maintenance (potholes, patching, *trips*, etc.)	2633	817	—	—	3450	Statutory duty to maintain road in a safe condition. Category 1 is reacting to potentially hazardous damage; category 2 is repair of damage which would cause expensive deterioration if left.
Extended mainte-nance (reconstruction of carriageways and footways)	4266	1195	674	—	6135	Statutory duty to maintain roads in a safe condition; council policy to maintain capital assets cost-effectively. Category 1 is reconstruction to prevent failures within one or two years; category 2 is preventive treatment at optimum time to minimize costs; category 3 is reconditioning on routes where traffic levels etc. justify basic maintenance only.
Winter and emergencies	1220	570	430	65	2285	Statutory duty to maintain safe passage; council emergency plan. Category 1 is for salting/gritting runs on the approved strategic network; category 2 for the approved major routes; category 3 for the approved school accesses, bus routes and special areas; category 4 for custom and practice runs listed in the emergency plan but not otherwise approved. NB. allowance is for average winter with no snowfall; no contingency allowance for emergencies.
Total:	13 775 (65%)	4821 (23%)	2004 (9%)	585 (3%)	21 185	

legal obligations, however unpopular or unnecessary they may appear to be, must be included complete, fully costed and free from any suggestion that they are optional or amenable to short cuts. Conversely, discretionary activities should always be accompanied by an assessment of the consequences of the authority exercising its discretion to abandon or delay, while indicating clearly that it has that choice. The comments column in Table 6 illustrates how this information might be presented.

Strategy

Table 7. Accident prevention programme — Western area

Site	Works	Cost (£)	Estimated 3-year accident savings
Gypsy Lane: St. Thomas Church to Community Centre	Surface dressing	35 000	7
Smith Street: Market Cross to Boundary Bridge	Surface dressing	27 000	4
Fairwood Estate	Traffic calming	33 000	5
Heath End College	Pedestrian crossing and refuge	15 000	3
Beech Hill Station	Supplementary lighting	5 000	2
Binford (North End)	Village Gateway feature	7 500	2
Old London Road/Western Avenue	Right turn lane and traffic islands	19 000	3

Table 8. Annual programme — reconditioning schemes (1)

Primary routes		Cost (£)	Failure	Rutting	Accidents	Complaints
A488	Westvale, Church Cross to County Boundary	250 000	****	***	*	**
A4455	Southbrook, link road to Motorway Junction	420 000	***	***	****	**
A397	Eastbridge, Jubilee Way Roundabout	160 000	***	**	**	*
A3783	North Fordham, Hospital to Mill Lane	380 000	**	****	**	****

Table 9. Annual programme — reconditioning schemes (2)

Major county roads		Cost (£)	Failure	Rutting	Accidents	Complaints
Middleton	Western Avenue, Railway Bridge to Kingsway	240 000	*****	**	*	****
Barchester	Riverside, Castle Road to Westgate (Stage 2)	110 000	*****	**	*	**
B4039	Beech Hill to London Road	90 000	****	***	**	***
B478	Binford, Chapel Street	130 000	****	**	**	**

Ranking

As a result of all this effort, and a certain amount of heart-searching, the complete range of services, programmes and projects — together with their budgets — will be assessed and categorized. The next and final stage of the process is to use the information to establish priorities that are a reflection of the authority's current and future objectives, not a knee-jerk reaction to the pressure of events, nor a complacent continuation of past arrangements.

First call on resources must go to the basic statutory obligations that the authority has to discharge. The next in order of importance are usually those contractual commitments that, while not part of the council's duties, are legally binding and cannot be abandoned or curtailed without penalty: these would include items such as construction contracts in progress, term maintenance contracts with time to run and so on.

Thereafter, the exercise becomes more fluid, for while the next priority on professional and technical grounds would be meeting the good practice level (as opposed to the legal minimum) on the statutory services, the many other competing demands for discretionary action will bring powerful political pressure to bear on the selection machinery.

Ranking the options is not easy and however much politicians may value flexibility in their choices, they will acknowledge — sometimes reluctantly, but more often positively — the benefit of a degree of professional objectivity in the process. So, a systematic approach to measuring the benefits and costs of particular options, weighting them and putting them into a ranked order is an essential technique for managing the delivery of public services. The simplest version ranks options of the same or similar type, and is usually based on a single measure, or set of measures, selected to highlight one end product, which is generally recognized as the key aim of the service or programme.

Accident prevention schemes (Table 7) are typically ranked on the personal injuries they will save over a three-year period, with the estimated expenditure on each scheme being brought into the calculation to give a *cost per casualty saved* as the basis of their relative order. This technique can be applied to specific types of accident prevention projects such as surface dressing to reduce skidding accidents, or street lighting improvements to cut down night-time casualties; it can also be used across a variety of schemes where it is agreed that road safety is the principal objective of that programme.

Carriageway reconstruction projects can be grouped into sets based on volume of traffic (measured perhaps in total numbers but more likely with some extra factor applied to the count of heavy goods vehicles), or some other criterion to reflect importance in the road network; then the schemes in each set are ranked by appropriate criteria, which may be relative (as in these examples) or numerical (Tables 8 and 9).

More complex objectives need more sophisticated ranking systems. One basis for assessing relative value will not be enough and a number of factors may be relevant: if they are all judged to be of equal importance they can be aggregated to give a total score; where this is not the case, different weights can be applied to each factor to adjust its contribution to the overall evaluation. Weighting is a matter of fine judgement and there is rarely a simple technical answer that can be applied. Often the best solution will be found by applying the pragmatic approach of trying out a first attempt on a few samples to see if it produces a ranking that feels right — and changing the weightings until it does. This is not quite the fiddle it appears to be: the whole purpose of different weights is to strike the right balance between the relative values of dissimilar factors, which is bound to involve some initial calibration of the results (or, in plain language, trial and error).

The rank order for a series of proposed priority bus lanes on existing roads could be prepared by taking projected time savings for peak hour journeys and multiplying by the peak passenger load and then adding the corresponding figure calculated for the off-peak period. Alternatively, if time savings for commuters were considered of special value, a factor of, say, 1·5 could be applied to the peak hour calculation.

The ranking of a programme of proposed cycleway schemes could be established by taking estimates of the usage in trips per year and the works cost, and then calculating a cost/benefit ratio. To reflect concern about child safety, the numbers of trips by schoolchildren could be given a weighting of, for instance, two to favour projects with this element.

Schemes in a footway improvement programme are ranked according to a scoring system weighted in favour of vulnerable pedestrian groups —

- for every 100 pedestrians counted between
  7 a.m. and 7 p.m.   1 point
- for every 50 pedestrians under age 16   1 point
- for every 50 pedestrians over age 60   1 point
- if no footway on the other side of the road   2 points
- for two-way traffic flow between 7 a.m. and
  7 p.m. of 5000–10 000 vehicles   3 points
- for two-way traffic flow between 7 a.m. and
  7 p.m. of more than 10 000 vehicles   5 points
- for more than 10% heavy goods vehicles   3 points

Any approach to setting priorities or allocating resources based entirely on a mechanical formula leaves politicians increasingly uneasy, and tends to enjoy little credibility with communities now much more inclined to reject the opinions of those in authority and argue for the primacy of public opinion, or, more specifically and perhaps more honestly, local opinion.

A classic case is the use of the PV^2 formula for calculating the pedestrian (P)/vehicle (V) conflict at proposed pedestrian crossing sites. If the result is above the guidance level of 10^8, all well and good. Otherwise, the contrast between the cold application of mathematics and the emotional pressure of potential casualties makes rational decision making very difficult. Each exception, however well-justified by the special factors normally recognized (high proportion of elderly persons, proximity of important public or community buildings, etc.) opens up the potential for other marginal cases and so on. Most highway authorities have recognized that the formula has to be supplemented by a limited range of discretion, in which special factors can be evaluated and applied, so as to introduce a degree of flexibility that will accommodate all (or almost all) the deserving cases.

While a systematic, strictly technical method of ranking may be criticized by politicians and public alike as bureaucratic and rigid, the other extreme of using subjective choice based on perceived public benefit is also, to say the least, open to question. Just as the path to hell is paved with good intentions, so the laudable aim of listening to local views can, without some objective framework to guide decision making, lead to an outbreak of lobbying in which priorities are set on a 'who gets in first' or 'who shouts the loudest' basis. As resources are finite and it is rarely financially or practically possible to accommodate every demand for action, the widespread sense of unfairness and resentment generated by this unstructured approach far outweighs the short-lived and local benefits its flexibility might provide.

The effective response to the failings of both approaches is to develop a methodical system which commands public acceptance as a fair and reasonable means of ranking options or competing bids. Such a system has to combine technical measurements, professional judgements and popular preferences, differentially weighted as appropriate, so that they produce more or less consistent results when applied to a set of alternative proposals or a list of possible schemes. The process must be transparent: there cannot be an invisible stage where some factor is applied which can change the score or order; and it must be understandable: the relevance of the different elements and their relative values have to be clear. Above all, the system itself has to be acceptable to those who will subsequently have to accept its results. So the key stage for the professionals is not simply getting their ranked order of schemes or programmes approved, but devising the methodology for ranking and reaching agreement on its use.

Tables 10 and 11 provide an example. Although some components of the system are of general relevance, much of it reflects the nature of the particular process — a review of a series of options for dealing with the traffic problems of a small market town ranging from 'do nothing' through to a partial bypass — and the relative importance attached by

Table 10. Casterbridge transport review — evaluation framework

Objective	Attribute	Measurable	Value	Rating*	Weighted rating
Traffic Movement	Congestion levels	Traffic volumes (veh km) Route length over capacity (km) Junction arms with delay > 3 min			× 3
	Rat running	Route length over desirable threshold (km) Change in speeds (± km/h)			
Public transport	Bus and rail	Bus network density index Arrivals in peak hour Average journey speed (km/h)			× 2
	Park and ride	Reduction in town centre car trips (±%)			
Cycling	Cycling	Change in time (existing routes) (±%) Length of new route (km) Safety etc. (index)			× 1
Walking	Walking	Av. journey time (existing routes) (±%) Length of new route (km) Safety (etc.) index			× 1
Environ-ment	Built	Properties demolished Properties blighted			× 2
	Landscape	Tree preservation orders affected Overall impact (index)			
	Pollution and noise	Residential properties ± 3 dB(A) Sites > 4 ppm CO			
Safety	Accidents	Forecast casualty reduction			× 3
Town Centre	Traffic flows	Route length over desirable threshold (km) Change in speeds (± km/h)			× 3
	Car parking	Spaces < 400 m from town centre			
	Servicing	Proportion with dedicated access (±%)			
	Pedestrians	Area transferred from highway (m²) Area landscaped (m²) Area experiencing ± 3 dB(A) (m²)			
Resourcing	Cost and fundability	Capital cost (£000) Net cost to council (£000)			
	Value for money	Benefit/capital cost = weighted rating ÷ cost Benefit/net cost = weighted rating ÷ cost			

* Rating:

*	...	Maintains current situation.
**	...	Improvement over 'do nothing'.
***	...	Significant improvement over 'do nothing'.
No 'stars'	...	Deterioration compared with 'do nothing'.

Table 11. Casterbridge transport review — option* 3 traffic management package

Objective	Attribute	Measurable	Value	Rating	Weighted rating
Traffic movement	Congestion levels	Traffic volumes (veh km) Route length over capacity (km) Junction arms with delay > 3 min	67 188 7·6 18	—	—
	Rat running	Route length over desirable threshold (km) Change in speeds (± km/h)	3·0 0		
Public transport	Bus and rail	Bus network density index Arrivals in peak hour Average journey speed (km/h)	1·0 20 14·3	*	2*
	Part and ride	Reduction in town centre car trips (±%)	N/A		
Cycling	Cycling	Change in time (existing routes) (±%) Length of new route (km)	−10 3·8	**	2*
				.	
Safety	Accidents	Forecast casualty reduction	15	**	6*
Town centre	Traffic flows	Route length over desirable threshold (km) Change in speeds (± km/h)	1·0 −10	*	3*
	Car parking	Spaces < 400 m from town centre	1256		
	Servicing	Proportion with dedicated access (±%)	0		
	Pedestrians	Area transferred from highway(m²) Area landscaped (m²) Area experiencing ± 3 dB(A) (m²)	350 200 0	:	
Resourcing	Cost and Fundability	Capital cost (£000) Net cost to council (£000)	450 300		
				Total	19*

Value for money	Benefit/capital cost: 19* ÷ 0·45 = 42 Benefit/net cost: 19* ÷ 0·30 = 63

* Option outline:
London Road traffic calming.
Church Road/Orchard Street traffic calming.
Market Place pedestrianization and limited access.
New traffic signals at Station Hill junctions with Oxford Street and School Lane.
New links in pedestrian and cycleway networks.
Revised parking schemes in Castle Street/ Victoria Street.

local representatives to the objectives that might be achieved. None of the evaluation results, least of all the summarizing step labelled *value for money*, is intended to be rigorous in any context other than for comparison between the options in this specific exercise.

———

At the heart of local government — as with most political activity — is the job of making choices. This is rarely easy, and in today's climate gets harder all the time. Providing a starting point broadly accepted as fair is the vital contribution that professionals can make to this difficult and often thankless task. The result, whatever it is, will derive some benefit from that sound beginning.

8. Council business

Committees do not enjoy a good reputation. They are seen as a means for wasting time, a device for fudging decisions, for cobbling together compromises and for concentrating on trivia. The ineffectiveness of collective decision making has passed into folklore, enshrined in tired old jokes typified by the one about the camel being a horse designed by a committee.

Yet a great deal of the activity of public authorities is carried out through the committee process. To some extent this is obligatory: the law of public administration, as has already been seen, requires local authorities to observe strict rules about the delegation of the council's power to make decisions. Furthermore, there are legal requirements about public access and accountability that make the formal processes of council business, constructed around a 'cycle' of meetings of the council, its committees, subcommittees, etc., essential to the proper conduct of public service. However, the need to consult, the benefits of clear communications, and the expectation of people and communities that there will be open debate on issues affecting them are all powerful enough reasons in themselves to justify the infrastructure of committees and their support. And effective committees do produce good results: the camel is, after all, a very efficient means of transport in desert regions.

Formal meetings

The committee and subcommittee meetings are the formal set-pieces, the embodiment both of bureaucracy and local democracy. Their procedure has already been discussed and is subject to statutory regulations as well as (in theory) the traditional rules of debate. They are a unique form of a meeting: usually in public, always infused with politics in all its forms, never entirely predictable. Officials and professionals attend in an advisory capacity only, and yet, while not in control of the meeting or the decision making, they can have a profound effect on the proceedings.

The basis of any committee's activity is the agenda and the reports which make it up. Some space will be devoted later (in chapter 13) to making the point that clear and effective report-writing leads to clear and effective action. The agenda itself can also benefit from good management. For instance, items which complement each other can be placed together and in the most logical order; those which might react badly can be kept apart. If complex or controversial items are placed early in the running order there is a likelihood that decisions may be taken before the committee has had time to settle into the rhythm of the meeting and not get the considered attention they merit. Conversely, taking such items late on the agenda may place them beyond the boredom (or fatigue) threshold from which all committees suffer, and so they get no attention at all. These approaches are sometimes used as risky techniques to get difficult decisions or badly-argued reports through on the nod without close scrutiny, although — and here is the risk — they may be treated to an equally swift and annoyed rejection or postponement. Managing an agenda is one thing, rigging it is quite another: the dividing line is a fine one and needs to be treated with respect.

The authority's professional advisers have the opportunity to speak at committee and subcommittee meetings, usually to introduce an item that has some special feature requiring emphasis or explanation, to give the latest available information on a particular topic or to answer questions arising out of the debate. It is as well to reflect this advisory rather than participatory role in a reasonable observance of the etiquette of formal meetings — addressing all remarks to the chaiman, not interrupting, distinguishing information from argument, etc. — although this approach should not be allowed to develop into the blend of exaggerated deference and pomposity that can still be seen on display at too many committee meetings, and only serves to make them seem more remote and inaccessible to outside observers, and many participants.

What the meeting (committee members and the occupants of the public seats) want to hear is clear explanation, briefly stated and with fact and opinion properly differentiated. Therefore, the professionals must be well briefed and confident of their facts. The reports should convey all the basic information clearly, and only a short scene-setting for major items should be necessary, with the introduction of new facts or the results of the latest discussions being the other good reason for speaking. Nevertheless, it is foolish in the extreme to rely on the report to provide all the ingredients for the debate and decision: not everyone will have read it or understood it; and the professional presenting it must be prepared to answer all the obvious (and some not-so-obvious) questions arising from it, expand on any of the data and justify the recommendations. The golden rule should be: speak briefly, firmly and with assurance, but when in doubt say nothing (or failing that, as little as possible). A frank 'I don't know, but I'll find out' is sometimes the only response to a genuinely unforeseeable question, but it should be used sparingly as, far from being seen as engaging honesty, this tends to undermine credibility. However, waffling is dangerous for it is almost certain to be detected or at least suspected, and it is more important to be credible than clever — although it is best to be both.

Wit can be an effective means of staving off boredom but has to be kept in its place and low-key; knockabout comedy is unacceptable behaviour, although there may be some committee members who choose to indulge in it. Similarly, while argument, in the sense of challenging assumptions and forcefully expressing unpalatable advice when the situation demands it, is both acceptable and necessary, ill-mannered disagreement is unprofessional and guaranteed to lose the case.

Clarity of information includes visual presentation. Any plans or drawings that are to be displayed must be clear and easy to understand. Colours, symbols, lettering size and layout should be chosen to convey data quickly and without the need for inspection at close range: members of the public (and of the council) will be quite justified in assuming that anything unclear is being kept secret, and be entitled to ask why! Each plan or drawing must have the number of the associated agenda item clearly attached to it, be properly titled and assigned a specific and unique reference number that can be used to identify it in the formal record of the meeting. Accessibility is as important as clarity but is often overlooked: plans must be displayed where they can be seen (not easy in some council chambers and committee rooms); if it is necessary to point out features or details, then drawings should be mounted where they can be reached (last-minute improvisation of pointers or vague arm-waving are guaranteed to distract both speaker and audience); all plans and drawings must be in place well before the start of the meeting to allow committee members and the public a reasonable opportunity to inspect them (otherwise the meeting is likely to be interrupted by frequent viewing breaks). None of this should cause a problem if everything is prepared well in advance.

Regular attendance at committee meetings will show that sometimes (although by no means always) important and expensive projects are disposed of with little discussion, while relatively minor and low-cost items are subjected to close scrutiny. C. Northcote Parkinson's Law of Triviality

> The time spent on any item of the agenda will be in inverse proportion to the sum involved
>
> *Parkinson's Law*

is a rather cynical observation on this aspect of committee work, illustrated by the author's tongue-in-cheek account of how a mythical committee deals with approvals for a nuclear reactor ($2\frac{1}{2}$ minutes) and a bicycle shed ($\frac{3}{4}$ of an hour). The account contains some important truths, but for all that is no more than half-true.

Large projects (e.g. a traffic management study, TPP package bid or park and ride project) have long gestation periods and most are considered in principle or in outline by working groups, panels, sections and other off-shoots of the decision making system long before the final, formal authority to proceed is sought. Small items (a no-waiting order or a petition for new street lights, for instance) frequently do not benefit from these preliminaries and so are completely new to the members of the committee. Minor matters — in technical terms — may yet conceal big political issues and because they are small, they may be less well-supported by facts and explanation than the major ones and so generate questions, and thus debate, to fill the gaps left in the report. Whatever the reason for it, professionals must be prepared to respond to close questioning on what they consider minor items, as well as on the large projects. Indeed, their credibility on important matters may depend on the impression created in dealing with the trivia.

Not all formal meetings take place at the civic centre or county hall. The nature of public works projects and programmes makes the site meeting a very appropriate way of exposing the practical aspects of an issue to the decision makers. Often it serves the equally important purpose of demonstrating to the public that the council is not remote and detached, and that its members and their advisers are prepared to see for themselves the concerns of local people.

Site meetings need to be very carefully organized. The location must be clearly identified: a plan should always be provided to avoid the embarrassment of a committee being spread out along a length of road, or scattered around the various entrances to a complex junction. The position of the meeting and the route of any tour around the site should be chosen to ensure that the key points are visible or accessible. If the issue under consideration is dependent on particular circumstances — time of day, state of the tide, school term, market day, etc. — be sure that the meeting is organized to coincide with them. If it is important to get attendance from petitioners, an action group or local people with a special interest in the subject of the site meeting, then details of the arrangements must be communicated well in advance and some thought given to the practicalities of achieving the twin aims of public accessibility and an effective meeting. All this, of course, must take place under the uncertainties of the British climate!

The serious point is to remember that a site meeting cannot be organized properly without attention to the specific requirements of the location (almost certainly involving an advance site visit to check that everything will work); nor can it be treated lightly, especially if local people, who see it as a chance to influence decisions that are important to them, are going to be there.

Whether in a committee room or on site, the essential feature of a formal meeting is that it is 'on the record'. The date, place and time of the meeting and the people who attend on behalf of the local authority (and others if they are present in an official capacity, such as the police, or by formal invitation, such as the secretary of a residents' association) are all recorded by a council official. The title of *committee clerk* is still widely used to describe this person, although job descriptions today are more likely to refer to *committee manager* or *members' services assistant*. Working in the secretariat or corporate support unit of the council these officers arrange and publish the dates of meetings, distribute the agenda and any associated papers, keep the official record of discussion and decisions, and notify all the appropriate parties of the outcome of the meeting.

About six weeks (sometimes longer) before the date of a meeting in the committee cycle a procedure begins to move forward that although subject to local variation and the use of slightly different terminology, follows a typical pattern.

- *Forward look list*: a review of the expected or planned agenda items, usually with a short summary of their content, is prepared after consultation with all the contributors and circulated to them, as well as to office holders and other interested parties such as the authority's solicitors and finance officers.
- *Draft reports*: initial versions are prepared for circulation, internal consultation and input from any subsidiary contributors, on, for instance, legal or financial matters.
- *Briefing/call over*: about three or four weeks before the meeting, the office holders and party spokespersons preview the agenda, using the latest draft reports, and assess them for their clarity, potential controversy and effect on the organization of the meeting (some may be

short items of formal business, others may involve petitioners and lengthy speeches).

- *Final reports*: the lead officer responsible for reporting particular items to the committee settles the content and hands it over to the secretariat.
- *Late or urgent items*: subject to a procedure normally laid down in the council's standing orders, the chair/chairman of the committee can agree to accept reports which have not followed the normal timetable, perhaps because information has been unavailable (a delayed response from a neighbouring authority, for example) or because the item has to be dealt with quickly (a brief government consultation period, for instance).
- *Publication and despatch*: the complete agenda is printed and sent out to the usual recipients in the council and elsewhere at least three full working days before the meeting; exceptionally, some items are indicated as *to follow* when there is good reason for a report, or some part of it, not being ready in time; these papers form part of the official record of the committee process.

In this preparation, the briefing plays a key part. Although held in private with a restricted attendance, it is a formal meeting, convened and recorded by the secretariat at which decisions are made about whether or not reports are taken forward, what items are to be confidential, and how the committee agenda will be organized. Equally important is the reaction of the members to the drafts. Professionals are wise to treat this as an opportunity for communication in two directions, not just one. In explaining the reports, they should note what runs smoothly and what needs clarification or additional information; that will help make the reports more effective, and the work of the committee more constructive. This does not mean that the briefing should become a political editing session, and professionals may sometimes have to tread a careful path between their duty to give advice to the council as a whole and not any particular politician or party group, and the need to recognize that they are serving a system based on democracy and not technocracy. By acting as a sort of dress rehearsal for the committee, the briefing will reveal some of the potential difficulties of presentation and give a preview of the tensions that might arise between the professionally sound content of a report and the expectations of its various audiences. It is often possible, with the benefit of this private exchange of views, to get a better understanding of how the professional components can play a constructive part in the public business of the committee.

The importance of ensuring that difficult-to-explain or controversial items are brought to the briefing cannot be overstated. It allows time and space for members to absorb the technical issues and do any political groundwork that may be necessary, and for advisers to adjust the professional input so as to make it as clear as possible and to minimize — it may not be possible always to avoid — conflict with the council's political aims. 'No surprises' must be the motto for officers and consultants who want to make the best of the committee process.

All the preparation in the world will not guarantee the outcome of a committee meeting and the final stage in its formal life is the preparation of a series of notes that set down key points in the discussion on each item and record the decisions made. These are the minutes. They will form the first item on the agenda of the next meeting, and will be the document relied on in future as the official record of the deliberations and actions of the committee.

Councils have different styles for the presentation of minutes — indeed, they sometimes vary from one committee clerk to another — ranging from a terse statement of the decision with only the most exceptional outburst or hotly-contested vote recorded, to a detailed narrative covering almost every contribution to the debate. Both approaches have their advantages and disadvantages, and the political 'personality' of the council — one dominant party with tight internal discipline, for instance, or a variety of party groups plus a number of independents — will have a significant influence on the chosen style.

One thing is true: the more words there are in the minutes, the more important it is to get them right. So, it is important to secure the cooperation of the committee clerk, and review them in draft to avoid the kind of ambiguities and omissions (or perhaps the incorrect use of technical terms) which can result in major problems in the unforeseeable future. This process can be time-consuming and tedious, especially if the committee clerk tends to be verbose. However, there are many occasions when the wording of a minute becomes critical in establishing whether or not the council's decision has been carried out, and Murphy's Law will ensure that the controversy will involve the item with the error or omission which was left uncorrected.

Writing up a good record of a meeting does not require any modification, subtle or otherwise, to the substance of what was said or decided. It should, however, involve the editing out of the digressions, false-starts and genuine misstatements, while retaining the sense and broad meaning of the discussion and accurately reporting the conclusions. The value lies in the reliability of the record and its acceptance by the participants, whether or not they agree with the outcome.

Getting the minutes to this state is a real skill, sometimes compared with the ability of a mortician to smooth away the wrinkles and blemishes on the face of a departed loved-one. If you can find a committee clerk who can do it, with or without your help, strike up a permanent relationship at once.

All the other meetings

Formal meetings are, of course, relatively few and less frequent in comparison with the steady stream of working meetings — internal, external, technical, consultative, etc. — which go on through the life of any public works project or programme. Although some may involve elected members (as, for instance, when the chairman and vice-chairman of the environment committee meet their opposite numbers from an adjoining authority to clear away any policy problems relating to the joint use of a refuse disposal site, or the identification of a preferred lorry route that crosses their boundaries), the vast majority are organized, attended, controlled and recorded by project managers and the members of their teams. Such meetings are not subject to the restrictions of statute or standing orders and their style ranges all the way from the quasi-formal (for example, meetings at which members are present, high-level discussions between officers of different authorities and progress meetings on major contracts) to the near-casual (site inspections with landowners, for instance, internal briefings for design teams or liaison with local staff of the utility companies). Formality demands an agreed chairman, an agenda, perhaps the circulation of discussion papers and the subsequent preparation of a record to be issued to all participants. A more relaxed atmosphere is reflected in the absence of a chairman, lack of paper and a brief note entered on a file to record the main points.

The differences are obvious, but they tend to conceal the fundamental similarities that must be present for a meeting to be effective. There are three basic purposes for meetings: to decide upon a course of action; to pass on or exchange information; to oil the wheels by personal contact. All three may be involved at once, but one at least must be present if the meeting is to have any value. Those calling the meeting have to be clear about what purpose or purposes it is planned to serve and take some common sense steps to make it effective.

- Whether it is a chairman agreed by vote or negotiation, or a leader who emerges during the course of discussion, someone must steer the meeting in a forward direction, keep talk on, or at least near, the point and ensure everyone with a contribution to make gets a chance to speak.
- A written agenda is not essential but it is vital to have a clear purpose and aim for the meeting, so that each participant knows in advance why the meeting is taking place (so as to come prepared) and what it is intended to achieve (so as to make a useful contribution).
- Meetings which are very large tend to be unwieldy and ineffective unless controlled by formal procedures and a powerful chairman: eight or ten people seems to be the limit for routine meetings.
- Long meetings rarely produce results in proportion to their duration and can generate bad decisions as boredom and fatigue take their toll on the participants: two hours is quite enough and probably too much.
- Some form of record must be kept, not necessarily in very detailed form but certainly summarizing all the topics discussed, the conclusions reached and the action decided upon.

Meetings whether formal or informal do not, in themselves, get anything done — that takes place in the design office or on the site — but they should lead to positive decisions about getting things done. These decisions must be expressed in terms of 'who does what and by when', otherwise there is a serious risk of either duplication of effort or complete inactivity. A meeting that results in no progress is simply a waste of time, and time is one of the project manager's key resources. Professionals may not relish the constant round of meetings that accompany the development of public works projects: lack of identifiable results just adds to the belief that talking is no substitute for doing, and sets up a vicious circle. If the project manager can show that effective meetings represent time well spent that will go a long way to ensuring that the meetings are effective.

Because a great deal of effort must go into the meeting and the subsequent actions, it is only sensible to ensure that the whole process starts from a good foundation. Yet in many cases, even for complex and important meetings, the elementary precaution of a briefing or pre-meeting is omitted. All too frequently, staff attend a meeting not knowing the project manager's views on the subjects under consideration and with no specific directions on what matters they should discuss or whether they should speak at all. The usual excuse is that there is no time for such preliminaries, but if a meeting is worth staff time in attendance, it should be worth time in preparation.

Getting things done

In any local authority, there are few procedures that are entirely self-contained within a committee or service department. The processes of decision making, approval and implementation can only go forward with the proper involvement of the appropriate officials and the necessary subsidiary action of other committees. It is vital for project managers to ensure not only that these steps are built into the timetable, but also to recognize that their priorities may not be seen in the same light by other parts of the council's organization.

Particularly important in the life of most public works projects and programmes are the contributions of the finance, legal, planning and property functions.

Finance

Virtually every scheme will have some costs associated with its preparation and execution and, perhaps, over its subsequent life. At the very least estimated figures will need to be checked against budget provision to ensure that properly allocated funds exist, and regular monitoring reports agreed to identify potential under or overspending. In the case of large, long-term projects the phased release of funds and the various borrowing approvals must be cleared by the policy/strategy and resources committee or by the finance department which is often given delegated power to authorize (or, conversely, to veto) financial commitments such as the letting of a contract. When special funding arrangements — developers' contributions or capital receipts, in particular — are involved, the money has to be released and its use accounted for in accordance with the latest government regulations and guidelines. In most authorities committee reports have to indicate the financial implications of the proposed action, and failure to get this section completed by, or agreed with, the finance officers in time for the meeting is a sure way to cause delay or even cancellation of the project. (Similar controls and procedures exist when authorities act as agents, whether for another council or a government body such as the Department of Transport.) A quick review of chapter 4 will provide a reminder of the power which rests with accountants, auditors and the financial regulations they operate.

It is planned to use contributions and capital receipts from town centre redevelopment to fund the installation of a closed circuit TV (CCTV) system to monitor junctions and car parks. The financial appraisal indicates that all costs are met from external sources, but not all the expenditure can be classified as capital — the long-term charges for telecommunications links, for instance — and the direct use of the funds cannot be approved. The solution depends on the expertise (and cooperation) of the finance department in reallocating these external capital funds to suitable schemes that are presently earmarked for funding out of revenue, thus freeing up the right sort of money to be available for the non-capital parts of the CCTV project. Easy when you know how . . .

Legal

Public authorities, as has been seen in chapter 1, can only act within clearly defined limits, and then they are often required to follow specific procedures for notice, consultation, consideration of objections and proper publication of decisions. In many cases, the implementation of projects and programmes is achieved by letting contracts for works or services, which will range from standard documents through modified versions to special legal agreements drawn up after complex negotiations. The timing, content and conduct of council and committee business, and the operation of schemes of delegation are all governed by legislation and regulation. In an environment where open and accountable government is subject to continuous and well-informed scrutiny, it is essential that *due process* is followed. Similarly, when agreements and contracts are ever more frequently put to the test in court or arbitration, it is vital that they are based on sound advice.

Before signing a long-term contract with a waste disposal company for the provision and operation of a new high technology plant to treat domestic refuse, the council needs to safeguard its position. The lawyers will want to ensure that the firm, which is a subsidiary of a large conglomerate, is guaranteed by the parent company for all its liabilities; that there is an enforceable clause making the contractor, and not the council, responsible for alternative disposal arrangements if the plant fails to work; and, among other things, that the council is not liable for any claims for damages if the new process causes any local nuisance or pollution. Drafting a suitable set of contract conditions will take time, and they will be bound to have an impact on negotiations even when they are brought forward at an early stage. But if they are introduced late, or when the contract is about to be signed . . .

Planning

Large projects, and some small ones if they affect sensitive locations such as a conservation area, need planning consent before they can proceed. This is true regardless of the fact that they may be promoted by the same local authority as will consider the planning application, and approval should never be taken for granted. Although a council can consider its own project and give itself planning permission, the full process of public notice, consultation with affected residents and interested parties (including other local authorities), and consideration of responses must be followed before any decision is made. The

.decision making body — the planning or development control committee — will not be the same as the service committee promoting the scheme which is, in fact, the applicant. Not only is it essential to build into the programme the time needed to take an application through the planning committee's normal cycle, it is equally important to do what any sensible developer does and seek pre-application advice on the council's planning policies and their requirements. Even then, because planning decisions are often much influenced by local factors and not just the professional opinions of planners, the project manager must be ready to accept conditions attached to the consent.

Although the reconstruction of an existing road, with some minor realignment to improve visibility, did not require planning consent, the demolition and rebuilding of a river bridge at one end of the route was of sufficient extent to warrant an application. The position of the structure on a section of the river classified as having high landscape value made its appearance an important issue; the use of local building materials and styles, and the preservation of public access along the riverbank were other high priority planning policies relevant to the proposal. The sensitivity of the location, the presence of an active local conservation group and the need for the council to be seen to be acting with particular care over its own application led the planning committee to organize a site meeting, with a public display of drawings and artist's impressions in the nearby village hall, before making its decision. The project timetable had allowed only two months for the entire process, apparently based on a minimum consultation period followed by a rubber stamp decision. It took four months, and only by shortening the time for preparing the final documents through the use (and expense) of extra staff was the contract let in time to carry out works in the main stream during the period when the Environment Agency would permit disturbance to the flow. The project manager should have known better ...

Property

The management of a council's property stock and the activities necessary for acquisitions or disposals is a complex business with far-reaching effects. Property — land and buildings — is a valuable and tangible asset and is invariably subject to close supervision by the council, usually through a separate committee or a subcommittee of the powerful policy/strategy and resources committee. Acquisition of land for a project may proceed by negotiation, using the services of the local authority's own professionals or external chartered surveyors, subject, initially, to approval of the requirements and, subsequently, of the final deal. Although agreed purchases are common, the statutory compulsory purchase powers that local authorities are able to employ are often needed and it is always prudent to set the procedure in motion, if only to hold it in reserve should negotiation fail. Again, the activation of a compulsory purchase order (CPO) requires a specific process of approval, publication, consultation and consideration of objections that can lead to a public inquiry. Getting the details, and the potentially extended timetable, right is essential and requires close cooperation between the project manager and the property specialists. Two vital ingredients that clearly rest within the responsibility of the project manager are the accurate definition of the land-take and the comprehensive justification for the need. Inputs requiring particular cooperation are the modification of non-critical design features to eliminate objections and the agreement of reasonable accommodation works to mitigate the impact of the project and/or act as a more acceptable substitute for a cash transaction. While acquisition is always more contentious than disposal, the sale of land surplus to requirements at the completion of a project can be an important source of funds, and care in the design will maximize this potential (so will the basic act of remembering where surplus land exists!).

The construction of a car park, access road and a series of junction improvements for a park and ride project involves the acquisition of 75 plots of land. They range from ten hectares of low-grade agricultural land, through the purchase for demolition of a modern detached house, to the setting back of the front boundaries of a row of cottages by two metres or less. In addition, about 80 residential properties are possibly affected by increased noise levels on the improved bus route; 60 householders consider they will be injuriously affected by noise and other disturbance from the adjacent car park; and a further 15, although less directly affected, are indicating that the scheme will blight their properties and depress sale values. The use of CPO procedures is clearly essential in such a case, and every aspect from the justification of the benefits of the scheme as a whole to the detailed layout of sight lines at the improved junctions will be open to close and hostile scrutiny. The project manager has a decision to make: instruct the council's property department (which knows the scheme but is deeply involved in a programme for the disposal of redundant school playing fields to generate major capital receipts for a prestigious new sixth-form college), or put the main body of the work to a private firm (which has a well-respected local office and has worked for the council before, but will need close liaison and guidance). Which would you choose ...?

These descriptions and examples, are based on the theoretical, and unlikely, situation in which there is a self-contained relationship between the project manager and just one of the major participants. In practice, there will be a network of inputs, contacts and processes that will need to be managed through the life of the project. Because properly authorized financial, legal, planning and property activities may all be needed (and the first two are almost always necessary) the project manager will be well advised to draw up a 'route map' to chart the path through what can be a maze, and too often becomes a minefield. The signposts will identify the essential decisions, who can make them, what timetable they require and the contingency action (if any) should something be missed. Even relatively simple projects will benefit from this exercise.

Canalside cycleway: £30 000 approved in current year's capital programme; £40 000 in the following year. It is mid-November.

- Since resolution at November council, no capital schemes with an effect on next year's budget can be committed without endorsement by the director of finance and approval of the special budget management section set up by strategy and resources committee — next meeting, first week of December.
- Traffic regulation orders drafted by solicitor's department, approval to publish already obtained; minimum 28 day objection period extended to six weeks for this scheme by resolution of last subcommittee; if no objections, delegated power with solicitor to make the order, otherwise consider at highways subcommittee — third week of January. (NB if modifications and report back needed, next available meeting in third week of February.)
- Three signs needed to be fixed to buildings in the canal basin conservation area; district planning officer can exercise delegated powers subject to local consultation — allow seven weeks instead of normal four because of Christmas, with formal clearance by mid-January. (NB if delegated approval not forthcoming, report necessary to district planning committee at next available meeting in first week of February.)
- No land acquisition necessary as British Waterways Board has confirmed it will grant a licence for three cycle parking areas and for two viewing points in the canal basin area for a nominal fee plus some repairs/replacement to railings and fences along the route; property officer has delegated powers to agree terms and accommodation works; solicitor to check documentation etc. — allowing eight weeks to cover Christmas holiday, agreement ready before end of January. (NB include railings/fence repairs in contract for cycleways works.)
- Select tenderers from approved list; subject to price being not more than 5% above estimate — standing orders allows officer action with subsequent information report to highways subcommittee — invite tenders after budget clearance in second week of December with return by end of January (NB any changes to signs or railings/fence works notified by tender amendment); award, subject to no outstanding objections etc., at the end of first week of February for a start date of 1 March; sixteen week contract period

---

9. Politics

There is a tendency to consider local government as being all about politics, and paradoxically to maintain that 'public service has nothing to do with that sort of thing'. This is based on a mistaken and rather naive view that politics is defined by party strife and the clash of ideologies, by manifestos and debates and elections. Such a view passes lightly over the political processes that go on within any organization, group or community. They are as real and immediate in, say, a cricket club or a management team as they are in a council chamber or a party conference, because politics is about balancing competing interests and influencing the environment which those interests occupy, whatever it might be. Thus, every project or programme, whether controversial or not, is affected in some way by the politics of the community or organization in which it exists.

So, while professionals working in, or for, the public service are wise to have no party allegiance, they cannot claim to be above or outside politics. Successful project management requires working with politicians, being politically sensitive to the local communities and interest groups and, when the occasion demands, getting involved in the politics of organizations.

Party politics
There are local councillors who belong to no formal party and sit as independents, either as individuals or as part of loose local groupings. However, they represent only a small proportion of council membership, as the vast majority of elected representatives are voted in under the label of one of the established national parties and join a (more or less) cohesive group seeking to implement its policies at a local level.

Some may express regret at the demise of independent councillors who cast their votes on the basis of local benefit and not party dogma, although it is questionable whether they were quite so numerous, or so disinterested, as is often claimed. Certainly, the municipal corporations in the great Victorian cities were run on party lines and played an important role in the national political scene; similarly, the growth of the trades unions in the coalfields, mill towns and railway workshops was marked by their enthusiastic participation in local democracy. Although the squirearchy which dominated the shire counties served out of obligation, and neither followed nor proposed any organized policies, it nevertheless represented a community of interest and tended towards a general conservatism (with a big and a little *c*).

So, local government has not suddenly become politicized in the recent past, but has always had a strong element of party politics in its character. It is true, however, that in the last 25 years or so national party politics has come to exercise a greater influence on local politics; party discipline and organization have tended to be strengthened; and council elections have become transformed into giant public opinion polls on the popularity of governments. All this has created a sharper emphasis on party groups and a markedly parliamentary style in most local authorities, where coalitions form administrations, oppositions demand free votes, whips are active and documents are leaked.

Whatever its origins, party politics is now a fact of local government life, and must be acknowledged as part of the environment in which public services operate. Parties have a purpose: they provide a focal point for opinion to be channelled into policies and, perhaps, action; they allow resources to be organized and mobilized in mutual support and coordinated activity; they provide channels of communication into, and out of, the formal processes of government. It is easy for professionals to scoff at the way this neat theory operates in practice, and criticize as bad management (or worse) the splits, U-turns, special cases, exaggerated claims and avoided decisions that are ever-present in all parties and political organizations. This ignores the fundamental difference between the largely quantifiable and calculable factors to be dealt with in project management and the altogether less controllable components of the politician's trade: imperfect institutions; insufficient money; infinite demands, and human nature.

Before affecting a counter-productive cynicism of, and isolation from, the politics of local government, project managers should try to understand how these factors shape political activity and learn to appreciate the ground rules that underpin it.

- *Politics is about reconciling conflicting interests.* All political parties are to some extent coalitions representing similar, but rarely identical, views; to secure and keep wide support they must operate through consensus and not by extremes; the permanent mismatch between expectations and resources makes compromise a constant feature. Even Bismarck, who dominated late 19th century Germany and was not called the Iron Chancellor for nothing, recognized the practical limitations when he coined the phrase 'politics is the art of the possible'.

- *Political priorities must be flexible.* While basic principles and key commitments cannot easily be abandoned, the timing and relative importance of specific elements have to be variable; the pressure of outside events and the emergence of unforeseen factors may delay one objective, or bring another urgently forward, or render yet another impossible to achieve; the continuous balancing of finite resources against virtually unlimited requirements means that no future plan or programme can ever be unchangeable. Queen Victoria's favourite prime minister, Benjamin Disraeli, believed that 'finality is not the language of politics' and almost a century later another occupant of No.10, Harold Wilson, said much the same thing when he remarked that 'a week is a long time in politics'.

- *Politicians must work with the grain.* Parties that do not reflect the general trend of opinion do not, in the end, command public confidence and their representatives do not stay in office; delivering popular policies is easy, and real political skill lies in consulting, persuading and convincing enough people that a tough or difficult decision is, nevertheless, the right one; changes in direction are rarely accomplished by sharp, sudden reversals but by a series of gentle shifts that the majority can accept, or even feel part of, as they occur. Every practical politician would recognize the risks of being too far ahead of, or too much at odds with, public opinion, though few would go as far as Alfred Bonar Law, one of the lesser known 20th century Prime Ministers, who explained his approach with the words 'I am their leader, I must follow them'.

So the workings of party politics have their own internal logic; complaining about it will be of as much use as complaining about the weather, and prudent project managers will try to accommodate both in their plans. A little specialist knowledge always helps.

Party groups on a council are usually organized around a nucleus of influential members: the leader, his or her deputy and a small number of key supporters. If the party is in power, they will all probably hold important committee posts, but that is not always the case and there may be some members of a 'kitchen cabinet' who do not take a very public role but prefer to operate within the group or perhaps through working parties that meet in private. These are important people in the council: their views on a programme or project, on the credibility of the professionals promoting it and the relative priority it might achieve are crucial. Briefing meetings which they attend are significant, therefore, as opportunities both to learn of the group's current position and forward plans, and to advocate the benefits of a scheme or service.

Not that the leadership is always free to act. Factions within the group may limit its freedom to make decisions. The group may be affiliated — by loose connections or formal constitutional arrangements — to a local branch of the national party organization and subject to some direction, ranging from the nods and winks variety up to an official mandate or instruction. The changing patterns of party support in local government elections have added a new dimension: the hung council where no single group has overall control, and various accommodations, agreements and (not a word openly used because of resistance at national level) pacts are developed to maintain one party or (less common) a formal coalition in power. These arrangements may be well known and open or they may be covered by a cloak of secrecy and deniability, and in any event are unlikely to have been so thoroughly codified as to deal with every contingency. Managing professional services for elected bodies requires reliable and up-to-date intelligence on the workings of all these components of the political machinery. This can only be obtained by diluting an understandable cynicism with a large measure of respect for the political process, and by keeping close to it rather than holding it at arm's length.

There is no restriction, legal or ethical, on the provision of professional advice and information to a party group, provided that the same service is available to all the groups in the council. The ruling party will tend to have, through its control of the committees, a close day-to-day working relationship with the professionals, especially the senior council officers. Nevertheless, the opposition is entitled to, and should receive, the same standard on routine service delivery matters and the full range of advice on policy issues. The realities of political power make it inevitable that the majority group will be seen by the opposition as enjoying the support of the professionals, simply because they will be actively engaged in promoting its (i.e. the council's) projects and programmes. Paradoxically, the realities of human nature will frequently lead members of the ruling party to speculate, when the run of political events goes against them or when mistakes are made, that the opposition is getting special help. If the professionals can be accepted by all parties as neutral for 90% of the time, and for the other 10% fall out with them in roughly equal shares, then they have probably got the balance right.

The dividing line between professionalism and politics in local government is not always easy to see, and specific attention will be paid to it in a later chapter. What is important at this point is the recognition that party politics and politicians have a role to play in public services, which must be accommodated for project management to be successful and professional advice to be productive.

Take the example of a rise in town centre parking charges which is being prepared for approval by the council, principally to fund the cost of major structural repairs to the multi-storey car parks. In straight technical terms, this is a solution based neatly on the user being asked to pay. But town centre car park charges are almost always controversial. There are a number of potential political issues: concern over town centre trade; incentives to switch to public transport; restrictions on car-generated pollution; improvements to security and safety in car parks; standards of maintenance, past and present; good financial housekeeping, etc. Party groups may well have different positions on them. By understanding the politicians' need to justify and sell the increases in the face of potential powerful non-party opponents — e.g. motorists, commercial interests — as well as the opposition, a package of charges and offsetting benefits can be assembled that satisfies both the practical and political aspects. Ignore the politics and the proposed increases may have to be withdrawn, leaving the repairs to be funded by a transfer from the hard-pressed road maintenance budget — hardly a satisfactory professional outcome.

The fundamental duty of the professional, whether public servant or consultant, is to provide sound advice within the framework of a code of ethics. The basic objective of party politicians is to win — and having won, maintain — power, within a somewhat looser set of moral guidelines. If (as will be shown in chapter 16), both recognize each other's position, then they should be able to coexist on reasonable terms.

Interest groups

Sociologists and political theorists have spent a lot of time analysing the development of interest groups, their composition, methods and relative success at representing the opinions and needs of their constituents. In recent years the rise of a particular variant — the pressure group — has opened up a new field of study, evaluating the concentrated effort and energy, in the shape of publicity, protest or persuasion, which it can bring to bear to serve its aims.

Interest groups and pressure groups are familiar at a more practical level to public service professionals. They all share the common feature of seeking to influence events from a position outside the machinery of government, but beyond that there is a clear distinction between four different types.

- *Causes.* Cutting across generations, location, socio-economic groupings (i.e class) and sometimes even political loyalties, such groups stand for a goal or ideal that is wider than the interests of the group or its individual members; the classic examples are the Campaign for Nuclear Disarmament and Shelter. In the field of public works causes are represented by environmental groups such as Friends of the Earth, Greenpeace and Transport 2000, that take a prominent part in issues of waste recycling, water pollution, congestion, etc.

- *Sectional groups.* Such groups are more narrowly based in terms of age and class of membership, less politically-involved, but generally still free of any specific geographic focus; the models are the Council for the Protection of Rural England and the Childrens' Society. Public works managers will find the Ramblers' Association, the Royal Society for the Protection of Birds and the AA and RAC among their active contacts.

- *Economic interests.* Formed to protect and enhance the economic position of their members, these groups are bound to be focused on a specific territory, although not necessarily a geographic one, and they may or may not have strong political linkages; they are typified by the trades unions and the National Farmers' Union. In public works projects and programmes the British Road Federation, Environmental Services Association, local chambers of commerce and the British Asphalt and Coated Macadam Institute are the sort of groups most likely to be encountered.

- *Local groups.* Established, sometimes with a very short life span, to represent the views of people (although not necessarily the majority) living in a particular area (which can be large or small), these groups are the most diverse and volatile; the standard case study is a residents' association. In the management of public works the geographic base may be a street where a pedestrian crossing is wanted; a housing estate demanding traffic calming; a village wanting a bypass (with a corresponding stop the bypass action group also in operation), or a whole district campaigning against proposals for waste disposal.

To a significant extent groups such as these have become an alternative to parties: Greenpeace has more members than any one United Kingdom political party; the Royal Society for the Protection of Birds has a bigger membership (almost 900 000) than all of them put together. They have come to play a prominent role in local government in a way which would have been difficult to imagine a generation ago. To challenge the views of the authorities was not just difficult in practical terms, it was generally considered unacceptable behaviour — not now. Most local councils encourage contact and dialogue with interest groups, and many have set up procedures to involve them in consultation and give them access to committees. This brings them into the political process; although not every pressure group will want to take up that opportunity, because being outsiders is seen by many of their members as an advantage, not a disadvantage. Indeed, it is very important for professionals to recognize that interest groups are even less likely than party politicians to adopt an objective approach to an issue. It is a contradiction to expect a pressure group to see both sides of the argument. It is unrealistic to anticipate that logic or figures will prevail over the weight of emotions. It is dangerous to underestimate the persistence and determination of a motivated group, or its ability to command attention, sympathy and publicity. Above all, it is foolish to assume that they will play by the rules. Why should they?

Petitioners for a traffic calming scheme will not be impressed by explanations that priorities for limited funds must be based on accident records. 'Do we have to wait for someone to be killed before anything is done?'

An action group campaigning against a park and ride site in its suburban neighbourhood will not take much account of an assessment of the benefits from reduced congestion to be enjoyed by people living near the town centre, or of more environmentally-friendly transport in a general sense. The campaign will focus on 'concreting over green fields' and 'destruction of the countryside'.

Residents opposed to a landfill proposal near their village will not acknowledge their part in the production of the waste it will receive, nor accept arguments demonstrating its suitability on transport, hydrogeological or any other technical grounds. 'Don't let Binford become the rubbish bin of Westshire.' 'Fight the Dump — take your rubbish to county hall.'

Slogans are the stock-in-trade of pressure groups and professionals must never be patronizing about them nor provoked by them. Their purpose is to catch the eye or ear of their target audience and if they do that they are working well, however silly or inaccurate they may appear. The only response is to be patient, respond courteously and keep the debate (or at least your side of it) at an objective level, well-supported by facts and confirmed opinion. After all, the aim cannot be to persuade the pressure group that it is wrong, but rather to demonstrate to a wider body of opinion, and particularly the decision makers, that its demands are partial and, therefore, may be unacceptable.

This is not to imply that local pressure groups employ only the headline-grabbing, mud-slinging, 'don't confuse me with facts' variety of argument.

Long-established interest groups typically employ, directly or indirectly, their own experts to research and present their cases: anyone who has come up against, say, the well-informed opposition of the Council for the Protection of Rural England will be well aware of that. Similarly, the more vociferous and overtly political national pressure groups such as Transport 2000 are just as capable of mounting serious technical resistance to a proposal as of putting on a banner-waving demonstration. Nowadays, these resources can also be found in active use on local issues. Widespread concern about the environment and road safety in particular, coupled with what are often unspoken but, nevertheless, real (and, if selfish, still justified) fears about the value of property, have spurred many people into supporting local collective action with money as well as time. Professional and technical advice, as well as data, may be obtained from within the group itself or purchased from outside, thus raising the discussion on to a different level.

The petitioners for traffic calming carry out their own count, identifying vehicles using the road as a through route; a relative who is a retired engineer uses his professional institution's library to check out the latest technical guidance; a day spent at the local library reading through the minutes of the road safety subcommittee for the previous two years reveals a number of special cases where councillors have voted to introduce schemes although there was no record of injury accidents. Persistent counting gets a record of a particularly busy day, the guidelines indicate areas of discretion for the use of some calming features, and the minutes are full of precedents: a strong case is being built up to underpin the emotive threat of an accident waiting to happen ...

The Save Southfield Meadows Action Group includes an economics lecturer who, with the help of other university contacts and some computer time paid for by a fund-raising barbecue, prepares a cost-benefit analysis which predicts the park and ride scheme will be a costly failure. Another member of the group is an accountant who is the honorary treasurer of the County Natural History Society, and she arranges for an authoritative report on the importance of the flora and fauna of the meadows. A third member works in a local solicitor's office and secures help to look over the orders to see if there are any points worth challenging ...

After a meeting in the parish hall attended by almost the entire village, the Binford defence committee is set up with a fighting fund big enough to commission a hydrologist to prepare a report on pollution of the groundwater by putrescible waste in the landfill, and from a pathologist on the risk of Weil's disease being carried by rats into the nearby river and lake. A villager is an associate in a large advertising agency and another is the former editor of the local weekly newspaper, so the reports are strikingly presented and get excellent publicity ...

The skills and self-confidence that our modern, media-conscious society has developed so widely among the population, and the willingness to challenge authority which is now found throughout the community, make all interest groups worthy of very careful attention. Whether working subtly through established channels or bringing vigorous protest to bear in spectacular form, their ability to influence decision makers can be significant. It is important to recognize that politicians will be unlikely to ignore or miss political pressure aimed directly at them, and will tend to respond. They may also see such alternative sources of advice as a refreshing and attractive change from the voice of the council's professionals, and tend to listen. So, it is essential to be aware of what is going on and keep a steady stream of facts and technical recommendations flowing, both to maintain the council's confidence in its policy or project and to give it effective counter arguments. Do not, however, get drawn into the action: this is one time to be energetic in support, but leave the politics to the politically active.

Office politics

If politics is who gets what, when and how, then the internal workings of organizations — private and public — are intensely political. Managers may well prefer to play down the importance of the balancing of interests, the competition and conflicts that are always present, at both small-scale and large, in their working lives, but that would be to underestimate their effect on organizational culture and outputs.

Businesses have their fair share of internal wheeling and dealing, tensions and turmoil, and the issues of profit and production, far from always providing a unifying aim, are just as likely to be their cause. Public authorities, however, with their wide range of responsibilities and lack of a single core function, tend to find it even more difficult to focus their managerial priorities. This is complicated by the close proximity of party political activity, the uneasy relationships between very different services coexisting in the same organization, and between service delivery and central support.

It is not the intention to produce a survival manual for use in the office jungle, nor any master plan for waging a successful campaign in the endless power struggles of bureaucracy. Rather the objective is to point out where office politics can be a relevant factor in the promotion, planning and implementation of public works projects so that the effects can be taken into account. The close relationship with local government politics invariably means that, to some extent, the credibility and status of officers will be reflected in the support and priority afforded the services and functions they represent. The pecking order may be much influenced by the perceived helpfulness, flexibility and reliability of the chief officer; or perhaps the subjective assessment of the performance of the department at its tasks; or the reflected glory of the publicity and popularity its services generate. It can also have something to do with the political awareness of senior staff and the belief that an official is one of us.

There is nothing wrong — and a lot that is right — about being regarded as reliable, credible and sensitive to the political environment in which local government operates. It is important to understand what will attract the support of politicians and, within the bounds of reasonable professional conduct, provide it. If good news publicity is valued, then ensure your projects and programmes get it. When there are difficult choices to be made, you should be careful to explain clearly and confidently all the consequences of the options, giving room for manoeuvre and privacy for decision making. As for the key members who influence the setting of priorities — well, it is only sensible to make sure they experience high levels of service and cooperation. The benefit to be gained is a firmer hold on the managerial initiative in the ever-changing climate of a politically-driven organization.

Remember that many public works programmes and services inevitably involve more demands for action — on traffic calming, road safety, environmental improvements, etc. — than it is possible to meet and this means saying 'no' rather more often than politicians like. Conversely, it is hard to imagine a politically unpopular library service or fire brigade. The lesson here is that it needs greater care, more effort and better public relations to maintain a positive image for public works with members than for almost any other activity, so work hard at it and take nothing for granted.

Different services are not only perceived differently by politicians, but they also operate with different values and within entirely different professional cultures. This makes the coordination of their activity inside one organizational strategy or plan very difficult. Chief officers and their departments have been compared with the feudal barons and their retainers, owing only nominal allegiance to the king but in fact intent on carving out their own territory. Chief executives have sought to impose order and corporate working on this potential chaos with varying degrees of success and bloodshed.

Alliances, conspiracies and loose federations may come and go, empires may be built, and revolutions plotted (and sometimes even carried out). The prudent project manager will not take a leading role in this, but will not ignore it either. At budget time in particular, and at any other time when reorganizations or management reviews are in the air, constructive involvement and inside information will be the best protection in the almost inevitable conflicts that result. Thus, it is important, for instance, to participate in corporate reviews where priorities are set across all services: this is the time when, whatever politicians may choose to do later, the professional playing field should be kept level and inflated calls for resources or commitment challenged. It is equally necessary to take an interest in the information presented to brief the council or party groups, to ensure its freedom from bias or, when necessary, to correct any imbalance which might have crept in. In spite of all the claims to corporate working that are commonplace in local government, many officials see themselves as advocates for their services — and advocacy does not involve putting anyone's case but your own.

This is not an argument against cooperating with other departments — not only is that what professional officers are supposed to do, but it is also a useful source of information — merely a caution about the motives and objectives of colleagues who may be working under pressures and imperatives very different from yours. Professional empires have tended to decline with the advent of more integrated management structures, but they have certainly not disappeared.

The property department's workload had been decreasing steadily with the sale of the council's land stock and the delegation of maintenance budgets to local schools and service managers. Following some dramatic overspends on new-build projects in the education department, however, the opportunity arose for the property department to take over the client role and provide external project management/value for money services. The logic of extending this to social services projects was soon accepted, but there was insufficient activity from both sources to justify a full-scale in-house project management unit. The Director of Property suggested that all capital works, including new highways and major road and bridge maintenance, should be covered by the new arrangements. The County Engineer drew a distinction between education and social services where the core business was personal services rather than the building of schools and residential homes, etc., and his responsibilities which included effective construction and maintenance of highways. The Director of Property sought support from the Finance Director, pointing out how much a rigorous external challenge could reduce the costs of over-specified projects; the county engineer responded that for relatively small extra construction costs, both routine and long-term maintenance expenditure could be significantly reduced. At this point, noting these arguments about initial capital costs and revenue expenditure over time, the Director of Finance began to feel that a value for money audit was really an area where he should be taking the lead.

The tensions between individual services can come to real confrontations which may even surface in public — when, for instance, infrastructure or property development plans of the council come up against its planning policies — but these are usually incidents rather than constant themes. Very different is the relationship between services and the corporate centre.

A somewhat awkward and unstable equilibrium exists between the central functions and the service departments in their relationship with members. Service departments need the cooperation of the centre, particularly on legal and financial issues, as a word (or, just as importantly, a silence) from that quarter can alter the feasibility or priority of a project; the staff at the centre are close to the politicians, advising or warning them about what they can or cannot do with the authority's powers and money. This, service chief officers would say, gives the corporate centre a privileged and protected position, exaggerating its importance over that of the council's real reason for existence — service delivery. When, they would go on to ask, has a central function been subject to the kind of internal review regularly applied (usually by officers from the centre) to service departments? When (the sacrifice of the occasional chief executive excepted) has a central department made any significant staff or budget reductions?

There are — somewhere — some robust answers to these questions, but the problem of perception remains. To a large extent it is for the centre to demonstrate its value as a support for the services as well as a check on them, and to make its activities, particularly where advice to the political processes about service issues is concerned, more cooperative. However, the services need to recognize the difficult task which has to be done and their own reluctance to play as part of a corporate team. This is particularly important for public works projects and programmes, which often lack the emotional appeal of other service priorities, and tend to be more complex legally (traffic and side road orders, for instance) and financially (utilities' diversions, contractors' claims, etc.) than would appear to an outsider. Good working relationships with the centre can smooth these and other potential difficulties, and generate a mutual understanding of each other's requirements. Quite simply, this means identifying the people with influence so that help and advice can be got quickly, and finding out what keeps them, and other contacts involved in progressing your projects, happy in their work, e.g. regular expenditure returns, committee items delivered ready-typed in advance of deadlines, acknowledgement of assistance in reports, etc. To have the positive support of an accountant, a committee clerk and a solicitor should be every project manager's dream, and you should be working to make it come true.

10. Making contact

The nature of politics, as has been seen, has changed considerably over the last 20 years. It is less structured, more responsive, and to a large degree polarized between the very central and the very local. Regulations, codes of practice, citizens' charters and, above all, public expectations have made a high level of communication essential. Furthermore, the traffic now has to be two-way and there is a strong presumption, particularly in local government, that the public interest cannot be properly served unless the public is fully involved.

It is, perhaps, rather churlish to draw comparisons between these expectations and the continued low turn-out in council elections, and it may be that this only proves the point about the shift of attention from party politics to the politics of interest groups. Nevertheless, in the current climate making contact with the public and those who represent their views is only the start, and probably the easiest part. The real difficulty comes in striking the balance between the relatively few but active joiners, and the usually much more numerous and passive non-joiners, to get a cross-section of the community. And then the challenge is how to engage people in choosing and decision making, and what share to offer them in the powers of action and influence that local authorities can wield.

Consultation

Consultation is about getting the response of the public and their representatives to a proposal or set of alternatives. It is more — much more — than the simple 'here are the facts, do you want to object?' exercise carried out when, for instance, a traffic regulation order such as a parking ban on part of a residential street is advertised. This represents consultation in its minimal form; informing but not involving. A public works scheme can affect many people, not only those who live or work in its immediate vicinity and thus feel its impact or benefit directly, but also those from much further afield whose involvement may be indirect (through use of the facility perhaps, or through the effects it may have on development). However many they are — and it could be dozens or thousands — there will always be some who will feel deeply affected and will want to be involved.

There will be, as with any expenditure of substantial public funds, a political dimension too, possibly extending far beyond the locality and its inhabitants, and involving more than just the proposed scheme or its alternatives, to embrace fundamental questions about priorities and relative values: maintenance before new construction? cars before public transport? roads before schools?

The public expect to be consulted on these issues and expect the job to be done properly. The first requirement is to identify who should be consulted. The following list provides some general guidance and, more importantly, indicates the size of the task.

- *Elected councils:* every council within whose boundaries the project will lie including, if it is a suburban or rural area, the appropriate town and parish councils, and any neighbouring authorities that are likely to be affected by the proposal or have an interest in it (not necessarily the same thing).
- *Official consultees:* Government departments (Departments of Transport and the Environment, Ministry of Agriculture, Fisheries and Food, etc.) and other agencies or bodies that have special status conferred on them by law or by their function (the utility companies, British Rail, British Waterways, Forestry Commission, Police, Fire Brigade, Countryside Commission, Royal Fine Arts Society, English Heritage, etc.).
- *National interest groups:* those which may have an opinion on the specific impact of the scheme on their particular activities (National Trust, Royal Society for the Protection of Birds, etc.), and those taking a factional view on behalf of a particular lobby or pressure group which may go beyond the details of any specific proposal (Friends of the Earth, Transport 2000, Council for the Protection of Rural England, Freight Transport Association, British Roads Federation, and so on); in either case such bodies are best approached through their local branch if one exists.
- *Local interest groups:* mainly in the form of residents' associations, but also including trade and business organizations (Chamber of Commerce, London Road Traders' Association, etc.) area-based special interest societies or clubs (County Natural History Society, River Thames Society, Friends of the Ridgeway, etc.) and local pressure groups (Casterbridge Cycle Campaign, Binford Defence Committee, etc.).
- *Individuals:* most obviously, the owners and occupiers of the land and properties, residential and commercial, which may be physically affected by the proposals; also those indirectly affected but likely to suffer from noise, visual intrusion, severance, and so on; less obviously, those individuals (people and businesses) whose patterns of living and working may be affected by the presence — or perhaps the absence — of the proposed scheme or one of its alternatives; finally and most difficult of all, those who, in spite of appearances to the contrary, genuinely believe they are obvious subjects for any properly conducted public consultation.

No list can be exhaustive. Local interest groups in particular may have an erratic life cycle, lying dormant for long periods until revived by a new, controversial issue. Some pressure groups will only come into being as a result of the consultation process. It is impossible ever to be certain that all the organizations, groups and individuals have been identified, and there is no master directory to which a project manager can refer: the only way to partial success is to think hard, look carefully and make thorough inquiries locally — and then wait for those left out to get in touch, and bring them into the consultation.

Having identified the consultees, the next step is to involve them in the process of consultation itself. This is not as easy as it may appear. Contacting local councils, official bodies and large-scale representative groups should present no problems and communication can go ahead through the normal channels (formal consultation should always be done in writing to eliminate any possibility of misunderstanding or misrepresentation), but the smaller local groups and some individuals (absentee landlords, holding companies, etc.) may prove difficult to track down. Most elusive of all is the general public.

The secretaries of residents' associations and similar local organizations are not to be found conveniently listed in Yellow Pages, but councils — not forgetting parish and town councils — usually keep lists of contacts, although they are unlikely to be comprehensive. The electoral roll will provide helpful details on the occupiers of specific properties. Armed with this information, and the latest revision of the Ordnance Survey, a mail drop can be organized. The most effective method is a combination of the post (to official bodies and representative groups) and hand delivery (to the individual premises likely to be affected by the proposal). This latter element which may involve many hundreds or even thousands of drops, can be contracted out to a specialist firm.

This still leaves a large and ill-defined collection of individuals and groups who should — or feel they should — be consulted. Reaching and involving them in sufficient numbers that the silent majority is represented as well as the activists and pressure groups is a difficult task. Advertising, by posters or in the press, is unlikely to be effective: it is the wrong medium for this sort of message, and is also surprisingly expensive if done on a large-scale. A good story in the local newspaper with some eye-catching photographs or drawings is a much more successful approach, and is free. A cut-out slip on which the reader can indicate a preference or make comments is often just enough to stimulate the non-joiners into action. However, not everyone reads the local paper, and a column or two is a very limited space in which to explain fully and objectively the issues and alternatives, particularly if the news editor has had a go at livening up the story.

Bringing the public and the information together is an essential step in the consultation process, and the most cost-effective and popular method of achieving this union is by mounting an exhibition. The size and style of the exhibition will depend upon the nature of the project, but some basic features apply to all cases.

- *Publicity:* through the mail drop, press coverage, public notices and announcements on local radio, all timed to give adequate advance warning of the event, but not so much in advance that it will be forgotten.
- *Accessibility:* the location should be easy to reach, and if the catchment area for the consultation is large more than one site may be necessary; the hours of opening must extend well beyond office hours to allow people to attend after work; for a big exhibition at least one Saturday session should be included to permit family visits.

- *Quality:* however much we might wish it to be otherwise, first impressions do count and for many of the public the exhibition will be their first contact with the project and its promoters, and it is little short of negligent to cut corners or accept low standards; this does not mean extravagance (although quality rarely comes cheap), but it does mean that the presentation material must be as carefully designed, specified and put together as any engineering component of the project itself.
- *Clarity:* the information must be presented in a logical sequence, with well-lit and clearly printed display boards; everything should be easy to read, both in terms of print-size and language; any plans or drawings should be as near self-explanatory as possible and, where preliminary proposals are shown which affect property, due warning must be given about the possibility of subsequent changes during detailed design.
- *Durability:* a successful exhibition is one which attracts a large attendance, and so the display material will come in for a lot of rough treatment. Plans should be produced to withstand heavy finger-prodding; display boards should be robust enough to survive several moves; anything portable should be bolted down ...
- *Availability of advice:* staff should be available to explain technical matters, answer queries and advise on the various ways of responding to the consultation; when appropriate, information on compensation procedures should be prominently displayed.
- *Availability of information:* although it is not usually practical to provide copies of the full study report or consultation document to every person attending the exhibition, some kind of summary or fact sheet should be available free to anyone who wishes to take more time to consider the proposals or discuss them with neighbours (Fig. 4 shows an example of a leaflet from the consultation on a traffic management scheme).
- *Opportunity to comment:* the obvious presence of quantities of printed forms can be an effective encouragement to the public to express their views; this is particularly so in the case of the silent majority and the non-joiners who might otherwise never make the unfamiliar effort of putting their views in writing; a higher response can be generated by making arrangements to collect completed forms on the spot — an election ballot box is a powerful stimulus and well worth the trouble of borrowing one from the local returning officer (the council's legal department will tell you where to get one).

In most cases, the exhibition should be complemented by some form of public meeting. This gives the opportunity for the promoter to present the information in one piece, thus ensuring that as large a proportion of the interested public as possible get the benefit of sharing the same briefing and so establishing a common basis for their reactions. The consultees have a forum in which to debate the issues live, where the human factor can be properly introduced and where the promoters and their advisers must, in a very real sense, face the people who are affected by their proposals.

These worthwhile benefits can be lost all too easily. Meetings are often no more than a boring recital of facts that fail to produce any worthwhile response,

NEWTOWN PARKSIDE - BUS & CYCLE IMPROVEMENTS

BACKGROUND

For many years Westshire County Council and Newtown Borough Council have been concerned about the levels of traffic and congestion in the town centre and the pollution and environmental damage they cause. Both Councils are convinced that the solution is to encourage more people to use buses and cycles as well as their cars.

This means making travel by bus more attractive so that people will use them instead of taking their cars into the town centre. To make this happen, we need to shorten bus journey times, ensure that they run on time and improve bus stop facilities and service frequency. Making cycling safer and easier will also help relieve congestion.

IMPROVEMENTS TO TRAFFIC CIRCULATION & THE ENVIRONMENT

Last year a temporary one-way system operated in Parkside, running clockwise (northbound London Street, southbound Westfield Road and westbound Brookside Road). This improved conditions in Parkside, reduced morning and evening peak hour delays and assisted bus services using the area. It is suggested that this system is made permanent, to provide improved pedestrian facilities and traffic circulation with a reduction in pollution and better parking arrangements for residents.

If this one-way system were introduced it would be possible to widen footways in London Street to benefit pedestrians and to provide some on-street parking on this busy shopping street. Similar measures would be possible on Brookside Road. Longer term aims would be to provide significant environmental improvements to enhance the streets.

TRAFFIC SIGNALS & PEDESTRIAN CROSSINGS

Town bound buses using Park Road would be helped by the introduction of traffic signals at the Church Street junction which would include special equipment to detect the buses and allow them to join the main road without delay. The existing zebra crossing on London Street would be converted to a pelican crossing which would also enhance pedestrian safety, and signal timings at other junctions would be modified to help buses.

BUS STOPS

The Parkside shopping centre is a focal point of the local bus network but existing arrangements for passengers are not ideal. Relocation of the town bound bus stop from Park Road to Church Street removes the need for shoppers to cross the main road and concentrates all town bound services at a single well lit stop.

WAITING RESTRICTIONS

General assistance can be given to buses by the introduction of waiting restrictions at locations where buses suffer delays from parked vehicles, such as Chapel Hill, Park Road and Brookside Road.

CYCLING

Cycling facilities need to be provided for commuting, shopping and leisure trips. Routes which are safer, quick and direct are needed and some proposals are shown in the exhibition.

The County and Borough Council Cycling Working Groups will be considering cycling facilities in Parkside. If you have views or suggestions please let us know so that these can be considered.

YOUR CHANCE TO HAVE YOUR SAY

The Councils' ideas are displayed at this exhibition, but we want to hear from residents, local businesses and interest groups. Your views on the current situation and any problems you may be experiencing, together with your suggestions as to how these can be solved are welcome. Remember there will be a public meeting on the last day of the exhibition - Friday 10 February, 6.30 p.m. If you have any queries about the proposals or would like further information please contact John Davies on 230558 or Pat Smith on 230813.

THANK YOU VERY MUCH FOR TAKING TIME TO HELP US

YOU CAN WRITE YOUR VIEWS IN THE SPACE ON THE OTHER SIDE OF THIS LEAFLET AND PUT IT IN THE COMMENTS BOX AT THE EXHIBITION, OR SEND THEM TO ONE OF THE ADDRESSES SHOWN OVERLEAF. PLEASE MAKE SURE WE HAVE GOT YOUR VIEWS BY FRIDAY 24 FEBRUARY.

Fig. 4. Typical traffic management scheme fact sheet.

they can degenerate into confrontations, or be 'hijacked' by small, vociferous but unrepresentative groups. They must be well-prepared and well-managed, and three basic ingredients must be right.

- *The chair/chairman:* preferably an experienced councillor, perhaps an office-holder on an appropriate committee or subcommittee, well-used to the procedures of public meetings and without a specific local interest in the outcome of the consultation.
- *The speaker:* a sufficiently senior professional to reflect the importance of the consultation, an effective 'platform speaker', well-briefed and — if necessary — well-supported by technical experts; in most cases, the presentation will involve display plans, slides or other visual aids which must be clear and readable if they are not to distract the audience from the speaker.
- *The mood:* the chair/chairman and the speaker, and to a degree the audience as well, have a responsibility to ensure that the meeting is an exercise in two-way communication; each must recognize that the others have a right both to be heard and to listen.

Just as the standard of presentation at exhibitions should be high, so also for public meetings. In particular, the speaker must be confident about the information and judgements he is putting forward and be prepared to defend their quality from any attack. This should make for a lively and robust debate, which is one of the main purposes of the meeting, and help identify the strong challenges or counter arguments that may play a significant part in the final recommendation or decision. The speaker will need to handle this aspect of the meeting with care. It is wrong to ignore other views and suggestions and it will do positive harm to give any hint of 'talking down' to the audience, but it is just as bad a mistake to let unjustified criticism — especially of the destructive kind — go unanswered. This is where effective chairing and presentation skills come into their own: the best approach is to recognize that everyone has a right to their opinion, and even a right to be wrong, but not a right to be rude. Equivocal or evasive replies can seriously undermine the credibility of the project and the consultation. For the same reason, promises should never be made if there is the least doubt about their fulfilment and assurances that matters will be given 'further consideration' or 'taken into account' must not be confused with commitments to action.

An informal note of the meeting should be taken, both to guard against misinterpretation afterwards and to feed the views expressed during the discussion into the consultation process. A well-organized debate will yield a very good sample of opinion and a great deal of useful information, and a contemporary record is the most efficient way of preserving it for future use. However, and although a well-attended meeting is an excellent opportunity to collect the comments and views of the public, pressure to 'take a vote' should always be resisted. A consultative public meeting has no power to take decisions and it is only likely to lead to misunderstanding and disappointment if anything is done which gives the impression otherwise.

The process of consultation will — it is to be hoped — lead to an informed decision in which the views of interested parties are not only brought into the process, but are seen to be treated seriously. That means that reports and presentations to the decision making body must give prominence to the results of the consultation exercise and explain the extent to which the views expressed have been accepted — or, if not, the reasons why they have proved to be unacceptable. The final stage in this dialogue should be to tell the public the outcome through a general statement and, where particular groups or individuals have been deeply involved, by specific responses. Consultation succeeds only when it is perceived as a process with a beginning, a middle and an end; for that to happen, the result — even though it is not going to satisfy everyone — has to be made known, otherwise all the effort will have been for nothing.

Participation

Consultation aims to ensure that the public is encouraged to consider the issues and comment on them, so that the various elements of public opinion are available to assist decision makers. It gives people a voice. However, participation implies a part in the decision making, and thus a vote. Despite the apparent fairness and democratic logic of such an arrangement, it is very rare that genuine participation is implemented. There are two major problems. The first concerns the difficulty of identifying a representative public to engage in the participation.

Suppose there is a major radial road which it is proposed to widen to carry increased traffic flows. The frontagers along the road are an obvious group to participate in the decision and, with the exception of the operators of any filling stations, or other commercial premises interested in passing trade, their reaction is also likely to be obvious. Equally predictable, but opposite, would be the vote of the residents of a nearby housing estate which presently suffers from large-scale and dangerous rat-running by vehicles seeking to avoid the congestion on the main road. And what about the inhabitants of the larger local community who believe that traffic congestion on the approaches to the town centre is driving business — and scarce jobs — to new greenfield sites, leaving the inner areas to decline and decay? Or the public transport users who feel that too much money is being spent on accommodating car-based commuting at the expense of a properly supported bus or train service?

Even if it were possible to define all the various constituencies who should have a say in a decision, the second problem remains: how are their votes counted? Easy to answer when there is an overwhelming majority in favour of one option, this question becomes much more difficult when opinion is divided, or more than one alternative commands support. How much better to canvass the opinions of these groups through a consultation exercise, put them forward for open consideration and leave the voting to those whose right to do so rests on well-established and generally-accepted principles: the elected members of the appropriate public authority.

As true participation is rarely feasible, the term should not be applied loosely to the exchange of information or consultation. The public and their representative bodies must never be left in any doubt as to the nature of their involvement and any misapprehensions should be corrected as soon as they arise for it will only become more difficult and unpopular to do so later on.

While the idea of local communities taking part in decisions on issues of more than local significance is fraught with danger, and could be said to undermine representative democracy, there is real potential on truly local schemes, or the local aspects of a larger project, for active participation. Local knowledge, coupled with the focus which comes from having to live with the results, makes for a positive combination that adds value to a project, encourages its acceptance and strengthens its support. By bringing local people into the process of developing the project, as early as the design brief stage, the fit between key technical requirements (such as visibility and safety standards) and local preference (street furniture and planting, for instance) can be explored. It will not be possible to meet every wish but it is very likely that many of the local suggestions or options can be accommodated, and some sensible compromises achieved.

The environment committee's budget has an annual programme of £150 000 for cycleways. For two consecutive years it had not been spent in full due to difficulties in progressing projects and lobbying by cycle groups for changes to schemes, and for different options. A cycling forum was established with representatives from all groups in the highway authority's area. The current programme was put to the forum, with the council's advisers attending to cover issues such as design standards, cost estimates and legal requirements, for it to consider the contents, rank them in priority order and suggest any alternatives. This was not an easy exercise but eventually, and after expressing strong concern over the limited funds available to promote cycling, the forum endorsed a new two-year programme which the council accepted. The details of individual schemes were examined and many useful, practical improvements incorporated. While funding restrictions remain a source of controversy, the cycle lobby is now helping to shape the council's plans not disrupt them.

To make this approach work it will be necessary to identify what is generally agreed as the community and set up an acceptable machinery for participation. It may be that one already exists: the organizers of a petition, the residents' association or village amenity society; the town or parish council. Take care, however, to try and assess how representative each group really is; check that its aims and objectives are widely shared and see if it is too local and likely to generate opposition from neighbouring areas. Local councillors will be helpful in this exercise, as will a reasonable helping of common sense. Human nature inevitably brings with it a certain amount of selfishness and it is unrealistic to expect a group pressing for an improvement in their street, estate or village to take fully into account the views of near-neighbours who might feel that the problem, far from being solved, is being passed onto them.

That is the project manager's task and it requires diplomacy and firmness, together with the kind of political backing that is only possible if elected representatives have been kept fully briefed. There will be times when the participation of all local people is not a practical proposition, because there is no consensus and the needs of one group will have to be put before those of another. That means people will feel dissatisfied and even disadvantaged. In circumstances such as these it is far better to keep everyone informed, consult with all shades of opinion, take into account as much as possible the concerns of those who will be disappointed, but make it clear why the decision has to be made. False hopes, mixed messages and raised expectations are the ingredients for professional and political disasters.

Changing patterns of travel resulted in an increase in traffic on a B-road running through a small village. The highway authority decided to ask the villagers for a solution. To the frontagers on the High Street — many of whom had their front doors opening directly onto the road — there was only one solution: a physical closure allowing access from the north and south but no through traffic. To those living in properties on the half-dozen side roads, the resultant diversions, adding four or five miles to regular journeys, were unacceptable and their proposal was for traffic calming by road humps, width restrictions, etc. The High Street residents were all totally opposed to the noise and disruption which they felt would come from the calming measures and entirely sceptical about any reduction in traffic or increase in safety they would create; for them the diversions were a price worth paying. The attempts to encourage participation simply split the community, with rival action groups petitioning the council and both claiming that promises of involvement in the final decision had been broken. An experimental closure was abandoned before it had run its trial period, and some limited, and not particularly effective, calming measures installed. It was two years before the council returned to the problem with a consultation exercise on a traffic management solution.

Empowering

In modern local government, *empowering* is a popular concept, not least because it does not have a specific definition. It is, in a general sense, accepted as conveying the idea of sharing power and decision making with the people affected, and is widely applied both to the management within organizations as well as the relationship between public authorities and the public.

The variety of models for empowering offer opportunities for misunderstanding and failed expectations, so it is helpful to attempt to set down some characteristics of an empowered group.

- Its existence and membership are clear to all, its methods are open.
- It is accessible and fosters two-way communication.
- It works through agreed objectives rather than by instruction or command.
- It gets its status from its own credibility and not from position in a hierarchy.
- It cooperates with other groups and does not try to establish and protect its own territory.

All of this relates to an ideal world where values and priorities are shared, and lively debate takes place between open-minded people who are willing to support the outcome whatever it might be. Reality is rather different and local authorities in particular, with their legal and financial obligations and restrictions, cannot honestly offer full empowerment to local communities. That does not invalidate the concept, and the approach can be tailored to the practical world of local government and successfully applied to many services and projects.

Highway authorities have to make strategic decisions about policies and priorities in transportation that inevitably cross the boundaries of local communities and involve winners and losers. Not every project or programme falls into this category, however, and it is important to avoid applying the same broad, objective overview approach that would be right for, say, determining the funding strategy for road safety over the next three years, to the implementation of accident reduction plans at a community level. The establishment of local groups to deal with specific highway-related topics is a means of offering a practical level of empowerment. Typical features would be

- *constitutional arrangements designed to bring in local representation*: elected members of district or perhaps parish and town councils given membership and some voting rights (although the highway authority would have to retain a majority to guard against decisions being made that go outside its legal powers)
- *terms of reference defining the programme/service areas covered, for instance*: local highway maintenance, traffic management, road safety, street lighting
- *financial regulations delegating some budgets and funding decisions*: giving, for example, five area sections 10% each of the budget for accident prevention schemes and retaining half under central control, and leaving the sections discretion to select schemes and let contracts
- *policy guidelines and best practice indicating the extent of the freedom in decision making offered by the highway authority*: thus, priorities for maintenance works on a specified network of major routes might be set centrally, with other roads coming under the local section; or the choice of which cycleway schemes to

progress could be made locally provided the selection was from within a pool of approved projects in the authority's cycling strategy; or decisions on pedestrian crossings can be delegated within a standardized procedure for assessing need

- *accessibility and communication made easier than at the more formal meetings of the council*: petitioners, local groups, objectors, etc. encouraged to speak and present their views; agenda items proposed locally; outcomes of meetings reported back to interested parties.

Groups such as these can engage the local community in issues of real local significance, and bring about a partial, but nevertheless genuine, sharing of power and influence. The cost must not be underestimated: the amount of time and effort — and therefore, as far as professional/technical resources are concerned, money — which are involved is proportionally very much greater than for traditional, centralized council processes. Issues, which in highway or traffic engineering terms would be considered trivial, may need very considerable discussion because of the local interest and perceived importance they attract; proposals, which are non-starters for financial, legal or technical reasons, may require full debate and explanation to satisfy local people that they are not being dismissed out of hand. Reports, whether written or oral, must be in language which avoids not only the jargon of technology (85 percentile speed, positive drainage, TRO, etc.) but also that of local government (CPO procedures, *ultra vires*, capital receipts, etc.). Acceptance of the authority's internal norms and ground rules cannot be taken for granted and some straightforward and potentially difficult to answer questions have to be faced.

This scheme cannot be progressed as there is no budget for highway drainage improvements — Why?

The centre is not a sufficiently important tourist destination to warrant special direction signing — Who says?

Patience is an essential requirement, and an acceptance that where there is discretion or an open choice available, decisions may be made which are not the right or best ones on a professional basis; that will not make them wrong or bad as far as local people are concerned.

Empowerment, like consultation and participation, is labour-intensive and time-consuming; it is far less predictable and controllable than conventional arrangements for involving the public, and it is here to stay.

11. Funding

Of all the changes, for better or worse, in public service over the last 20 years, the most far-reaching has been the realization that it all costs money. The public may, to a large extent, still be unaware of the true cost of the functions and programmes of work carried out on its behalf (see chapter 4 on how the structure of local government finance makes such understanding difficult to achieve), but for the elected representatives and professionals involved in operating the system there can be no escape from their financial responsibilities.

It has long been the boast of the engineering-based services in local authorities that they were used to tight financial controls because of their experience of supervising works contracts involving tough commercial organizations. To some extent this claim was justified, but only as it applied to a relatively limited area, i.e. the individual major projects in the capital programme. Elsewhere, in the large and continuing expenditure of the revenue budget, there was less reason for self-congratulation.

All this has now been overtaken by events on a wider stage, and the pressures of managing with severely restricted, and often sharply reduced, financial resources have become part of the normal environment for public service professionals. That means taking an interest and playing an active part in all aspects of funding, from start to finish.

Estimates
The fundamental importance of the budget process to all that goes on in local government, and the very limited flexibility which managers — and indeed members — have these days to revise programmes and their funding once they are set, makes accurate and specific spending forecasts vital. The estimated cost will not only affect the chances of an individual project appearing in an approved programme, but will also have an impact on the management of that programme and the progress of all the schemes in it.

The first imperative, therefore, is to get the estimate right. The story is told from the days of the Victorian railway boom of a contractor who decided to submit a tender of £18 000, but, having talked it over with his wife, increased it to £20 000; worried that it was too much of a risk, he doubled the figure and then slept on it; after further reconsideration, he put in his price at £80 000. He won the job.

For all its success on that occasion, this is not a technique to be recommended. The obvious restraints of a public bureaucracy, the requirements for traceable audit, both financial and quality, and the structured methods of project management systems, all work against anything approaching such a free-wheeling style. But it is not just about procedures. The importance of assessing the cost of a project is a good deal less critical in a time of growth and expansion than it is in a period of retrenchment and cuts. Cash limited no-growth budgets are the common denominator of most public works programmes, with the result that authority to start a project will depend on tender prices being within estimated costs, and regular checks on actual expenditure against forecast will determine progress on other starts, as any overspending must be balanced by corresponding reductions.

Getting the estimate wrong can have wide ranging effects. At its simplest it can prevent a project going ahead. If the particular scheme has a special priority, technical or political, then another will have to be postponed or cancelled to release the necessary funds to cover the shortfall. Should the initial price and estimate match, but the forecast prove to be different from reality as the scheme progresses, the project manager has to understand the reason to take the necessary corrective steps. If extra costs, unforeseen or omitted at the planning stage, are coming through then prompt and firm action will be needed to stop new commitments being made elsewhere in the programme. If the departure is a result of faster than expected progress, then some fine-tuning of starts and agreement with the finance department on spending profiles may be sufficient, as the overall total spend is not affected.

Even though the greatest difficulties for managers come with underestimation of costs, overestimates are not without problems. The funds freed when the price of a project comes in well below the forecast will not necessarily be available for use on additions to the programme. Fortuitous savings of this kind are often required to be returned to a corporate pool, for redistribution according to priorities set centrally. Thus a programme drafted with a number of overgenerous estimates will have fewer schemes in it than would otherwise be the case, and might lose to another service the difference between the forecast and the actual costs.

Getting the estimate right, and not just the overall cost but the timing and pace of the expenditure, depends on a thorough and systematic review of all the components.

- *Works cost*: provided a reasonably accurate estimate of quantities has been prepared, the critical step comes in applying relevant unit rates for materials and operations to build up a forecast of the probable tender price; remember to check the price base of the rates being used, and if it is different from the one on which the budget is based, make the necessary adjustment; make a realistic assessment of the total time to carry out the works and of the profile of expenditure over that time; pay particular attention to the municipal year (which runs from April to March) and any spending which extends beyond a single year, because strict financial controls have their sharpest effect at the year end and it saves a lot of trouble to get the bottom line correct for each accounting period.
- *Utilities cost*: two factors have increased the significance of this element in recent years: the development of high technology apparatus, such as

fibre-optic cables, has made the cost of diversions reach levels which can overshadow the value of the works themselves; and the commercial priorities of the utility companies are unlikely to match those of public authorities, so that the timing of key activities, with their consequential effect on the expenditure profile of the whole project, may be uncertain and require some careful risk assessment.

- *Land acquisition*: the swings and roundabouts of property transactions have made valuers notoriously reluctant to provide specific estimates on a project-by-project basis, preferring to work within overall figures for a service or programme; tighter controls on priorities and costs mean that project managers have to insist on more precision even though some of the information will have to be categorized as confidential to avoid prejudicing negotiations; expenditure on property transactions has to be monitored closely as a delay, underestimate of purchase cost or overestimate of sale value can have a dramatic effect on projects and programmes.
- *Fees*: ever-stricter separation of client and consultant costs, and the clearer identification of the resources used in preparing, designing and supervising projects have made estimates and profiles of fees (whether paid to external firms or charged against internal units) as important as that for the works; the shift from the large infrastructure projects of the past to the more local and small-scale schemes of today has also seen a shift into labour-intensive programmes where consultation, consideration of options and design work takes up a much higher — and, therefore, more visible — proportion of the overall cost and requires tighter management; these costs should cover not only the staff but also travelling, plan printing, publication of documents, etc.
- *Other charges*: along with the consultant's costs for engineering design etc., come the professional services ancillary, but nevertheless essential, to the delivery of the project, e.g. the preparation of legal agreements and the processing of any planning application; these can add up to a significant amount, particularly where projects are complex and their preparation is relatively expensive compared with the physical works required to implement them; although service level agreements can now be found widely distributed in local authorities to govern the charges and standards of service for work done by one department or unit for another, experienced project managers will take personal hands-on control of what colleagues may be doing on their behalf, and at their expense.
- *Client costs*: in parallel with the direct and indirect charges to the project described above, there will be the costs of the client function in setting up the brief, supervising and monitoring the external or internal consultant, and carrying out the tasks which are not delegated to the consultant; while these costs may be spread relatively thinly over a number of projects and programmes (this is not necessarily so, particularly for large single schemes and recurring tasks where a significant degree of involvement has been retained by the client) the overall level of resources and expenditure can be significant and should be accounted for.

To be complete, the preparation of estimates must cover the sources of the funds that will be used to meet all these various costs. Public finance is, as has been seen previously, a complex subject and the different methods of funding, and of classifying expenditure, can assume considerable significance for both accountants and project managers (not to mention auditors).

Straightforward revenue expenditure, funded from the council tax or government block grant, is relatively easy to handle provided the estimate is accurate and the expenditure broadly follows the profile. If it does not, and runs over into the next financial year, then with reasonable notice, good working relationships with the finance department and no dramatic changes in the distribution of the authority's budget, things should be manageable. Capital projects are subject to tighter controls, especially on carry-overs between financial years, and government grants can be time-limited and subject to claw-back if not spent according to profile. Overspending on grant-aided projects may have to be met in full from the authority's own funds, with all the pain which gearing can induce (see chapter 4). Even projects funded by developers' contributions and capital receipts, for all their freedom from many of the external controls and restraints, need careful treatment, especially if their approval has been justified by their fully funded status: there may be no money to meet a shortfall caused by a low estimate or an inaccurate spending profile.

Putting together all these different pieces of the jigsaw is more than just good project management. Building a reputation for precise and reliable expenditure forecasts reinforces credibility and gives managers greater freedom to progress the schemes in their current and future programmes. The opposite situation — estimates that are wrong, expenditure profiles that go adrift and, worst of all, overspends resulting in requests for transfers from other budgets — is likely to lead to the kind of intervention and corporate supervision which undermines support for new projects or continuing programmes.

Whole life costs and benefits

In times past the most important steps in securing funding for a project were to get the estimated cost accepted as an entry in the budget and then to report a tender offer at, or below, that estimate: the contract would be signed and the scheme would go ahead. Even these limited rules applied only to significant capital projects; other large areas of works and services, such as highway maintenance, were progressed within annual programmes that were hardly touched by questions of financial control or cost-effectiveness. In very few cases, and certainly not for these rolling programmes, was any serious consideration given to the full cost falling on the public finances over the whole lifetime of a project or service.

It was the development of methods of evaluating the cost–benefit ratios of different options that first focused attention on the overall expenditure incurred during the expected life of an infrastructure project. As well as assessing the benefits accruing over a 20 year period in terms of journey-time saved and accidents avoided, the cost of maintaining the new length of road and its structures was also calculated and used in comparing the rates of return produced by alternative routes. As a result, and also as a consequence of efforts to make level comparisons between different methods of road construction, whole life costing became a well established and systematic process, built into the framework of cost benefit analysis (COBA).

Ironically, the development of this sophisticated system has coincided with a shift away from large bypasses or green field motorways towards programmes of public works in which smaller-scale improvements, maintenance and management of assets have assumed a much greater importance and share of available funds. The concept remains valid, however, and the closer and more specific control of expenditure has made it important for all projects and programmes. This is particularly so when cash-limits and no-growth budgets dominate councils' financial strategies and every local authority is under pressure — applied by central government through financial regulations and manipulation of the grant system — to reduce debt.

In this context, every spending decision has to be examined not just on the basis of what it will cost *now* but also on how much it will cost *later*. This brings us in the first instance, back to the fundamental question of the categories and, therefore, the source of funding: revenue, capital receipts or developers' contributions, means cash; anything else is borrowing and means debt charges. Thus schemes which can be paid for out of the authority's direct revenue income, principally the council tax, or better still with other people's money, such as property sales or development agreements, will bring with them no long-term burden in servicing any loans. The only difficulty — and it can be a major one — is finding the cash when it is needed. While borrowing may be easier — and for big projects it is often the only way of funding a very large and concentrated expenditure — the cost of repayment will form a substantial commitment over 20 years or even longer, and can count against the authority in the complex calculations that determine government support. Approved borrowing, such as that to cover the council's share of funding transport supplementary grant schemes, comes with an allowance for the debt charges in the revenue support grant which the local authority receives: in other words, the cost of the loan is met. Finance directors will give this apparently good news a cautious reception, pointing out that for these debts which will take 20 years to pay off there is no commitment of similar duration from the Government to continue to include repayments in its grant calculations. As for borrowing, which is without the benefit of this support, the costs become a priority that have to be met out of future budgets, denying new projects their funding by tying up revenue income or taking a proportion of any capital receipts, as required by government regulations. Small wonder that schemes requiring a significant element of borrowing are scrutinized with some care, and their long-term costs critically examined.

It is important, therefore, to assemble a strong case, identifying loans which receive government support (albeit not guaranteed indefinitely) and demonstrating in full the benefits which will accrue over the life of the investment, because if it is a good scheme, that is what it will be.

Projects or programmes that are paid for out of revenue income, or are otherwise fully funded and so involve no burden of debt, still require to be costed over their operational lives. Competition for funds and priority within approved spending plans is increasingly dependent on a complete assessment of financial viability.

Benefits from new or improved infrastructure, while relatively easy to predict and quantify on the basis of established models, are not necessarily convincing to budget-conscious public authorities. Reductions in congestion and accidents undoubtedly save the community significant sums, but they will not appear as savings in the council's budget, nor will they be available as real money to be spent on new projects or improved services. They should still be emphasized as positive contributions to the economic development and environment of an area, and as a genuine relief from the pain, suffering and waste of road casualties, but their capacity to prove claims of the 'this proposal pays for itself within five years' variety is dubious. That is not how local government funding works.

More convincing are quantified projections of the running costs that will be reduced or avoided altogether by the new project, or the improvement or refurbishment of the existing stock. These need to be clearly associated with the results of the expenditure under consideration, predictable with some accuracy as to both amount and timing, and preferably identified with costs that are already having to be met.

One of the most persuasive demonstrations of this approach is the use of depreciation curves (Fig. 5) to justify preventive carriageway maintenance on the highway network. A technical assessment of pavement condition can be combined with traffic flow data to provide decision makers with a strong financial case for funding a programme of proactive regular prevention rather than reactive cure. The costs of the two scenarios can be assessed and their effects projected as future maintenance budgets. The argument that good housekeeping is a more economic policy than dealing with failures can be strengthened by including a risk assessment of the costs of meeting claims (both for damage to vehicles and personal injury) which are likely to arise from low standards of maintenance and repair.

The replacement of obsolete street lighting equipment — lanterns, switches and control systems — can be justified not simply as necessary refurbishment which avoids expensive call-outs to repair breakdowns but also as part of an energy-saving policy. Such a policy would not only be environmentally friendly, which is a good reason in itself for promoting it, but would also generate reductions on the electricity supply account from the introduction of more economic light sources and more efficient patterns of use.

Alongside the benefits must be considered the direct costs, which will arise in future years and will have to be found from within tightly-constrained financial resources. It is all too easy to assume that once a new project or improvement has been funded, there are, debt charges possibly excepted, no further costs to meet. This is rarely the case, however, as most schemes involve running costs and charges which start, if not at once, then quite early after commissioning and accumulate, and perhaps escalate, through their operational lives.

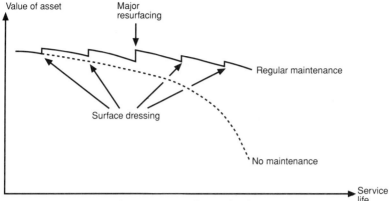

Fig. 5. Maintenance and depreciation of a road (after J. A. Bergg)

New lengths of highway and improvements such as the installation of positive drainage, new street lights and traffic signals, will generate operating and maintenance costs. Some of these — sweeping the road, cleaning gullies and drains, electricity supply charges for lights and signs — will begin at once; others such as replacement lanterns, repairs to accidental damage to street furniture, minor surface defects to carriageways and footways will come in over time; and eventually the long-term maintenance tasks of patching, resurfacing and reconstruction will be required. Each addition to the stock of infrastructure will, unless it is a particularly large one, generate a marginal increase in the running costs, but in total, and over time, the extra becomes significant.

Brand new installations, particularly those involving new systems or technology, can produce operational charges which are not only substantial but which also fall outside all the current budget provisions. Absorbing additional costs by minor incremental increases, changes in priority or redistributions within existing budgets, is difficult enough. Setting-up a new provision is extremely difficult, especially if it comes to the council's attention after the project which generates these costs has been committed on the basis of what was thought to be a complete financial assessment.

A closed circuit television system was approved as a means of assisting traffic control and road safety on a busy town centre network, and of enhancing security in adjacent pedestrianized areas. The cost of the equipment, including mounting columns and a fully equipped control room at the town hall with remote direction of the cameras, video recording and links to the local police station, amounted to over £2 million (spread over two years) and was partly supported by transport supplementary grant. Existing staff would operate the control room which was sited within the Department of Technical Services' current office space, so no additional personnel or accommodation costs were involved. In a difficult year for funding, the project was given the go-ahead because of its benefits in reducing congestion and accidents by making better use of the computer-linked traffic signals and its contribution to crime-prevention; the availability of approved grant to meet over half the cost was a further important factor. In the second year of the project, the committee received a report explaining that the telecommunications links on which the system depended had rental charges of £25 000 a year and the specialist maintenance contracts for the cameras and other ancillary equipment required annual expenditure of £35 000; neither item had been identified previously. Unable to cancel or reduce the scale of the much-publicized project the committee had to make compensating reductions in the annual programme for improved lighting and security in town centre car parks.

Selling the project

It should be clear by now that securing approval for a new project or programme is not just about promoting its features, nor is it only a question of identifying the full extent of the value for money it will offer. Important as both these items are, they are not, even when effectively combined, a guarantee of support. To give and maintain its approval, a public authority has to be more than just satisfied with the cost–benefit analysis: it has to accept what is fashionably called ownership of the project, which implies that there has been a successful sale.

Making a sale, as any business text book will tell you, involves finding the person with the money and the authority to spend it, who needs the service or product you can provide. In local government it is rather more complex than that, but the principle is still valid and the key aim has to be the establishment of a priority for the service, and for specific projects, in the places where decisions on funding are made.

It is important, therefore, to put together packages of benefits, properly costed, which match the needs or aspirations of those who will make choices about priorities and those (they may be different groups) who decide on the allocation of funds.

In developing an urban transport package as a key element in the submission for transport supplementary grant, the initial stages involve the preparation of a series of interrelated projects which will meet the highway authority's objectives, command broad support in the community and reflect the latest guidelines laid down by the Department of Transport in its advice on TSG bids. The eligibility of the package for grant is clearly a crucial issue, as the scale and timing of the programme would be very different if it were being considered for funding without TSG support. Nevertheless, value for money remains a factor, as the council will be expected to demonstrate its commitment to the overall aims of the package by funding some parts for which TSG might not be available in a particular year, and without that involvement, grant support might not continue over the life of the package. In addition, questions of relative value will be at issue: grant may cost the authority nothing (or very little), but there is only so much grant available and, therefore, there will be competition at a local level over which bids get priority for inclusion in each authority's submission.

Assuming a successful completion to this part of the process, and agreement on a package which meets the council's requirements, the next stage is to assemble (or reassemble) the components to attract the best response from the Department of Transport. It will still be necessary to incorporate and emphasize benefits that will meet policy and service objectives, although those of the Department of Transport may not coincide exactly with those of the council, nor will the local dimension be so important relative to wider goals. So, while enhancing public transport and reducing pollution may feature as priorities for both the council and the DoT, the former will have given considerable attention to the site of the proposed park and ride facility and the projected improvements in air quality on some sensitive local routes, while the latter will be more interested in the forecast fall in traffic making local trips on the nearby motorway network and the associated reductions in peak hour congestion at the interchanges. Value for money will play a very significant part simply because the funds are from the DoT and all bids are competing for limited resources. Therefore, the total cost of the package, and also the way in which it is spread over time (too long and it becomes a semi-permanent commitment, too short and it concentrates large sums into specific years; in both cases restricting flexibility), and the potential for additional or alternative funds from the council and other partners (neighbouring local authorities, developers, private finance sources) will all assume prominence in the presentation of the case.

In promoting the benefits, the emphasis should be on the results which are delivered rather than the technical means of achieving them. It is easy for professionals to assume, for instance, that employing the latest technique or technology is a justification in itself for a project. Similarly, there is a tendency to assume that ever higher standards in materials, equipment and capacity should be pursued in preference to lower and cheaper alternatives which may entail only a marginal reduction in service or operational performance for the user compared with the top of the range. Not everyone, especially not councils faced with hard financial decisions, wants the best or newest solution, and certainly not one they find hard to understand.

So, while members of the highways committee will want to know that SCOOT means Split cycle offset optimization technique (if only because they are going to be asked that when they get home), they will not be impressed or convinced by details of the capacity and response times of the computer system, nor the assurances of their traffic experts that it is the most advanced available in Europe. The questions they will want answered before giving approval to the £3 million urban traffic control project will be

What will be the reduction in journey times in the morning peak?
How does the green wave giving priority for emergency service vehicles work?
Can it detect buses?
Does it allow pedestrian phases to be altered?
Will it cure the terrible tailbacks at the junction at the bottom of Station Road?

In other words, they will be looking for credible forecasts of tangible, measurable benefits from the funds they are being asked to provide.

———————

Clearly, if decision makers like a project, they will have a positive attitude towards funding it. The textbooks will stress the importance of finding an individual or collective champion to support the project, influence other key figures in its favour and widen its appeal as a preferred option when choices have to be made. In general, this is very sound advice and applies to public projects as much as to the more commercial aspects of selling. Indeed, there are many examples of proposals which have secured such a measure of popularity as to become virtually unstoppable despite severe financial restrictions. However, these are more likely to be libraries, fire stations and swimming pools than transport, drainage and highways projects, thus demonstrating that there are schemes which, provided someone likes them enough to get them started, are very difficult to dislike thereafter (in public at least). It is certainly true that the more controversial the service — and transportation infrastructure will attract infinitely greater conflict than a public library — the harder it is to recruit a champion. Yet the need is greater, so project managers must be energetic in building positive, attractive cases for their proposals, which will encourage the support of champions enthusiastic and well briefed enough to take them forward. Here, liking the product and the salesperson is not the whole issue: the need, and the value for money being offered, have to be firmly established too.

Champions are not always where you might expect them to be. Professionals can give a project real drive, and a good reputation for delivering effective work on time and in budget will be very helpful. However, this benefit may be limited to the service area and not carry the same weight in the wider political and corporate arena. Support from key persons or groups in the political process will be more important, provided that their influence can be brought to bear, and in the right quarters. Thus a committee chairman may be a well-liked, respected public figure skilled at representing the council's policies to the community; but the vice chairman may be the person who sits in the leader's kitchen cabinet where the decisions on political and financial priorities are made. A subcommittee or local section may give wholehearted backing to a new programme; but the parent committee which coordinates all funding requests will have to share that enthusiasm before it passes a suitable recommendation into the council budget process. And, as has been observed, not all politics in public authorities is party political: the support of an internal group such as the corporate project evaluation team, or perhaps just the finance director, may be critical even though it will be exercised behind the scenes.

For some programmes, behind the scenes support is all there is likely to be, as there is little or no obvious visible benefit to show the public for the results of the funds spent on them. Preventive maintenance of ancillary equipment (the replacement of old street lighting columns, for instance, or the refurbishment of a drainage system) typifies this category of work in which the prime objective of the expenditure is to keep things working much the same as they always have been. Attractive benefits are not available to help sell these projects, and a credible, persuasive justification has to be made to fund such 'out of sight, out of mind' activities. Here, as for many public works programmes which produce long-term value by avoiding tomorrow's problems rather than in solving today's, success is not so much about being liked as being believed. Public service professionals have to work on trust: it comes with the territory.

12. Project management

Everything is a project. Not just the traditional individual schemes (bypasses, pumping stations, car parks), but also programmes comprising a series of small but similar works which stretch over time or are repeated in a cyclical pattern (traffic calming, street lighting refurbishment, surface dressing) and the provision of professional/technical services (road safety data collection and analysis, development control advice, carriageway condition assessment, etc.).

A project does not always have a clear start and a finish, nor is it necessarily represented by a physical object. Its main characteristics are its inputs, outputs and outcome. All of them require management.

Starting up the system

While some projects are continuous, being rolled forward or repeated on the *painting the Forth Bridge* principle, and so do not have a starting point in the same way that entirely new pieces of work may have, every one should be covered by a management system which is based on a start up procedure. The aim is to get clear from the outset of the project, whether it be the very first step or the beginning of a new period in a continuing activity, the basic information needed to ensure its effective control and direction.

- *Title:* without a clear statement of what the project is to be called, it is fascinating (but also frustrating) to observe how a range of variations on an appropriate theme can develop and correspondence, data and charges, consequently, go astray. A corresponding job code will eliminate — in theory at least — all possibility of confusion.
- *Client contact:* the individual (it may be a person or a named appointment) who is to be the client's representative needs to be identified to establish the proper channel through which instructions, variations and new information will flow, the point for addressing queries and delivery outputs, and the authority for acceptance and — very importantly — approval for payment. This requirement is just as important with in-house arrangements as it is for a commission with an external consultant.
- *Brief:* this is the client's description of what is required and, depending on the client, may be very specific and detailed or vague and open-ended (see chapter 5 for an example). It is often the case that the brief is drafted with the involvement of the consultant and it is arguably true that these

are the best ones — or, at least, those most likely to be delivered to the mutual satisfaction of all concerned. It is important that both parties understand the consequences of the different approaches to briefs: the more detail, the tighter the control and the less freedom to vary the content within the price; the more general the description, the looser the control and the greater flexibility to change within the agreement.

- *Project manager:* the named individual who is running the job and has (or should have) the authority to direct resources corresponding to the responsibility carried. It is reasonable to change project managers as different stages are reached — when design is complete and the contract preparation and supervision phase begins, for instance — provided that it is made clear to everyone involved what is happening and when.
- *Complexity:* it is worthwhile assessing each project against a simple scale — high, when the nature of the work is likely to involve the client in frequent discussions and decisions; medium, where there will need to be regular or pre-planned checks with the client to maintain direction and control; low, in which the client's involvement is not expected to be necessary between commissioning and acceptance.
- *Timetable/key dates/milestones:* while these may be covered in the brief as far as the important steps for the client are concerned, there may be other critical times — the availability of technical specialists, for instance, or the preparation period for artwork for an exhibition — which are essential to the management of the project and need to be agreed, recorded and adhered to.
- *Resources:* the timetable and the brief should between them determine the resources to be applied (the target cost may have a part to play, but that is dealt with separately below); the input of professional, technical and other support staff should be identified by grade or level to ensure broad compliance with the quality standards of the brief and effective cost control; there may also be specific requirements for the identification and approval of key managers or specialists; the delivery of some works supplied by a separate contract with a third party (a construction company, for instance) may form an integral part of the project and the method of procurement and estimated overall cost will need to be covered in such cases.
- *Change control/variations:* the authority of the client contact (see above) to make changes, and the mechanism for recording variations to the brief and evaluating them — including means for the consultant to claim unforeseen changes — must be identified.
- *Interdependencies:* the project may require formal links with other organizations or contractors which must be specified, including the channels of communication.
- *Target cost:* the method of payment and agreed rate, formula or price for the project itself (but not any third party contracts, which are covered under the resources entry, see above) will be one target; there may be another which will be the objective set for the project manager and, as an internal and, therefore, private matter, can reflect judgements about income and expenditure, profit and loss; for this reason the resources

actually applied — to a prestige project, for instance — may not be directly related to the agreed price, and the project manager's target may not be set in terms of immediate profit.

- *Special features:* there may be particular aspects of the project (or of the client organization itself!) which are not fully covered in the brief but will affect its management — a particular emphasis on wide consultation affecting the planned schedule for that stage of the work, for example, or a very strict approach to the checking of documents by the council's solicitors before issue; special requirements for insurance may be involved, particularly where potential pollution hazards are involved; the project manager may be required to arrange some extra activity such as technical publicity, visits by professional bodies, etc.

The start up procedure is not a project management system, but it represents the first step in initiating the organized running of the project. Without it no system, however sophisticated, can be effective.

What follows will depend on the methods of project management required by the client and operated by the supplier of the project. Many large clients in the public sector have their own well-developed systems, tailored to their purposes and mandatory on any provider of professional services. Other inescapable commitments, such as the Construction (Design and Management) Regulations, will introduce their own routines and processes.

The extension of quality assurance, both as a client requirement and a feature of well-managed professional/technical organizations, has put QA procedures for project management into place on a wide scale. Many proprietary systems exist and, for those wishing to start from first principles, there are shelves of books and manuals on the theory and practice of project management, covering a variety of methods which will offer various levels of detail. All of them can work, provided the system is operated conscientiously and project managers satisfy themselves by periodic checks (not necessarily regular ones) that the information it is providing is synchronized with the real world, and reflects what is happening and not what people would like to happen. Some systems work better than others on different kinds of projects; some need careful adjusting for each project to get the level of detail right; some rely on particular computer facilities and some are based on simple but effective paper forms.

Whatever the particular arrangements, the system will provide for the management of time, money and quality. As long as it does that, the only other essential requirement for a project management system is simply that there is a manager operating it.

Specifying

Systems should be of general application. Specific instructions of what is expected in the detailed execution of every relevant part of the project come in a different form. Involvement in the drafting of documentation for works contracts, and their supervision on site, will have introduced many engineers to the concept of defining the various components, materials and operations which are required for satisfactory completion of the job. There are two basic types of specification, namely

- *method:* where the ingredients of a particular element are set out so that by following the recipe, compliance is assured (for example, the number of passes to be applied by various classes of roller on a range of layer depths to achieve compaction)
- *performance:* where the finished result is the standard for compliance, and the supplier can choose any reasonable working methods and/or materials to use in the task (surface texture on a carriageway is an example of the end product being the measure of acceptance, as is the surface finish to an exposed concrete feature on a structure).

These are used, separately and in combination, in a number of widely-accepted standard specifications which give comprehensive cover for most engineering and building works. These specifications, with their accompanying *notes for guidance*, provide all the material generally needed to translate project management into detailed implementation through construction contracts.

Not every project, however, is for works construction. The collection and analysis of data with recommendations for action, a feasibility study, the organization of a continuous programme of inspection, and the preparation and presentation of evidence to an inquiry or tribunal are all examples of the wide range of professional services projects that are required by public bodies. For them to be managed effectively requires the same degree of specifying as, say, a reinforced concrete bridge or a subway lighting installation, although the project manager is not going to find standard documentation as readily available as for works projects.

The brief may go a long way to specifying the project in full, particularly if it is of the detailed sort. However, some briefs do not have that kind of detail, perhaps because it is available elsewhere, or is assumed to be known, or has just not been covered. In these cases a supplementary specification is necessary, ideally produced to accompany the brief, but in any event the project manager should ensure that one is in place to define the work. The contents could be a mixture of extracts from standard procedures, documentation of local custom and practice and original definitions specific to the project. The approach can be method, performance or a combination of both models.

- *Tenders.* A minimum of four tenderers are to be chosen from the council's select lists on the basis of capability, availability and previous performance; if no appropriate list exists or European Procurement Regulations apply, public advertisements will be placed through the council's press office; where no competitive list is drawn up approval must be obtained from the Head of Technical Services (up to £20 000) and the Finance Director (over £20 000) for single tender action. Documents, which must include the standard instructions for tendering, are to be approved by the Head of Technical Services and one set issued to each tenderer with additional copies charged at full printing and delivery cost. Tender periods will be four weeks minimum; longer periods by agreement with the Head of Technical Services, whose approval is required for justified recommendations for extensions to the published submission date. Tenders will be received and opened in the legal department in accordance with the council's standing orders section 5.1. Tender evaluations covering compliance with the instructions, arithmetic checks, technical appraisals of any method statements, commentary on anomalies, potential errors and alternative proposals will be prepared in two weeks (or a longer period as agreed with the Head of Technical Services). Corrections to errors must be confirmed in writing with tenderers and cover any effect on the the overall tender price. Recommendations to accept other than the lowest tender must be accompanied by full justification and presented to the Director of Finance. Award of the contract will be in accordance with the council's standing orders section 5.3 and the scheme of delegated powers.

- *Accident records.* Three year personal injury records for all 0·5 km. long sections and numbered junctions on the network will be recorded both in clear tabular form on a suitable database and also graphically on a background of the council's network link diagram, all up-dated at weekly intervals, so as to provide data by section, link or junction at one working day's notice.
- *Correspondence from the public.* All letters will be answered in accordance with the council's code of courtesy and having regard to appropriate guaranteed service levels published in the current edition of its community charter. Response times will be as follows

  - reply based on information on file or record — 5 working days from receipt to despatch of reply
  - acknowledgement of information etc. — 5 working days has to be obtained
  - reply when inspection on site is required — 12 working days
  - reply when measurement, count, check or archived material, etc. is required — 17 working days.

Monthly returns will be published of totals and percentage compliance.

Method specifications are harder to write and easier to control than performance specifications. Performance versions give flexibility which can be used to respond to a variety of circumstances, but which can be abused by specifier and provider alike. Combinations, if balanced correctly, can give the best of both approaches: the skill lies in applying the performance element to the part of the job that is changeable, subjective and difficult to define, and the method element to the part where firm, quantifiable and consistent outputs are required.

Specifications are as important to consultants (in-house and external) as they are to clients, not only for having a clear understanding of what is expected to make up the satisfactory outputs from the project, but also as an essential means of managing the inputs.

Monitoring

Systems and specifications provide a framework for what *should* happen: monitoring tells you what *is* happening. It provides essential prompts on what needs to happen next, indicators for corrective or change action and an audit trail on the progress of the project. The client's brief and specification, if effectively prepared, will include the basis for monitoring, although the project manager, especially if a formal consultancy service is being supplied, will be conducting a supplementary and separate exercise against business-related targets.

Inputs as well as outputs can be monitored. Indeed, it is control of inputs which offers the most effective way of ensuring the required outputs, as information that the output is not up to the necessary standard may come too late for anything to be done. In any event — and perhaps for this very reason — many briefs and specifications include requirements for inputs and the project manager will certainly be keeping a watchful eye on them. Typical categories are as follows

- *level and amount of resources at specific stages*

The brief may require the design team to be set up under a chartered structural engineer approved by the Chief Technical Officer with at least one chartered engineer to deputize and support and one incorporated engineer, or equivalent with computer-aided design experience, to manage the production of drawings etc. — these personnel to be available full-time and no substitution or withdrawal permitted without consultation and approval.

The specification may stipulate that an experienced, suitably-qualified hydrogeologist will attend each inspection and sign the site log recording the readings from the boreholes.

The project manager will want to have time sheet returns on a weekly basis to review actual commitment of resources against the plan.

- *timetable for actions*

The client may specify that the land survey team is required to make entry and start work not more than two weeks after possession of the site has been notified.

With specialist computer time booked in advance, the project manager will want to know one week ahead that all data are ready on disk to start as planned.

- *links with other participants*

The brief may indicate that the full list of all plots, ownerships, tenancies etc. affected by the proposed scheme will be made available by the county property department by week 16 of the project programme — this information will be essential to the preparation of compulsory purchase plans for approval by the committee at its scheduled June meeting.

The final estimate, on which approval to commit funding depends, must cover all costs, including utilities' diversions, and its accuracy is a performance measure that affects the fee — the project manager will need to be sure a last check has been carried out with the electricity company (the biggest diversion cost by far) in good time for any amendment to be made, and also for peace of mind.

The value of monitoring inputs notwithstanding, it remains true that outputs are the focus of most activity. They represent the deliverables (or parts of them) which the project exists to provide, and they are what the client is paying for. In terms of demonstrating service delivery and certifying payment, output measures have tradition and convention on their side and do reflect a common sense approach to project management. This is only true, however, if the right outputs are being monitored in the right way. Thus

- *volumes and quantities*

Numbers of street lighting lanterns replaced quarterly — measured against annual programme target.

Hours (outside normal working hours) operating the urban traffic control centre — to cover additional activity for which extra payment may be due.

Total of committee reports prepared — of limited value without more precision (some reports may be recording readily available facts, others may involve extensive data collection and analysis) and evaluation (quality of reports, achievement of deadlines).

- *frequency, punctuality and response times*

Average interval between street lighting inspections on primary routes and high risk sites — for assessment against specified standard

Actual publication dates of consultation documents on transport plan — for comparison with schedule in the brief but subject to adjustment for any delays due to extended consultation, deferred committee decisions, etc.

Percentage of letters answered within ten working days — for evaluation against a 90% target provided that the standard distinguishes between straightforward correspondence which can be given a full response from readily accessible data and more complex topics requiring an inspection, site measurement, etc. which can only be acknowledged within the specified period.

- *efficiency targets*

Proportion of street lights operational — indicates effectiveness of inspections, preventive maintenance and response to faults.

Reduction in casualties from programme of accident prevention schemes — valid over a sufficiently wide group of projects and suitably long period of before and after comparison.

Success rate for decisions on winter maintenance operations — measures accuracy of forecasts, sensors, thermal maps and local knowledge both in avoiding unnecessary salting/gritting and in ensuring it takes place when needed.

Utilization rate for staff — tells the project manager whether the time booked against the job and accepted by the client for payment is more or less than anticipated by the target.

- *end products*

Completion of the programme of lighting column replacement within the financial year and the approved works budget.

Delivery of the final report on the Binford traffic management study to the September meeting of the transportation committee.

Designs, layouts, calculations (including bridge checks) and quantities to be handed over to the Head of Technical Services by 30 September.

Invoice for the final payment of the fee for the design stage issued to the client on handover of the documents and drawings.

Although satisfactory outputs are, if the right ones have been specified, a reasonable indicator of satisfaction with the outcome of the project, this is not necessarily the case. Outcomes tend to be subjective, and often involve issues only indirectly related to the works or service being provided. It is possible to deliver all the outputs within the requirements of the brief and specification, yet have an unsatisfactory outcome; conversely — and perversely — it may be that a good outcome results even though outputs do not meet specified standards.

A bus-priority project was approved, after consultation had indicated significant public support, with specific requirements to achieve a timetable for the traffic regulation orders, tender documents, start of works and commissioning date, all within a tight budget for fees and works cost. The orders were duly processed and, although some objections to the associated parking restrictions were received from local traders fronting the route, the high level of public (and political) support continued. Tenders were invited on time, and came in just below the estimate, but by now local concerns about the effect on passing trade were beginning to attract some wider sympathy. When the work started — on schedule — a general downturn in shopping activity on the route was becoming a well-publicized issue, even though it was much more to do with the opening of an out-of-town superstore than the reduction in on-street parking. At this stage, the scheme's perceived benefit was diminishing fast, it was seen as the reason for loss of business locally and potential closures, and the planned outcome of a popular and environmentally-friendly community asset was no longer achievable. The project, which was running to time and budget, had become controversial and was halted for further consultation and finally completed with some on-street parking retained: its popularity and environmental benefits had been compromised.

A programme of maintenance and refurbishment of the pedestrian footways on a long stretch of suburban road was due to start. The project was seen as straightforward with the ouputs — completion to a specified standard within a budget and timetable — effectively equivalent to the outcome. In accordance with the highway authority's customer charter letters were distributed to all frontagers notifying them of the start date and duration of the works so that the inevitable disruption would be minimized as far as possible. The result was a large and unexpected response suggesting items that required treatment, requesting changes in the planning and timing, and providing information which indicated that some of the survey data (on boundary details, entrances, etc.) was out-of-date or even inaccurate. The works programme was reviewed while an urgent check on the survey information was carried out; the contractor was instructed to delay starting on a large part of the road and issued with a number of small variations. Work commenced late and slipped further behind schedule; extra works and claims caused costs to rise; the project manager's own internal budget for resources was exceeded with only limited compensating increases in the design and supervision fees being agreed by the client. The highway authority received considerable praise for its sensitive and responsive approach to the needs of local people.

Here it can be seen just how important and difficult it is to monitor outcomes. The first example is of an outcome which, although clearly stated, became incompatible with the more mechanical outputs. Monitoring the changing perception of the project against what was intended made it clear that to press on with achieving the outputs (timetable and cost) would have made matters worse; the solution was to adjust both outputs (late completion and a small increase in cost) and outcome (community acceptance at the expense of some of the environmental benefits). The lesson to be learned is to check carefully that the outcome is achievable at the start and through the progress of the project, and be prepared to modify expectations rather than stick rigidly to a plan that has been overtaken by events.

The second case illustrates the way in which an implied outcome — customer satisfaction in its broadest sense — which had not been covered explicitly in the preparation of the project became an overriding measure of performance. The failures in project management (inadequate data collection) and process (lack of a consultation mechanism), and their consequences (increased preparation and works costs, late delivery), were perceived to be less serious than the benefits which flowed from achieving a good outcome. The lesson is to think through the outcomes carefully to ensure that they are fully and clearly understood, and that the inputs and outputs are compatible with what is expected so that everything, not just one element, can be monitored for performance.

Risk

Project management — or rather, the more difficult parts of it — is about risk. No projects are risk-free: identifying, assessing, minimizing, containing and avoiding risk are what makes project management more than mere administration and delivers its true added value. Managing risk is not the same as taking a chance: it is about probability rather than possibility; and it is certainly not about luck.

Project managers will look at the range of circumstances which might affect their plans, and the consequences that would flow from them. The aim is not just to eliminate from their plans those factors that are irrelevant or impossible, but also to form a considered judgement on the factors which, while still possibilities, cannot be cost-effectively covered. Decisions of this kind are made by assessing the cost of eliminating or minimizing these factors, the likelihood of their occurring and the effects that would result if they did. This means, for instance, that a risk which is very unlikely to happen, has only minor consequences and would cost a great deal to remove, can be accepted. At the other extreme, a risk which would have catastrophic results, albeit with a very low probability, must be properly covered even though the cost may be extremely high — indeed even if the cost may render the project non-viable.

Thus, in designing the car parking areas for a new riverside leisure and arts complex, capacity (based on two people per car) equivalent to 85% usage is provided as more would involve major structural works. On the few occasions in the year when demand is likely to exceed capacity, the result would be the need to hire nearby private parking areas and operate a shuttle-bus service: a potential cost which is, in this case, acceptable. However, the designers also recommend that site levels be expensively raised and culverts added to cater for a one-in-100 years flood, on the grounds that the impact of major flooding has a cost which significantly outweighs the expense of this provision. The potential damage to the investment made covering the risk essential.

Risk and probability are both aspects of the same calculation: the lower the probability of failure, the lower the risk. So, the ideal situation would be where the level of checking, inspection and monitoring was high enough to make it impossible for a fault, omission or breakdown to pass unnoticed and uncorrected. This is rarely possible and as a result systems are established that reflect the balance of risk and practical, operational reality. The objective of such systems — which may be specific to a single, time-limited project or for general application to continuous, long-running programmes — is to manage uncertainty and the associated potential ill-effects within acceptable limits. Risk management of this kind is embedded (often unrecognized and thus taken for granted) in every organization.

Structural designs are subject to a formal, categorized checking process in which the extent and degree of independence is related to the scale and complexity of the project.

Street lights are scouted to check for failures, and response times in maintenance contracts are usually specified, on the basis of a hierarchy, with safety installations on heavily trafficked routes, busy junctions and areas of pedestrian/vehicle conflict checked more often, and repaired more quickly, than amenity facilities in suburban areas or on lightly used rural roads.

Defects on the highway — potholes, trips in footways, damaged safety fences and parapets, etc. — can be dangerous and are a breach of the highway authority's duty to maintain safe passage: inspection should (in theory) be continuous and response instantaneous; in practice, the law has been satisfied provided an authority has made arrangements to inspect the highway at reasonably frequent intervals (which may vary with the intensity of use), supplemented by special plans to deal with sudden emergencies.

The number of new, or unfamiliar, items in a project increases the risk regardless of the scale of the project. Thus, a large and complex piece of infrastructure that involves no new technology and is virtually a repeat of a recently completed version has a lower risk factor than a small but innovative scheme which depends heavily on a prototype system.

Risk assessment and management not only cover physical damage or disruption to persons and property; although of a different kind, there is also just as much risk, and just as many potential problems, associated with procedures and processes. Indeed, much public works activity involves more procedure and process than works, with correspondingly more opportunities for things to go wrong and for external influences to have a significant effect.

This is particularly the case when timing and the availability of funds are interdependent, and where public approval (or at least lack of serious opposition) is essential to progress. The project manager must examine the critical steps in the programme for the project and evaluate the probability of failure, making contingency plans where it is feasible to do so. The complex network of committee cycles, financial procedures and consultation processes carries with it, as has already been seen, many uncertainties. Containing the risk, and more importantly identifying and correcting problems before they become serious, requires accurate, fast and relevant information, delivered through reliable systems and backed up decisive action when the system indicates it is needed.

This kind of progress chasing is especially important when the delivery of vital parts of the project is in the hands of people or organizations not under the project manager's direct control. Property acquisition, legal procedures and planning consent are typical pieces of subcontracting that can make or break the timetable, and even the whole project. It is a disappointing fact of life that the importance and priority given to these activities outside the project team is frequently not as great as the team might want or expect. It is the project manager's job — the delivery of the complete project is a responsibility that can be shared with no-one — to be satisfied at every stage that these subcontractors are on schedule. Effort, progress and a shared sense of urgency cannot be taken for granted: there are numerous examples of schemes that have been delayed, disrupted and cancelled entirely because, too late for anything to be done, the project manager has found out that the vital plot of land, contract or planning condition has not been dealt with as planned. Formal arrangements and written confirmations for each step in these subsidiary activities may seem excessive, particularly if the various parties all work for the same corporate body, know each other and (most awkward of all) may even be friends. The simple question for any manager who is personally accountable for the successful delivery of the project and whose staff may well be without work if the job goes wrong, is 'Can you take the risk?'

13. Giving advice

Although much professional and technical activity takes the form of information gathering, data analysis, design, document preparation and supervision of works, rather than the direct presentation of advice, this is not the basis for a sharply-drawn distinction. In practice, there is a clear, if not always direct, relationship between most tasks performed in support of public works projects and programmes and the decisions, made on advice, which public authorities take to initiate, undertake and pay for them.

Thus, by gathering information, analysing and processing it, the raw material is brought together for advice on the scope, nature and cost–benefit of the options for a new policy or project. Similarly, the designer assembles the components which will become the recommended proposal for some new or reconstructed item of infrastructure; and the site team supervising and measuring the works is compiling the facts which will justify recommendations on acceptance and payment.

Advice, therefore, is collected, coordinated and prepared from a variety of sources, even though some of them are at a distance — in time or space — from the point of delivery. That being so, it is, nevertheless, still true that the formal channels for delivering advice are the familiar ones of reports, presentations and recommendations. What has changed are the expectations of those receiving the advice: passive acceptance and dull uniformity are no longer the norms; a challenging approach and widely different styles are the characteristics of the environment for today's professional advisers.

Reports

The committee system, central to the British system of local government, drives the production of reports. At any rate, that is how it should be, although there are rather too many examples of the production-line of reports driving the committee.

Different authorities have their own standards for style and content. These range from very formal efforts to put all the relevant facts and opinions on the record as a basis for a thorough evaluation resulting in a considered decision, to a brief justification of the case in support of a decision which has, in effect, already been made. In some cases, a strict 'two sides of A4' limit is applied, in others this is relaxed by allowing appendices or annexes, and in others reports can be of any length. Where one authority adopts a narrative, even conversational style, another will want notes and key points, considering anything else to be unnecessary 'padding'.

While this author prefers short but readable reports, that is of much less importance than the preferences (or prejudices) of the recipients for whom the advice is being prepared. Choosing an unfamiliar or, worse still, unacceptable style will not create a favourable first impression, and may well set the readers against the topic from the outset. Thus, the reports prepared for different authorities reflect their varied 'personalities'.

However, there are many elements in the contents of an effective report that will be common, no matter what style is used to express them. This indicates that a framework can be prepared which has wide application for delivering advice, covering all the key requirements yet flexible enough to accommodate local needs.

- *Title:* a short but self-explanatory phrase which identifies what the report is about (Annual Road Safety Report; Binford Traffic Calming Study — Consultation Exercise).
- *Application:* the electoral wards or divisions affected by the report are identified (for a wide ranging topic or a policy report it might be everyone, otherwise specific to local areas — Binford etc.).
- *Purpose:* a brief summary of the content, enough for a reader to decide whether or not to continue into the more detailed sections, preferably not more than 100 words long (this should not merely be a repeat of the title, such as: 'to report on the results of the consultation exercise into the Binford traffic calming study' but be something rather more informative — to report on the consultation during March on the proposals for traffic management in Binford which showed strong public support for speed enforcement cameras and 'gateway' features on the village approaches, a majority against speed humps and chicanes, and opinion equally divided on a parking ban in the central section of the High Street).
- *Proposed action:* basically, there are three types
  - ○ the committee can note the report for information and do no more
  - ○ resolve (i.e. decide to exercise the powers delegated by the council) and do, or indeed stop doing, something
  - ○ make a recommendation to another committee or up to the full council, either because that is where the decision making powers lie or — to be brutally frank — to 'pass the buck'.

  These can be used in combination as needed, but care may be required as this is an element for which councils often have very specific forms of words drawn up by the solicitor or the secretariat and not to be trifled with. The committee is advised to resolve that
  - ○ the speed cameras and 'gateways' proposed in the Binford study be implemented
  - ○ no further action be taken on the speed humps
  - ○ a report be presented to the next meeting on a 'peak hours only' parking ban in the High Street.
- *Financial implications:* a section that has increased in importance and precision, so it is unlikely to be acceptable to state 'none — covered by existing budgets' as if funds, once allocated, no longer have to be accounted for; costs, sources of expenditure and any appropriate

categorization should be covered. (The proposals will cost an estimated £27 000 for works and £5 000 for fees, as detailed in the supporting information below, and are provided for in the approved accident prevention programme budget.)

- *Environmental implications:* an increasingly necessary section where the potential effects on the environment, good and bad, local and global, are set out as part of a discipline to ensure these issues are considered and publicized for all projects. (Reduced traffic speeds will decrease the noise nuisance for frontagers and pedestrians, and will contribute to the general community benefit of road safety; the siting of camera mountings and other street furniture will need careful consideration because of its detrimental effect on the Binford conservation area.)

- *Supporting information:* this is the detail which explains, supports and justifies the proposed action and its financial effect; it will be as brief or as long as the authority's reporting style requires, but it must fill in any gaps in the earlier sections. (The consultation exercise involved the distribution of 500 questionnaires of which 322 were returned ... 74% were in favour of enforcement cameras and 93% in favour of gateway features — see attached drawing 1164/TM/5 ... 34% were in favour of speed humps but 61% specifically rejected this option ... 80% of the respondents expressed a view on the proposed parking ban, 42% in favour and 38% against ... the cost of the camera mountings is £10 000 with all video equipment and operational running costs met by the police and the two 'gateways' are £8500 each ... to meet objections expressed in respect of the effect of the all-day parking ban in the High Street on adjoining streets and local shopping facilities a report on a peak-hour alternative will be prepared for the July meeting.)

- *Background papers:* to facilitate cross reference to any previous reports, documents or relevant to its subject, a list of titles, dates and sources is provided (Road safety in Binford — Petition, Highways Committee, December 1995; County Transport Plan 1995 edition; 'Safer by Design', DoT 1994, etc.).

- *Contact:* the names, job titles and telephone numbers of the relevant people — not necessarily the official who is nominally responsible for the production of the report — who can provide further information and clarification on the topic (Joan Smith, Traffic Management Team Leader, 234511).

- *Drawings etc.:* any figures, tables, schedules, drawings, etc. mentioned in the report should be bound in with it wherever possible, clearly described and marked with the report's title and its reference number in the committee agenda (Figure 1 — Accident locations and types, Binford traffic calming study, Item 15; Table 1 — Summary of responses to questionnaire, etc.).

- *Appendices, annexes, etc.:* sometimes because it is a useful but separate piece of information, an appendix is attached to the report rather than listed as background; the report should, however, be able to stand on its own and such an attachment ought not to be a means of getting round a limit on the length of reports (Annex A — Binford parish council's response to the traffic calming study).

Fig. 6 illustrates the framework in use for a complete report.

Presentations

Most reports are presented to committees, sections, panels, etc. in the normal run of business: the contents frequently being taken as read or briefly introduced by the professionals with the follow-up questions and debate (if any) leading to a decision taking account of, though not necessarily accepting, the advice set out in the proposed action. That process has already been reviewed in chapter 4.

The routine of committee reports is broken occasionally by the arrival of a subject that warrants a more elaborate treatment. A major project, a new policy statement, or a strategy for redevelopment may require a more extensive and comprehensive report than the usual format, and a style of presentation more elaborate than normally necessary.

In these cases, the substance of the report may become a free-standing document, prepared for wider circulation than within the council — perhaps for distribution or sale to the general public — and designed and printed to a high standard. A short 'covering report' will then appear in the agenda, containing the appropriate purpose, proposed action, financial implications, etc. but instead of providing supplementary information, the reader will be directed to the separate document.

The subject of such a presentation might be

> the highway authority's transport policy and programmes submission to the Department of Transport — because of its scope, complexity, long-term effects and high public profile as a comprehensive bid for substantial funds
>
> the response to a major consultation exercise on a series of park and ride options — to summarize a wide range of opinion and demonstrate that the council is honouring its assurances that public reaction would be given full consideration
>
> the description of plans for a new development proposal, with extensive associated infrastructure — to coordinate and publicize the committee's position.

Presenting advice to the council at this level justifies staging a properly prepared session in which the main points of the report, supplemented and supported by suitable visual aids, are delivered in a lecture-style format. The aim is to take the audience through the key elements — data, options, public response, costs, alternative actions — so that everyone shares a common understanding of the professional advice, rather than their individual interpretations or impressions of what may be a large document. It also creates the opportunity to display striking images — pictures, graphs, pie charts — in combination with effective delivery of the spoken message. Equally, it provides

5   Of all accidents throughout the Council's area, two-thirds occur on urban roads (i.e. those roads subject to a speed limit of 40 mph or less) and, of these, two-thirds occur at junctions. Over the whole of the Council's rural and urban road network nearly 60% of accidents occur at junctions. Whilst these predominate at 'T' junctions on public roads there is a significant number at private accesses.

6   In the main, accidents occur during the working week when roads are busiest. During the day, accidents peak in the morning and evening at the times of travel to and from work. Accidents peak in the autumn. This is due to the end of British summer time and to the seasonal conditions.

7   Inexperienced road users are more likely to be involved in accidents and young drivers are at greatest risk. Over one quarter of all accidents involve drivers in the 17-24 age group. Male casualties are predominantly higher than female casualties throughout all age groups.

8   Human error is a factor in over 90% of all accidents and the main cause in over 70%. The use of excessive speed is the most common contributory factor to deaths and injury on the county's roads. In 1995 over one quarter of fatal accidents involved a driver or rider going too fast for the prevailing conditions.

9   The Annual Report recommends specific action to bring the trend in casualties back into line with the projected target, as follows:

   ● a campaign to strengthen safety awareness amongst school children
   ● additional speed deterrence measures, especially enforcement cameras, in urban areas
   ● a priority test of junction improvements.

   These measures are proposed as priorities for the Committee's draft budget at an overall cost of £450,000.

10   The publication of the full report with a print run of 300 copies is advised. Distribution to Members, libraries, neighbouring local councils and the interested parties approved last year will require 150 copies, the remainder will be available for general sale at £5 a copy. Total net cost is £300.

11   The draft public information leaflet can be printed and distributed via schools, libraries, local councils and interest groups free of charge at a cost of £1,400 for print run of 3,000.

APPENDICES etc. The full copy of the Report has been placed in Party Group Rooms and copies are available from the Department of Technical services. The draft public inspection leaflet is attached as Appendix 1.

BACKGROUND PAPERS:

● Draft Public Information Leaflet (attached)
● Full text of Annual Report (in Party Group Rooms and available from the Department of Transportation and Planning)
● Annual Road Safety Report for 1994 (January 1995)
● Road Safety Plan 1995/6 (April 1995)
● Budget Working Party, October and November 1995 ... Draft Categorisation of Budget Priorities.

Contact: John Brown, Group Leader Road Safety, direct line 234648.

Fig. 6. Document depicting elements common to an effective report.

TRANSPORTATION COMMITTEE — JANUARY 1996

ANNUAL ROAD SAFETY REPORT 1995 (All divisions)

PURPOSE: To present to the Committee the Annual Road Safety Report, recording casualty trends in 1995, particularly the increase in accidents to child pedestrians, and identifying remedial measures. A draft public information leaflet is tabled for approval.

PROPOSED ACTION: The Committee is advised to RESOLVE to:

(a) accept the Report and authorise its publication;
(b) endorse the recommendations, supplemented as necessary, for the 1996/97 Road Safety Programme and advise the Budget Working Party accordingly;
(c) approve the public information leaflet, amended as necessary, for distribution.

FINANCIAL IMPLICATIONS: The publication of the Annual Report and the printing and free distribution of the leaflet are covered by a specific item of £1,700 in the current Road Safety Budget; the estimated cost of the recommended remedial measures is £450,000 which will require consideration as part of the Budget process.

ENVIRONMENTAL IMPLICATIONS: The identification and minimisation of the causes of road casualties contributes positively to a safer environment in the community.

SUPPORTING INFORMATION:

1   As Highway Authority, the Council is required to monitor accidents on the road network and work to reduce them. The Annual Road Safety Report provides the basic information for this task and offers recommendations to assist in its implementation. This information is available to decision-making for the Council's Budget, and for input to the Road Safety Plan which is submitted, as part of the TPP process, to support the Council's case for grant aid.

2   The Council has adopted the target set by the government of reducing the overall level of road casualties by one third of the average 1981-1985 figure by the year 2000. In 1995, there was an increase of nearly 7% in casualties on the Council's roads compared with 1994. 2,741 accidents involving personal injury were recorded by the Police and accounted for the following casualties:

48 fatal
347 seriously injured
3,506 slightly injured

3   In 1995 the total number of fatal and serious casualties increased by 3% over 1994. However, this still represents a 64% reduction over the 1981-1985 average figure.

4   Car driver and passenger casualties have continued to increase during 1995 and are now 18% above the 1981-1985 average figure. Whilst most other road user groups have seen a downward trend in casualties in recent years, 1995 saw an increase in casualty numbers in almost all groups. This is particularly evident with child pedestrians where casualties increased by 53% over the 1994 figure.

Fig. 6. (contd.)

an occasion to be boring, patronizing and unintelligible. The guidance on meetings and consultation in chapters 8 and 9 applies just as much to these events.

The result should be an informed debate. It will be important to clarify, in the briefing for office-holders before the meeting, the points which are known to be of interest to the committee to ensure that they are fully covered. Equally valuable will be some advance knowledge of the issues which members of the council want to raise in the debate, so that appropriate 'hooks' can be provided in the presentation on which members can 'hang' their debating points.

Recommendations

Advice can come in a variety of forms and styles of delivery. The most important distinction, however, lies in whether or not it is accompanied by a recommendation for action. There will be occasions when no action is necessary — when reporting, for instance, the reorganization of functions in an adjoining local authority, or the issue of national transport statistics — and the recommendation is simply to note the information. Other issues will come forward with the expectation, perhaps an instruction, that they will be accompanied by a professional recommendation which will form the basis for a decision. For example

---

To approve the list, in priority order, attached as Appendix A to be the annual programme for carriageway reconstruction, with the schemes in Appendix B held as reserves.

That the Director of Technical Services prepare detailed designs and invite tenders for the demolition and replacement of the central pier of the Meadowvale bridge as shown on drawing 1163/B/5.

Although many of these decisions are taken 'as recommended', there may be some amendment in detail (repairs to make a bridge safe are unlikely to be challenged; the maintenance list probably will be, and one or two substitutions may be made by the committee on the basis of its own brand of 'local knowledge').

At the other end of the spectrum are the issues where the action is clearly and solely a political one: a message of support or opposition to a new government policy; a self-congratulatory statement publicizing the council's achievements; a 'negotiating position' in respect of some other authority or organization. Thus

---

This council welcomes/deplores the success/failure of the Government's transport strategy as demonstrated by the cost-effective/underfunded proposals and positive/damaging initiatives in the White Paper.

To endorse the continuation of the council's successful plan to regenerate the Middleton valley, creating new jobs and community infrastructure.

The committee rejects the proposals for the new membership of the joint working party, which have been put forward without consultation and instructs the council's representatives not to attend further meetings until discussions on other options, including the status quo, have taken place.

———————

These will be prepared by members or their political advisers and put forward as free-standing recommendations to what would otherwise be a 'noted item', or as additions to a professional recommendation. The source of the proposed action, however obvious it might be to an 'insider', needs to be made clear, although in most cases the politicians will be more than willing to take the credit!

In the middle ground lies a whole range of recommendations that are neither wholly professional nor entirely political. In these cases the advice must be technically sound and also take account of the political environment. It is essential that *take account of* does not become, as far as professional advice is concerned *give priority to*, for, as was seen in chapter 2, professionals serve the whole council and not the political party in control.

Naturally the policies of the council, set by the party group in power, will form a framework within which professional advice is given, and they must be taken into account. Putting forward recommendations that are contrary to an established policy, or are likely to undermine its aims, is more than foolhardy — it is unprofessional. Equally wrong is the presentation of biased or partial advice to justify policies that have no basis for professional support. There will, in reality, be very few of these, in the vast majority of cases the advisers' task will be to prepare recommendations which make progress towards the objectives the council has set for itself and which can be implemented by the normal processes of a professional organization.

This does not mean that the recommendations will always be the first choice or preference on technical grounds, because earlier decisions in the council's political machinery may have eliminated those options.

———————

Budget reductions in highway maintenance to fund programmes in social welfare and education may require recommendations to cut desirable, but non-essential, preventive repairs; it would be wrong to pretend that there were no long-term consequences, but the lower priority work could be identified and ranked.

A policy decision to give priority to accident reduction measures near schools might not be the most cost-effective use of road safety funds in a particular urban area. Nevertheless, within that guideline an action plan with a ranking of the best sites can be prepared.

———————

The professional advice will be constrained within the political priorities (to increase standards in one service at the expense of another, for instance, or to respond to a public perception of need rather than a technical one), but it will still be sound.

The question often asked, especially in respect of politically delicate issues, is 'should there be a recommendation?' To some extent the answer lies in the style of the local authority: some prefer not to have the consideration of a sensitive or controversial matter given too obvious a 'steer' by a professional recommendation; others welcome, perhaps expect, their advisers to recommend a course of action, even if it is to be heavily modified or rejected. Indeed, there may be cases when, because of the likely unpopularity of a decision, the politicians will see great benefit in a firm and unavoidable recommendation from a professional source!

As a general rule, and excepting obviously party-political topics, the presentation of a clear recommendation is the best approach because it puts on the record the objective technical advice and provides some foundation for the subjective debate that may follow. Occasionally, where equally acceptable solutions — in professional terms — may be available, the recommendation could take the form of a choice between two or more options which can be left to the council. Only rarely can there be justification for leaving a public authority without guidance, and such cases must run the risk of leaving the impression that its professional advisers do not know the answer — or worse still, know it and are staying silent.

14. Communications

Communication is the feature of modern life that technology has raised to remarkable levels of speed, coverage and quality; and which most of us believe is generally done badly, insufficiently, or not at all. No organization, particularly one which provides public services, can afford to ignore the need to communicate its objectives, activities and successes to those it serves and to its own people.

A great deal of effort is needed for effective communication. It can easily be misdirected if it takes no account of the audience and the purpose. Communicating internally is part of the basic task of management, and will be aimed at ensuring that the organization's tasks, processes and objectives are known and understood by the people in it, who in turn feel in touch with their managers and able to make a full contribution. Communication with the world outside the organization can be done directly by informing, educating and advertising, all of which comes under the broad description of public relations; this is, of course, distinctly different from the kind of external communications which the press and the broadcast media provide where the end product is under outside control. Each aspect needs its own approach.

Internal
Every textbook on the management of people (or human resources as the jargon has it now) stresses the importance of good communications in organizing, motivating and leading the men and women whose efforts and loyalty make the difference between success and failure in today's working environment. This is good advice. Nevertheless, the best lessons come from our own experience, and we will all benefit by asking ourselves: how many times have we felt uninformed? ... misinformed? ... ignored? ... confused? ... taken for granted? ... and what effect did that have on our performance?

The first and fundamental rule of communication, therefore, is: do it. Too much communicating is, on balance, less likely to cause problems than too little. It still needs to be effective, however, and that requires a systematic approach to avoid the kind of uncoordinated jumble of messages which leads people to switch off. Passing information clearly and quickly within an organization is important enough to warrant some guidelines, and while styles will differ, there are several common features that provide a basic framework.

- Use the cascade principle for spreading information by briefing teams or small groups through their leaders; it reinforces the responsibility of

157

managers for communication and provides clearly understood channels for messages.

- But do not rely on it. Some managers are much better communicators than others (for all sorts of reasons) and the performance of the system will need frequent checks, especially where 'blockages' are known to occur; the cascade principle is also much better at spreading than collecting information, and there will be data and ideas which do not get through to the project manager unless more positive efforts are made.

- *Management by walking about* is a concept that can produce results ranging from the highly creative to the dangerously chaotic: it provides a good check on whether or not the normal processes of communication are working, and can generate an atmosphere in which managers are seen as approachable and open, thus freeing up the flow of information; it may result in mixed messages or out-of-context pieces of information being given undeserved importance and attention; it can confuse otherwise effective channels of communication and result in some people feeling left out.

- The principle of two-way traffic has to be constantly reinforced. A dialogue between managers and the people performing all the other roles benefits any organization, but most channels of communication tend to flow in one direction unless active steps are taken to show that messages from the shop floor are received and acted on; equally, managers must sometimes make hard or unpopular decisions and in such cases it is vital to be clear that action, and not discussion, is what is expected.

- Agendas and papers in advance of meetings are incentives to ordered progress. People attending — and those who will not be present — can prepare their input with some forethought; clear structure and content, helped of course by good chairing, will make for cost-effective discussion and communication.

- Notes of meetings and information bulletins are a useful discipline: they disseminate information quickly (if done promptly); they serve the dual purposes both of keeping those not present at a specific meeting or not involved in a particular activity fully informed, and also of ensuring that those who were present or involved agree on what happened; they form a record of actions to be taken by whom and by when; they encourage those managing meetings and projects to think about what has actually been achieved.

- Using clear language in speaking and writing is the single most productive route to efficient communication: avoid initials unless they are genuinely understood by all, and jargon too; use everyday words and phrases; be as concise as possible without leaving anything really important out, remembering that ten minutes is a long time to listen and two sides of A4 is a lot to read; on those occasions when words have to be chosen carefully, try not to be so careful that the message ends up so bland as to be meaningless.

- Consistency in the message, and when it is delivered, helps enormously in achieving effective and credible communication. Slight differences are bound to be irritants, even on minor issues, and when the matter is important they are likely to be analysed and investigated to detect the subtle reasoning behind what are, in fact, accidental variations; spreading information to different people at different times may sometimes be necessary, but it usually produces problems ranging from concerns about status to the almost instantaneous generation of rumours and misrepresentation; wherever possible communication should be simultaneous or in accordance with a declared timetable.

There is in our modern world of faxes, networked personal computers, electronic mail, video conferencing and all the other marvels of technology a presumption that communications in organizations can make life better at work and, by so doing, improve the services being produced and delivered. Technology, itself, does not achieve this, of course, and the warning *rubbish in–rubbish out* applies not just to the input to computer programs. Managers have the responsibility to develop the channels of communication, check that they are working and, above all, feed in the essential raw material — what the project is about, the strategy for carrying it out, the targets against which performance will be judged — without which there will be no meaningful flow of information.

Public relations

Projecting, promoting and explaining what we do to the public at large is not a task that engineers do particularly well. Indeed, there are times when we seem to take a perverse delight in getting on with the job at the cost of our public image rather than to its benefit. The specific requirements of customer care — dealing constructively with the people directly affected by projects and services — are the subject of the next chapter and certainly involve communicating, but this section will deal with the establishment and maintenance of positive perceptions among a wider audience.

The scale, variety, complexity and value of public works projects and programmes is little understood by those not involved in their preparation and delivery. The resources, technology and sheer effort are all too often reduced to the level of the comfortably familiar — a pothole to be repaired, a new set of traffic lights, a parking ban — or just taken for granted. There is really no-one to blame for this but ourselves: there are plenty of interesting and constructive messages to send, which reflect well on local government and the people who work on its behalf.

Getting these messages across requires some creative thought, and there will be occasions when expert help is needed in packaging and presenting information. Exceptional cases apart, and always accepting that the help and support of a good public relations team will make a difference to the effective distribution of information, there is still no substitute for first-hand knowledge as the raw material. Public service professionals make the best publicists for what they do.

Typical public relations activity might include

- press statements giving the council's views on local issues; encouraging participation in consultations; announcing particular successes, decisions and new projects; and any other matter which is newsworthy (though be prepared for disappointments as the news editor may not agree ...)

- advertisements when the topic may not get coverage as a news item (these are, of course, in addition to statutory notices such as the publication of a traffic regulation order)

- newsletters for general distribution in an area; or directed at particular audiences such as town and parish councils, residents and businesses affected by a major project etc. to provide regular information and early warnings

- booklets, leaflets and notices describing the council's service standards (for example, its consultation procedures or customer guarantees); explaining its policies (a summary of its waste management plan, for instance); promoting particular aims and objectives (such as recycling advice and maps of tourist walks) and providing information about its operations or projects (schedule of car park locations and charges, descriptive boards at a historic site, etc.)

- public information/education material such as a road safety campaign; traffic news on the local radio; advance warnings in the press and by leaflet drops of diversions; maps of winter salting routes distributed via libraries and garages, etc.

All publicity must be subject to the law's restrictions on political content; so it cannot overtly promote the party aims of the council's ruling group nor any specifically political activity and it must not involve itself (for or against) in national politics. Politicians can find plenty of alternative ways to do all these things without using the authority's official machinery, and any potential conflict should be referred to the council's monitoring officer (see Chapter 2), leaving the professionals dealing with service-related topics.

There is a fundamental principle on which good PR is based: be positive. For most public works activity the benefits are relatively clear, although this does not mean that every item is going to be good news. It is in the nature of public service that there will be times when the news — of a budget cut, of a programme postponed, of a regulation restricting freedom of action — will not be good, but this should not result in a totally negative message. The critical task is to take the constructive elements — the work that will still go on even after the budget cuts, for instance — and give them prominence in the overall picture. With that basic proviso, there are three rules to follow

- make it simple
- keep it short
- time it right.

In most case the audience for the planned publicity will not want or appreciate complex, detailed statements. The simpler the message, the more widely it will be understood. Technical or local government terminology would be inappropriate, except when addressed to professional groups who will know what it means. It is important to focus on one or two unmistakable key points and not dilute them with additional, but subsidiary, messages. Simplicity does not mean talking down, which is very counter-productive, but it does require clarity of thought.

Brevity is not only the soul of wit, it is a practical way to ensure that your message is given some consideration. In a world of slogans and 'sound bites', competition for what are inevitably short attention spans is intense. Tight editing ensures the important points stand out and the whole message gets across, not just bits of it. It is important to say all that needs to be said, but not a word more. News editors and advertising copywriters make it appear easy — it isn't; and, once again, clear thinking is needed about what the message is trying to achieve.

Timing is everything in making the most out of any communication, and particularly so when the recipients are external and so not subject to direct organizational control. The most carefully prepared and clearly expressed message will be wasted if the intended audience is looking the other way or listening to someone else, so find out what might be competing for attention and adjust the visibility, volume or timing accordingly. When the aim is to coordinate the message with an event or activity, remember that memories are short: advance notice should not be given too early otherwise it will be forgotten; following up must be done quickly or no-one will remember what it's about.

If all this seems to imply that public relations and publicity will tend to go wrong rather than right, there is a degree of truth in that assumption—particularly where public service is concerned. The fundamental problem is of expectation, and it is no more than realistic to recognize that today's attitudes to public authorities are inclined to be critical rather than supportive. This makes external communications something of a thankless task but, nevertheless, an essential one which requires constant effort. 'No news is good news' does not apply.

Press and other media

In considering the world of journalists and reporters, it is worth remembering that the fundamental task for their management is selling newspapers. This depends on a vital balance between newsprint and advertising space: the former will encourage people to buy papers which, if purchased in sufficient quantities, will convince advertisers to buy space. Newspapers need to sell copies and space in them to be viable. The same goes for commercial TV and radio: viewers or listeners tune in for the service, and audience figures are used to sell advertising time. Even the BBC works, indirectly, along similar lines as it is in the same competition for ratings.

So the media have to be popular. This needs at least one (but preferably more) of the following ingredients

- up-to-date news (exclusive/latest report/our reporter at the scene)
- human interest (humour/sentimentality/scandal/tragedy)
- the unusual or the unexpected (man bites dog etc.)
- crusading or campaigning themes (*The Post* reveals yet more cases of heavy lorries cheating the ban on trips through the city ...)
- quotable quotes ('our kids are in daily danger' warns head)
- eye-catching pictures (our photographer, perched on a tower crane above the new multi-storey car park ...).

Getting in the news is not automatic (except when you want to avoid it!) and it is simply unrealistic to expect reporters to pick up on things that public service professionals consider important. The most effective way to make positive use of the press is to generate the stories yourself. For that to be successful some combination of the ingredients already listed is required, and the application of other well-tried methods.

- *Personal contacts:* cultivate journalists so they will come to you for information and stories; remember this is a two-way bargain and you must be a reliable, accessible source all the time and not only when you choose.
- *Interviews:* more formal versions of the personal links; you must do your homework first to handle the probing questions that are very likely to arise, and to be sure of getting your message across in easy-to-understand form (regardless of what questions you are asked).
- *Press releases:* they must be short, sharp and in popular language (no complex theories, no long sentences, no big words), contain at least one good quote and above all be about today's or tomorrow's news and not yesterday's.
- *Photographs:* every picture tells a story. Editors like them because they are not only good page-fillers but also help to break up the text and make the paper look interesting and attractive. It is worth arranging a photographer to cover your important photo opportunity in case the paper cannot send one, but make sure you get a professional because a holiday snap is unlikely to look good. Although it might seem obvious, news stories are more likely to get on to TV if they are visual; facts and figures without images are usually non-starters.

Above all remember that helping journalists and editors with their task is the best way to get a good press. Complaining that you do not speak to reporters because 'they always get it wrong' is a self-fulfilling prophesy. If you have nothing to say, then that is how much of your side of the story will get printed — nothing.

Leaving aside the alleged excesses of the more lurid end of investigative journalism, reporters have a simple approach to information and are invariably reliable at following their rules.

On the record means you can be named and quoted, and this applies to everything spoken or written, unless it is clearly stated to be ...

Off the record/on background which means it may be used in preparing a story but not as a quotation and not traceable to an identifiable person.

There are some variations on these basics.

- *Unattributable* information is on the record as far as quoting is concerned, but the source cannot be named except in a generalized way, e.g. 'a senior council official', 'an experienced structural engineer', etc.
- *Spokespersons* give quotations on the record but this is not the same as the more newsworthy direct quotes from attributable sources. Reporters are usually unenthusiastic about spokespersons simply because they are not authorized to give their names, and so are assumed to be either unimportant or a diversion from the real story.

- *Leaking* is a special sort of off the record contact involving something confidential: it can be constructive (flying a kite on a potentially controversial option, or paving the way for a major policy change), or destructive (when the secret belongs to someone else) and, contrary to their popular image, reporters do not like being involved in too many leaks because of the risk of being left out on a limb.
- *Embargo* is the well-established device of issuing information under confidential cover with a specified release date for its publication, thus helping reporters to put a story together in reasonable time and meet their deadlines without any advance publicity to embarrass the providers of the news. This convention is usually honoured although there is always a risk of it becoming a leak.

It is essential to make clear beforehand the terms on which information is given to a reporter. It is no good saying something sensational, revealing and highly secret to a journalist and then asking for it to be treated as background or embargoed, it will be on the record unless other arrangements had been made first.

Remember that, in spite of all the concerns that your words may be used against you, quotations are the most effective and attention-grabbing method of getting the message across. They combine immediacy, human interest and an identifiable source in one attractive package. Just consider a news report from the point of a view of a reader, listener or viewer and you will see why.

Same situation but four different stories.

No-one was available from the council to comment on the congestion at the Riverdown crossroads.

A senior council official defended the new traffic signals at the Riverdown crossroads, claiming that they would reduce casualties.

A spokesman for the Council's Technical Services Department said: 'the new signals will cause very little extra congestion, and they will prevent many of the injury accidents which now occur at Riverdown where there is a very poor safety record'.

John Smith, head of road safety in the Council's Technical Services Department, responded to criticism of the new Riverdown traffic signals. 'They are causing very little extra delays, and that is a small price to pay for the much greater safety at the crossroads', he said. 'The site has a bad accident record and the signals will definitely cut casualties', added Mr Smith.

The media operate on tight deadlines — newspapers have to be printed and news bulletins broadcast at regular and fixed times. Effective working relationships with the media require knowledge of, and respect for, the time constraints under which reporters and editors operate.

163

Local evening papers, for instance, typically work on a mid-morning deadline for the first edition, with only limited changes — usually to the front page and perhaps one inside news page — possible up to midday. It has to be an eye-catching piece of local news that gets into the paper after 11 o'clock. Weekly papers (and technical news magazines) normally come out on a Thursday or Friday, and most are 'put to bed' on Tuesday with some parts, such as the letter page or a featured interview, closing a day before. Press releases, media events, calls to reporters, letters and any other items must be timed to meet and preferably beat these deadlines.

Find out exactly what they are for the various news outlets. Make use of contacts with reporters to learn what last-minute openings there might be for hot news, but do not expect these to be available for anything routine. Remember that you can give advance, confidential notice of a news item under an embargo if this means the reporter will have more time to prepare good and extensive coverage, with graphics or pictures, rather than a short, rushed piece just ahead of deadline.

Above all, never forget that a missed deadline probably means no story. What seems newsworthy on Friday lunchtime is not going to impress the editor of the local evening paper on Monday, nor his colleague at the weekly which goes on sale the following Thursday afternoon! Old news isn't even used to wrap fish and chips any more.

15. Customer care

After the financial revolution, reviewed in chapters 4 and 11, the second great change in local government and one which has occurred more recently, is the shift of focus away from providing services to serving customers.

To some extent this reflects a strong move in the commercial world. Although customer satisfaction has always been set up as its major aim, the combination of a more assertive and affluent public and an emerging and lucrative market prepared to pay for added value directed the forces of competition towards customer care as a business prospect. The use of Marks and Spencer as a case study in drawing high margins from a strong customer orientation is so well established as to have become a self-fulfilling prophecy: when customers arrive at the food department of their local M&S to find the shelves empty of bread or fresh pasta, they do not blame the store for under-stocking, but themselves for being too late!

Public authorities have, with good justification, identified customer care as both a political and a managerial objective. Central government has reinforced this with the concept of citizens' charters which all parties support. Few councils, however, have approached the funding which the market leaders in the retail and service industries have applied to this aim, and, in some cases, the publicity attached to service charters, customer guarantees and similar commitments has been woefully detached from the reality of resources. Nevertheless, this is an issue that cannot be ignored, and everyone involved in public service has to be clear what it means for them.

What customers?

To a conventional supplier of goods and services, the customer is easy to identify: it is the person who might buy, is buying or has bought the product available for sale. Business development has tended to widen this description to include those potential purchasers whose requirements may not be fully met by the current market (indeed, who may not even be aware of their needs), but in any definition the customer has a direct relationship based on a transaction between a willing buyer and seller.

In the public sector, this means of defining customers is of limited use. Certainly, the council purchases the services of its professional advisers, either by paying their salaries if they are employees or their fees if they are consultants. Members of the public sometimes pay direct for a particular service they obtain from the council. However, the vast majority of services are neither offered nor provided, through a straightforward sale. The customer relationship is, at best, an indirect one based on the local council tax or (even more distant) on national taxation; often it rests on a perception of the way that local authorities should treat the public. So there are different kinds of customers — and not all of them are willing.

The easiest relationship to understand is the conventional one in which goods or services are offered and purchased.

Certain documents on policy (the highway authority's transport plan), of a technical nature (developer's guide to road layout) or of general interest (guide to long distance footpaths) may be published for sale; searches can be conducted to identify the effect of highway proposals on specific properties at a charge; design and supervision of minor works such as vehicle crossings for household access may be carried out for a price; car park users pay directly by the hour or the day.

In these areas the features of customer care are broadly similar to those any business would recognize: make the product and its delivery as attractive and user-friendly as possible; charge the price buyers are willing to pay; pay attention to what the customers want. Similar, but not always the same. Even in these straightforward examples there are the inevitable differences that come with the underlying purpose of a local authority: local government.

There is an element of monopoly when the council is charging for tasks only it can do (publishing details of statutory plans, consulting its own highway records). The legal duties of a public authority may cause it to turn custom away (not every vehicle access will get approval). Most significantly, there may be other priorities which are considered to be more important than the requirements of a particular group of customers (town centre car parking charges may be structured to deter long-term parking or even to act as a disincentive to private car use altogether).

When the customer is the council itself, the relationship is less clear cut and is complicated by its concurrent position as employer (of an in-house department) or client (for a consultant). The latter arrangement does not necessarily clarify the situation as will be seen in the final chapter. Nevertheless, individual members of the council, and corporate bodies such as the various committees and sections, are the recipients of a service and do see themselves in some respects as consumers.

Committees receive reports which are expected to meet certain criteria for delivery time, clarity, credibility and (from the point of view of the ruling political group) consistency with the council's aims; likewise the council expects its decisions to be implemented effectively, efficiently and promptly through approved projects and programmes; individual councillors want their queries, complaints and suggestions acted upon; members want a similar service for matters raised by their constituents which they have taken up personally or passed on.

———————

Thus, the transportation committee will consider itself as the customer for a road safety policy aimed particularly at children in accordance with its widely publicized objectives and delivered, with a programme of schemes, in time for the council's budget process; the committee will also expect to see the resulting list of projects carried out to plan; local members will be promoting safety projects in their 'patch' while also pursuing a wider range of issues on traffic management plus highway maintenance, development control, etc.; individual topics — a perceived hazard outside the local primary school raised by the parent teacher association, a residents' association complaining about speeding commuter traffic, a householder wanting a bus stop moved — which have been put by members of the public to their councillor will be passed on for an answer.

———————

The largest, and most difficult to deal with, population of customers is the general public. Every encouragement is given, quite rightly, to the development of a culture in which members of the public see the relationship with public bodies as that of customer and supplier in a market. This can only work, however, up to a point, and that point is neither easily nor consistently identifiable. Customer expectations ought to take into account the financial and legal framework with which local authorities in general, and individual councils in particular, operate; they should recognize the political priorities and objectives that influence local services; they need to have regard to the complexities of the requirements for consultation and communication which public authorities have to observe. In reality, the majority of the public know hardly anything (and perhaps care little — note the turn-out in local elections) about these things. It is hardly surprising, then, that this relationship is one which needs some effort to make it work.

———————

Local residents, concerned by a series of near misses and damage-only accidents on the road outside a local shopping centre, petition for road humps: they will not be much impressed by a response which informs them that, with no injury accidents on the record, it will need an exceptional decision by the road safety committee just to put the project on the priority list, let alone fund it and start preparation work.

A householder complains about a faulty street light: she is pleased to know that it will be repaired, but perplexed to be informed that, because it is classified as an amenity rather than a safety installation, it will take about two weeks to fix.

The residents' association for a new housing estate has excessive speed on the main distributor road as its biggest concern and it even has the answer — 30 mph signs on every lamp column; to be advised that Department of Transport regulations do not allow repeater signs in such a case, will not seem like positive customer care.

———

These examples are all, to some degree, negative and ignore the multitude of helpful, constructive cases which pass smoothly through the hands of every public service organization every day of the week. That these unhelpful responses are not the fault of the council or the people working for it is, of course, obvious to anyone with inside knowledge, but that will not change the perception of customers who will pass on their dissatisfaction via a multiplier effect which only seems to apply to criticism and never to praise.

This is unfair, but it is reality. It gets worse when the local authority has to do what no consumer-oriented private business would ever do: consciously pass on bad news which has a detrimental effect (whether real or perceived does not matter) on the interests of the recipient. Local government has to perform its statutory duties, meet its obligations to the community at large and often pursues broad aims which may disadvantage or antagonize individuals. Because they are public bodies, local authorities cannot ignore or avoid these hard cases. In such instances the consumers are not just dissatisfied, nor merely unwilling: they may well feel less like customers and more like victims.

———

Financial restrictions mean that the traffic management budget has to be cut; programmed traffic calming schemes, promised to start next year, are cancelled.

A factory closes down, cutting the traffic on a main road through a residential area, but one year later a developer seeks approval for a business park on the site and the residents' association demands permission be refused on road safety and pollution grounds, but because the predicted volume and nature of the traffic generated is less than from the previous use, the highway authority does not advise refusal.

New bus priority routes require widening at a major junction severely affecting the gardens of several houses; after long consultation and negotiations on accommodation works prove unsuccessful the council exercises its compulsory purchase powers.

———

So the conventional definition of customer does not apply. To some extent every person, business, voluntary society, interest group and public body (including the council itself, and its members) are customers, but their status and entitlement to service varies with different situations. As far as straightforward information or a response to a statutory obligation is concerned, then everyone is a customer and deserves proper service. However, no individual or group can demand that a service or a project which is discretionary be provided as of right, no matter how important it is to them, nor how regularly they have paid their

council tax! Similarly, officers (and consultants) cannot be expected to produce advice tailored to specific and partial requirements if that means that its content would be unprofessional or its thrust contrary to the council's policies.

Customers with these requirements are not wrong — customers never are — but they are not going to be as satisfied as they would like to be, and they will not get the same positive service which others in different circumstances, or whose requirements have a higher priority, might enjoy. Yet customer care is still relevant to them because in the public service sector every customer is entitled to at least one thing: a response.

Responding

This wide range of consumers and customers means a correspondingly high volume of activity. In a typical county or city the highways or technical services department will handle — in addition to its committee reports, consultations, programmes and projects — around 1000 letters and well over 3000 telephone calls a month. To deal with these quantities effectively requires a clear framework which is understood by all and puts the focus on the response, rather than on categorizing, recording, analysing and filing the customer contacts.

Making contact with a bureaucracy is, for most people, a difficult task in which expectations of facelessness and remoteness are waiting to be fulfilled. Recognition by people in the organization of the importance of being approachable and responsive cannot be taken for granted, and needs to be reinforced by the means which bureaucracies best understand: a policy. Most public authorities have drawn up charters, guarantees or service commitments which give general assurances

We will be courteous and helpful in all our dealings with the public.

We will keep local people informed of work that affects their neighbourhood.

We will consult, listen and learn from our customers.

and may make specific promises

All letters will be answers within a week.

Our helpline will be available to take your calls from 8.30 am to 5.30 am.

If you report a dangerous pothole our emergency team will make it safe within 24 hours.

The specific levels of service, assuming funding and other resources are there to support them, represent the mechanics of customer care. Systems, procedures and contracts can be set up to provide them. Harder to arrange and deliver are the aspects that depend on attitude — the assurances of courtesy, responsiveness and a genuine interest in people's concerns.

As members of our modern consumer society we all have first-hand experience of the best and the worst of personal service, and we know our reactions to them. Those reactions are the best foundation for developing the positive attitudes and setting the right standards which are needed in the public services we provide. Whether directly involved with front line customer contact or not, all staff should be aware of an overall commitment by the organization to the principles of customer care. For instance

We will treat our customers as we would like to be treated ourselves.

We will provide clear information about services and the standards customers can expect.

We will strive to ensure that our services are equally available to all customers.

On its own this is unlikely to be enough. Some practical guidance is required to translate what might otherwise remain fine words into real action. For example

Don't keep people waiting, be punctual for meetings.

Always reply promptly to correspondence — if you can't give a full answer within a week, send an acknowledgement saying why and giving a time in which you will respond.

Never ignore a ringing telephone — we should answer within five rings, and always be ready to pass on a message if we can't deal with the call ourselves.

Monitoring and publishing performance levels where quantitative data are appropriate is a necessary component of any serious customer care policy. Thus response times are critical — there is nothing more likely to generate dissatisfaction than an unanswered telephone or a long delayed reply (or no reply at all) to a letter. However, it is the content of the response, when it comes, which understandably assumes the most importance to the recipient. A positive and constructive approach must be used wherever possible, even — indeed, especially — in those cases when the reply is not going to match the customer's expectations. It is all too easy to produce, even with the best intentions, an officious and negative response which gives no balancing good news nor any hope for the future.

I am writing to advise you that your petition for traffic calming measures in Coronation Avenue has been considered by the traffic and road safety committee. Unfortunately, as the road does not have an accident record, priority cannot be given to such a proposal in the council's current programme. I regret, therefore, that your petition has been rejected on this occasion.

Although it takes a little longer and a bit more thought, the message can be delivered in a better way.

I am writing regarding your petition for traffic calming measures in Coronation Avenue, which has been considered and discussed by the traffic and road safety committee. As Coronation Avenue is fortunate in not having any personal injury accidents during the last three years, you will appreciate that it is difficult for the committee to apply funds from its limited budget to the measures you request. However, an assessment of the road shows that some SLOW markings should be provided and the Give Way signs replaced with more conspicuous new ones, which will go some way to easing the immediate problems.

Although you will be disappointed by this response, please be assured that the committee recognizes your concerns and will look again at Coronation Avenue when next year's priority lists are drawn up.

Variations on this theme are legitimate ways of attending to public concern: it is rare that there is not something that can be done, and very infrequent when there is really no case at all for a future re-examination. Similarly, passing out information and responding to complaints can be treated as opportunities for improving customer satisfaction rather than being reluctant or defensive.

Thank you for your letter enquiring about the traffic count which you saw at the Meadowvale roundabout last week. This exercise is part of an annual survey which is undertaken at key sites across the city. It provides data which the council uses to bid for government grants for road maintenance, and to decide where money should be spent to keep the heaviest used parts of the road network in good repair.

I am writing in reply to your telephone call on Tuesday regarding the fall which your mother sustained in the Broadway precinct. I was glad to hear that she suffered no injury although it must have been an unpleasant shock. These areas are inspected at weekly intervals for loose paving and other defects and I believe the slab on which your mother tripped became faulty since the last visit. It will be repaired as a priority. I enclose a form for you to return claiming for cleaning bills etc. and thank you for bringing this matter to the council's attention.

There will, however, always be the cases where the local authority has to deliver a response which is simply and uncompromisingly negative. It is best to be clear, raise no false hopes and give a proper explanation; if there is some means of appeal or compensation available, it should be specified.

With reference to your request for a mirror opposite the entrance to Home Farm, I regret that the Department of Transport does not permit such installations on the highway as they are considered on balance to increase risks for road users through confusion over distances, dazzle from headlights, etc.
I am sorry that the council cannot assist you on this occasion.

The council's environment committee has given very full consideration to the objections presented by you and your neighbours to the proposed widening of London Road at Church Hill. The committee considers that the benefits to the community achieved by the introduction of bus lanes outweigh the limited effects on frontages, and has decided to proceed with the scheme without further amendment. As you know, extensive accommodation works are on offer. If you wish to proceed with a claim for compensation, or to seek a local inquiry, the enclosed leaflets explain your rights and the procedures you need to follow.

All the examples are of letters. The same principles, of course, apply to telephone and personal calls, although they do present some practical problems as they are harder to monitor and leave more room for interpretation, misunderstanding and differing recollections than when the response is in writing. Clearly, this implies a need to put responses which are important and/or controversial (not easy to identify without the advantage of hindsight) into print whenever possible. Nevertheless, there is no reasonable way in which public contact can be limited to tidily filed letters, and customer care will not be meaningful unless it provides access through less formal channels.

Accessibility
Good customer care cannot exist unless there is some point of contact, some clear channel of communication between the organization and those it is seeking to serve. Local authorities, with all their resources, routine processes and at least

some general idea of where and to whom their services are directed, have problems in reaching their customers. Imagine how much more difficult it is for an individual trying to find a way into a large and complex body on an unfamiliar errand.

It may be disappointing, but it is, nevertheless, reasonable to assume that very few people have an accurate picture of the way local government is structured. Most members of the general public would be able to identify the appropriate functions in general terms — schools, roads, housing, etc. — but they would probably be unaware of the niceties of, for instance, counties and districts, department of transport and local authority agencies, and the operation of contracted-out services. The wide range of organizational structures and titles (not to mention the impenetrable jargon names) now found in local government would add to the confusion.

Providing information on an authority's services and who delivers them, with contact details, as part of each household's council tax statement, and by way of libraries, community centres, citizens' advice bureaux and prominent entries in the phone directory is helpful but not entirely practical. Callers will not always have those details to hand when needed, and in any case may not find an entry corresponding to their personal description of the matter in question.

The best method is the helpline or helpdesk: the single point of contact which will be available to any caller, on the phone or in person, who does not have a specific route into the organization. The job is simple to describe

- respond with information at the helpdesk (date of next road safety subcommittee, address of the government regional office, etc.) or by issuing standard material (leaflet on rights to compensation, public transport timetable, application form for a vehicle crossing, etc.)
- take enquiries, find out the answers and pass them back (forecast completion date for a cycleway, result of a committee meeting, etc.)
- redirect enquiries to the appropriate contact (the engineer in charge of a particular maintenance scheme, the administrator who deals with the registration of waste carriers, etc.)
- take a message and pass it on for the relevant person or unit to deal with (reports of faulty street lights and potholes, a no objection response to a local consultation, etc.)

In practice it requires considerable skill, patience and knowledge to handle large numbers of contacts, often with queries which are complex or cover more than one subject, and to do so with speed and courtesy. Finding and keeping the right people for this demanding role is hard, and they need proper support: high capacity switchboards; quick reference directories of names, phone numbers and calendars of meetings; up-to-date listings of projects and their managers; plentiful supplies of the leaflets, forms and fact sheets most in demand.

This sort of front of house operation is invaluable, but it cannot substitute completely for contact between customers and the project managers, specialists and administrators who are involved in specific service delivery. There will be occasions, and particular kinds of customer, which justify direct access. Sending a standard form, passing messages, repeating or handing out prepared statements will not be acceptable for residents whose property is affected by a major project, or a headteacher who has had a series of injury accidents outside her school — and it will certainly be unacceptable to councillors.

Access of this kind can be facilitated by directories listing contacts both by name and by function or project. Paper, computerized and teletext-mounted editions can be made available, perhaps with different levels of details. So, for instance, councillors, other council departments and neighbouring authorities may have a comprehensive schedule, whereas the version for use by the general public — through libraries, for example — would concentrate on the most-used services and a limited range of contacts.

Having a name or a job title as a starting point makes a real difference to first-time callers. Identifying the writers of letters personally, rather than using the title of the departmental head or a senior manager only nominally responsible for the particular service, also encourages accessibility as well as giving the recipient the feeling of being in touch with a person rather than an organization.

All of this requires careful management as customer care is an extremely labour-intensive service. To some degree access to professional staff must be rationed, otherwise the time for service delivery will be squeezed, resulting in delays, falling standards and missed targets. This should not be done in a rigid or obvious way, but by careful monitoring and a common sense approach to the value and management of time. Customer care is one of the tasks where getting it right first time pays very large dividends indeed.

16. Who serves?

Public service, public servant, service guarantees, serving the community: the language of local government is all about the concept of service. Some time ago, although not as far back as is often thought, the model for the public sector was rooted firmly in the development, provision and delivery of services through comprehensive in-house organizations. All aspects from the administrative framework through professional and technical activity to the work on the ground would be covered, even ancillary tasks such as printing, office catering and cleaning were included.

This approach tended, though sheer weight of numbers if nothing else, to produce a public service dominated by its officials and their working practices. The capacity of politicians to control and direct such organizations was limited, in their eyes at least, by the inertia which comes with size, complexity and established officialdom. As for the public, in whose service local government operates, neither members nor officers seemed to engage its interest. Apathy and cynicism combined to keep election turn-outs low and involvement restricted to topics of relatively short-lived local controversy. The silent majority stayed quiet, kept its view of the council as a well-meaning but remote and inefficient bureaucracy and appeared not to mind that its views went unrepresented.

This gloomy description, which was never universally true, has become outdated. The character of public sector organizations, the roles of politicians and professionals and the nature of local democracy have all changed. Whether for the better or worse is a question for which there is no single, simple answer: but we can say with confidence that the old certainties have gone.

A tradition of service

Local government has many links with ancient traditions. This is not the same as saying that it is part of our heritage, because the body we recognize as a public authority has a lineage of little more than 120 years. A city or borough may have a charter dating back to King John or beyond, and county sheriffs may trace their predecessors in office back 500 years and more, but the processes of local democracy and public services that operate in these councils are relatively modern.

Nevertheless, these historical associations invest the mechanisms of public service with an air of continuity and permanence which they do not entirely deserve. A surprisingly large proportion of the roles, procedures and processes of local government are not part of our unwritten constitution, but habit — *it's always been done that way*. These mechanisms should be the servants of the concept of local democracy and not its master, and they can be changed. The right of the public to put its views to the council, and question its decisions, is not limited to petitions, formal letters or channels of communication running through officials or members. Public question sessions at full council and committees are becoming the established practice for many authorities. Until recently, typical arrangements for devolving county functions to a local level comprised some limited agency agreements giving district-level authorities the management of activities such as maintenance and traffic regulations, but with almost all highway authority decisions retained by county committees. This tradition is gradually being replaced by the operation of local member panels, covering geographic areas and involving district as well as county councillors. Their terms of reference allow them decision making powers on local issues within broad policy guidelines, and the ability to select priorities within budget allocations.

Recognizing that established methods are not fixed does not mean they must be altered. There can be real value in custom and practice which is consistent, based on long experience and widely known and accepted. Change for change's sake may work in marketing luxury goods or impulse purchases, where the product needs to be repackaged and relaunched at intervals to keep its share of consumer attention, but it is irrelevant and damaging to public services where reliability, equity and cost-effectiveness are very important aspects. Tradition is not a bad thing, therefore, only a bad excuse for not improving things.

Of all the traditional elements in the local government environment, the one most admired and singled out for special protection from the forces of change is the public service ethos. No-one would argue that it was old-fashioned or unnecessary and it would come out top on many lists defining the essential attributes of a good public servant. But why is it important? Who has it? What is it?

These questions can go round in a circle. Public service ethos is what you find in a good public servant; you can identify good public servants by the public service ethos they display in their work, and so on. In a changing world where traditions have to be understood if they are to stay relevant, this is not enough.

Public service has certain defining characteristics, not unique in themselves, but together representing a special package which distinguishes it from other activities

- accountability to the public at large rather than a specific ownership or interest
- provision of service based on entitlement and equity, and not commercial transactions
- identification with a community defined geographically, not socially or economically
- openness and accessibility
- commitment to the principles of democracy under which the authority of elected representatives and majority decisions is accepted by all
- no profit motive, any surplus being remitted to provide extra or better service
- a presumption that the needs of the service come before the personal benefit of those serving in it.

Public services

These are all admirable features, but this list could only be applied in full to a world in which independent councillors operate without the discipline of party groups; career local government officers monitor themselves only against professional standards, and both are free from the constraints of cash limits and centralized regulation. If such a world existed somewhere, sometime, it has passed away, and these characteristics are now less clear-cut and specific. Some of the ideals of this tradition have had to be compromised and a realistic appraisal of modern public service has to acknowledge that.

Many professional activities are carried out under consultancy agreements, whether in-house or external, which not only require monitoring against economic targets but also set standards of acceptability that are not necessarily the highest achievable in terms of technical excellence. Certain grants on which programmes are heavily dependent — highway maintenance for instance — are bid for against criteria that are based on national and not local priorities. Similarly, scarce funds — highway maintenance again and traffic calming — may be given a priority which reflects political objectives rather than an equitable distribution to meet need.

The rationing of resources by price to the user (car park charges), by time (limited on-street parking and, rather less obviously, traffic signals) and by cost to the general community (priorities within programmes) is now an integral part of the delivery of local authority services.

The traditions of service have not, of course, disappeared, but altered to meet the times in which we live. They are certainly not the prerogative of officers any more, as the greater involvement of members, both personally and politically, and the community as a whole has widened the range of participants. Elected members and their local party organizations now play a much fuller part, but there is also a whole new cast of players

- voluntary groups, many of whom are relied upon for their support (principally in social welfare activities and education, but increasingly for work on conservation, recycling, road safety)
- private sector sponsors, who provide funds and also participate directly in campaigns and community initiatives (green issues depend heavily on this kind of public service commitment, as do road safety campaigns as well as those partnership initiatives such as town centre management where there is a clear commercial benefit)
- external consultants, specializing in providing public sector services through secondments, long-term contracts and sometimes the transfer of whole functions complete with staff (voluntary and compulsory competitive tendering for construction-related professional services, and the steady move away from in-house direct labour organizations, has been the most influential factor in developing this new area).

So, while the ethos of public service retains its continuity and validity, it can no longer be seen as exclusive to those employed in local government. Nowadays, many people, whether giving their time freely as volunteers, or working as employees under commercial contracts, contribute directly to the delivery of public services. As public authorities become more flexible and diverse in their responses to our rapidly changing world, it is essential to recognize that the key traditions of service — probity, equity and responsibility to the local community — can be transferred to the new structures and the new providers, as well as preserved by the long-established framework of the council and its full-time officials.

Members and officers

Elected representatives (MPs, councillors) set the direction, objectives and policies, which they do with the advice of officials (civil servants, local government officers and, working with them, consultants); similarly, it is the politicians who take the decisions and the professionals who carry them out. It is true that on many routine matters the professionals are given delegated powers of action, but this is only because the politicians have decided to operate in that way and this authority can always be withdrawn.

That is the theory. As far as the practice is concerned, it is known from sources as varied as Richard Crossman's *Diaries of a Cabinet Minister* and Jonathan Lynn and Anthony Jay's *Yes Minister* series that in central government the civil servants have an influence on policy and decision making that goes far beyond the theoretical limits. Local government is not so well-served with either memoirs or satire, but few with practical experience of its workings would deny the similarities. Although the situation will vary from one authority to another, and — depending on the personalities involved — within an individual council, officers are involved in far more than the presentation of advice and the subsequent and separate implementation of policies and decisions. They are often active and influential in the political processes and may play a significant part in determining what is done and, often just as importantly, what is not done.

Political appointments are, of course, not unknown in local government. Councils have the discretion, subject to funding and open disclosure of what the job is about, to employ political assistants to provide research, organizational support, information and ideas to their party groups: these people may be very visible and influential, but they are not supposed to be part of the departmental structure. More questionable in view of the local government officer's duty to the whole council, is the placing of individuals within the officer framework to ensure political aims are achieved. On the one hand, this can be made to look like the introduction of commissars; on the other, it is hard to see how a politically active group with a commanding majority in the council can work effectively with key chief officers who do not understand and share at least some enthusiasm for its policy objectives. The vital point is what happens to professional judgement: if it is suppressed or distorted to promote political ends then officers are in breach of their duty, legal and ethical; if it is presented and packaged to put the best case forward on behalf of the council and its ruling group, that is legitimate. The distinction may seem subtle, but in real life it will be much easier to recognize than to describe.

While politics overriding professional judgement is a serious matter, no less is the substitution of professional preferences for political priorities. The officer culture which is still deeply ingrained in some parts of local government tends to give significant — some might say excessive — weight to the professional view. Certainly, legislation requires the council to take account of appropriate professional advice when exercising its powers to formulate policy and make decisions, but it does not have to follow it blindly nor accept as definitive the view from its in-house advisers. Professionals can be as prejudiced as politicians, and just as unwilling to see alternatives.

Deeply worn tracks cutting across grassed areas and correspondingly under-used footways demonstrate the inability of the designers of many major residential developments in the 70s and 80s to produce layouts acceptable to ordinary people. More recently, the acceptance of the effectiveness of traffic calming by professionals was much slower than by the public at large, and very frustrating for local politicians who often suspected officers of rejecting small-scale, low-technology solutions as uninteresting. Similarly, there persists a belief, which professionals ignore at their peril, that engineers lack enthusiasm for public transport schemes, cycling projects and similar initiatives because they would rather see a return to extensive road building.

Officers who do not see the purpose of professional skill and judgement as a means to an end, but as an end in itself, are crossing the boundary into members' territory. They may think they know best, they may believe they know what the public needs (even though it may not be what the public wants) — but they will be missing the point. And the point is that, however low the turn-out, members have been elected and are the only — and, therefore, the best — representatives of the public in the local government system. By standing for election they take on a unique accountability to local people; they have a legitimacy conferred by the ballot box that officers cannot share.

Officers, who turn away deeply felt concerns about road safety from the residents of a busy suburban street because 'it is not considered to be a significant hazard', will not have to face the personal recriminations that the local member will suffer if an accident does occur. Nor do they have to respond directly to public demands for high standards in visible highway maintenance, such as minor pothole repairs, and the corresponding indifference — even antagonism — to long-term preventive maintenance schemes — even though, on these and similar issues, professionals bear a responsibility for failing to educate the lay public, and their representatives, in technical concepts that are capable of quite straightforward explanation.

Most dangerous is the perception that expressions of political priorities are inaccurate and unrepresentative, based on minority agendas such as cycling, or dual standards exemplified by the mismatch between the general opposition to road building and the lack of individual rejection of the private car. However accurate this assessment may be, it ignores two major factors: one of political theory — identifying forces for change at an early stage and working with them is one of the prime purposes of political action; and the other of practical politics — voters may practise a 'do as I say not as I do' approach, but that is how elections work. Officers might consider standing as the Cycling Facilities Are A Waste of Resources candidate, or the representative of the More Roads For The People Party and see how many votes they get.

The changing nature of public service and, in particular, the differentiation between purchasers and providers which will be examined in the next chapter, is beginning to isolate and eliminate (or perhaps drive underground?) the tendency of officers to make their own policies. Member involvement is also having a growing effect, although there is a concern that this could focus too much on implementation rather than policy. It is a question of balance. Policy cannot be made in the absence of professional advice, nor can members complain if, as has often happened, failure to take hard policy decisions leaves a vacuum that officers feel they have to fill. Similarly, members have a right to know what is being done in their name and how services are delivered, and officers must expect some involvement on the ground, and intervention if standards of customer care, consultation and other matters on which councillors can properly judge, are inadequate.

Officers and members can and should work together, recognizing the contributions both can make to the full range of public service tasks. One job, however, which professionals cannot do and should never usurp, is the role of representing the public — obvious as it may seem, only elected representatives can do that.

Representative democracy

The nostalgic picture of the days before local government became *political* portrays councillors, independent of any party allegiances, working for what was best for the local community rather than what national headquarters dictated. As has been shown, this is not an accurate portrayal: local authorities have been involved in party politics for generations, and the so-called independent councillor was more often than not representative of very narrowly based local interests such as small business, farming or trades unions. It is in the last 30 years that the public at large, both as individuals and in a bewildering variety of groups, has developed the confidence and awareness to expect its views to be represented and taken into account in the process of local government.

At the same time there has been a growing trend towards centralization. In the all-important area of public finance this has come from the national government; in the fields of health and safety, environmental protection, procurement and standards for products and services the initiative has come partly at the national and partly at the European level. Professionals, by their training, work within the new rules even when they find them oppressive or unnecessary. Elected representatives and the public have been much less inclined to accept what are often seen as unreasonable restrictions on the freedom of communities to organize their affairs locally.

The tension which these opposing forces of change have created cannot be ignored by professional advisers.

Ring-fenced grants for preventive maintenance on major routes have become a feature of highway authority programmes at the same time as the pressure on council funds has squeezed the money available for minor repairs on local roads. While there is a technical case to justify this ranking, it is not conclusive, as the two types of maintenance are assessed in isolation, without regard to relative priorities locally. To the public this can look like a total disregard for community interests and even a waste of money, as they will see apparently generous provision for routes which appear in good order while roads in poor condition (superficially at least) are left untreated.

Similarly, the regulations which tightly restrict the use of 30 mph speed limit repeaters, the limited but loosely defined discretion given on the provision of pedestrian crossings, and the greater flexibility available on certain kinds of signs create numerous situations where local priorities appear to clash with a wider framework of good practice. Residents, interest groups and elected representatives will expect their concerns to be given proper attention in the hope that it may lead to justified exceptions or, where that latitude is not available, to the gradual build up of a case for change.

Every professional working in or for local authorities has to understand this need for local views to be represented. It may not be successful, it may be a lost cause from the outset, but that is not the way to view the exercise nor to judge the value of the effort. The principal task is to ensure that the public have their say, and have it with the best technical support that can be given.

If the case fundamentally lacks any sound technical justification, then it clearly has to depend mainly on its emotive or political appeal, areas where professionals will not be playing a major role. However, if there is a technical argument to be run against financial restrictions, or if restrictive technical standards can be legitimately questioned, then it is no part of a public service professional's role to dissuade or deter local representative action, but rather to assist with information, advocacy and encouragement. The result will often be predictable, but the professional's response should not be 'I told you so' because if the cause is worth persevering for, then it is important to maintain enthusiasm for the next time. Representing local interests is not confined to separate specific issues in individual localities: it covers the whole range of topics that have a local dimension, and particular cases — whether successes or failures — are part of wider campaigns.

There is a growing body of examples to demonstrate the changes which local authorities have made to their own priorities and programmes, and those at a national level, as a result of representative action. The greater emphasis on traffic calming rather than capacity improvements reflects the success of public opinion, particularly expressed through local groups, in moving highway authorities to accept what are essentially obstacles rather than encouragements to traffic movement. Similarly, more flexibility in the design guidelines for traffic calming features such as road humps has resulted from pressure at local level to provide practical solutions rather than textbook specifications. Mitigating the environmental impact of major road schemes, by planting and other conservation measures, by positive efforts at noise insulation and reduction, and by more realistic compensation provisions for the effect of blight on property, has long been the aim of persistent and effective representations from individuals, pressure groups and local authorities.

No-one is likely to argue that democracy in general, and local government in particular, is the most efficient way to manage the affairs of people and communities. Giving the public a real opportunity to choose its representatives, and then to have its views sought, taken into account and expressed, is bound to lead to some uncertainty, inconsistency and changes in direction. That is the price we pay in our system for balancing local democracy against corporate management by the state.

This balance is a delicate one and takes special effort on the local government side of the scales to make it work. In particular, it has to be accepted that the position of the elected representative is no longer as clear-cut and distinct as it used to be: many groups and interests operate within the public service network and expect to have a say. They may be content to have a member or a party group speak on their behalf, or they may want to make their voice heard independently; they may be willing to work through the council's consultation processes or they may choose to express their views outside that machinery. Councillors have to live with this new aspect of local representative democracy, and professional advisers must respond to this, not as a nuisance, but as part of the job of delivering public services.

Officers — and consultants too — may at times be exasperated by the operational difficulties these 'untidy' arrangements may cause. The council's task, however, is to serve the public: professionals have to remember that their job is not to impose efficiency on local democracy, but to work efficiently on democracy's behalf — not the same thing at all.

17. The enabling council

As an institution, local government is seen by most people as dull, unimaginative, officious and much better at saying 'no' than 'yes' — a municipal version of the civil service. Sadly, some of the stereotypes with which popular imagination has filled both government and council departments do exist. But their brand of public service has no future.

Local government has been reassessing its purpose. For members, as has been seen, what is now required is a much greater emphasis on the task of representing the needs and views of local communities, not only in the council chamber as part of looking after the patch, but also on a wider scale through the processes of party politics or interest groups. For the council as an organization, it can no longer work on the principle that it should provide directly from its own resources all the service requirements for the local community: financially and managerially the goal is unachievable; nor is the public willing to accept the local authority as the sole supplier when alternatives are, or could be, available.

Recognizing that there can be, indeed need to be, other providers of services, and that there are many activities in which it can only participate in partnership or with the sponsorship of other bodies and organizations, the modern council does not see itself as doing things for — or to — the local community, but enabling the community to get things done.

In this new and still developing concept of the *enabling council*, there are new roles. The formulation of policies and strategic plans is a task in which members take a lead, with the advice and support of professionals, in-house or external. Purchasing or otherwise securing the services to implement those strategies and policies, and then ensuring they are delivered as specified is a job that the council's officers will do, with the involvement — to varying degrees — of elected representatives. Providing the services themselves, will be a mixed economy of in-house units, internal contractors and external commercial suppliers. These roles may overlap, individuals may play more than one, and there are no fixed definitions or rigid job descriptions: redefining the local authority means rethinking the tasks it does and who does them.

Strategists
The long-term aims and objectives of a local authority need to be set out in some detail and over considerable time periods if they are to be achieved effectively. In the political context this is necessary to ensure that the level of consultation,

the opportunities for development and amendment of details, and the groundwork for cooperation with other interests that all underpin the enabling approach can be accommodated. For the management of major projects and programmes, the lead times for authorization and preparation are long and advance notice is essential if broad acceptance is to be gained, and all the components — land, funds, regulatory orders — brought together. In addition, there are statutory plans that local authorities must prepare to secure government grants and to advance or protect their long-term strategic goals, and which have far-reaching consequences for the local community.

Strategies are an investment, of time and effort, that can provide a framework to enable not just the council, but also a range of participants, to work together to realize shared aims.

A small sample of corporate and service-specific strategies and strategic plans includes

- budget strategy: the classification of services by priority, with the consequences of expansion, reduction or withdrawal, including the potential for support from external sources, would need to be done almost a year in advance to permit consultation, much of it confidential, and the drafting and consideration of alternatives; the political as well as managerial effort involved in major redistributions of funds imply timescales of three or four years

- economic development: long-range plans to attract new businesses or provide support and assistance to existing ones will require contact and cooperation with individual firms, local chambers of commerce, government agencies and departments, the regional training and enterprise council, other local councils, trades unions, the general public and a range of interest groups; not only to find out their views and collect data but also to engage their commitment and resources in shaping and delivering the strategy

- the transport policy and programme: no longer just a bid for grant, but an opportunity to integrate many strands of transportation planning — a field in which interest groups and local communities are now deeply involved. Submissions have to be made almost a year in advance; to secure proper consultation on the overall policies as well as the specific contents of projects and programmes requires a start at least six months ahead; the time horizons extend to five, ten and fifteen years

- road safety plans: combine analysis of data and trends with proposals for works projects, publicity and education campaigns and training; voluntary organizations, schools, community groups and the police are all participants in action which has both immediate and long-term aims; results are assessed on three year comparison periods and targets for casualty reduction focus on ten years or more

- the local waste plan: its preparation is a statutory obligation, and an extremely sensitive political issue; although the guidelines the plan will set for treatment and disposal are intended to operate for up to ten years ahead, the consequences on neighbourhoods affected by landfill sites, incinerators, etc. will last for very much longer. Giving people a say, and still achieving a constructive strategy, is a major challenge in explanation, justification and the generation of a sense of community responsibility.

The preparation of such strategic plans and policies requires a combination of professional and political input.

The professional component must be based on a capability to look wider than the relatively narrow confines of engineering project management, although feasibility assessments and order-of-cost estimates will often be required. The content will eventually be presented to the council, and, therefore, must pass through the authority's decision making machinery. The limits on delegation in the Local Government Act 1972 mean that it will need to be the responsibility of a council officer, whose involvement will extend beyond professional *due diligence* to taking account of the political environment. These legal niceties and practical considerations apart, there is no reason why external consultants cannot be used as part of the strategic planning team. Indeed, there are topics (a study of the integration of road and rail-based public transport in a major city, for example) for which specialist expertise is best obtained from outside the local authority, and there may be occasions (for instance, a proposal to merge engineering and planning departments) when an external view is essential to avoid bias and special pleading — whether real or imagined. Equally, there will be subjects on which, for reasons of political sensitivity, members will want to restrict professional involvement to a very few senior officers whose understanding of the authority's inner workings (and their discretion) can be relied upon.

Only the largest authorities can maintain a dedicated corporate strategy team of any size, and such an arrangement always runs the risk of being remote from the realities of service delivery. More common is the use of specialists in departments or from outside for service related strategies (the TPP, for example) and corporate teams drawn from central and service departments, again with external support if required, for council-wide planning (such as the budget strategy). Member working parties provide the means of directing the professional activity, serve as the link with local interests and the public, and introduce the political factors which are essential if the council is to see any strategy as its own rather than its officers'.

Strategies take time to prepare, but they should be made to last — so being a strategist is not usually a steady job, but a role that different persons or groups may play at different times.

Purchasers and providers

Having a strategy is important, but delivering the council's part in it is essential, whether it is a major new initiative or the routine delivery of day-to-day services.

In the traditional local authority model of not so very long ago, officers would organize, order, provide and accept projects and programmes, in many cases entirely within the resources of their own department or unit.

The classic example of this approach is represented by the area or divisional surveyors in shire counties: remote from head office and working on a budget rolled forward year after year, they would use their local knowledge and judgement to decide on priorities for repair and minor improvements, and carry them out using the direct labour gang based on the area depot. It would do many conscientious officers a disservice to suggest this approach was wrong; it worked for times of greater stability — in funds, traffic and public expectations — than today, but it has been overtaken by pressures for cost-effectiveness and accountability which necessitate a much more open and systematic way of working to replace the very personal benevolent dictatorship of the area surveyor. If any still exist, they are the last of a vanishing breed.

Today, the typical arrangement is based upon a distinction between the role of deciding what services are needed, how they are to be delivered and whether or not they are acceptable, and the job of providing those services. The term *purchaser* is widely used, although *procurer* or even *facilitator* might be more accurate as not all services are bought in, some being the output of partnership agreements with voluntary organizations and commercial sponsors.

The purchaser role involves taking the projects and programmes identified in the council's strategic plans and securing their implementation through one or more service providers. How strictly the role is defined depends on the policies of individual authorities, but it certainly covers the preparation of the brief for the project, setting an estimated cost, inviting tenders or quotations, selecting the supplier, placing the order, acceptance of the end product and authorization of payment.

In a major infrastructure project, the purchaser might carry out the following tasks

1. prepare design brief and commission consultant
2. monitor design process, accept work when complete and authorize consultant's fees
3. secure relevant committee approvals for project and estimated cost
4. commission legal and property activity
5. arrange any design modifications resulting from committee decisions, land acquisition, etc. authorize professional fees
6. invite tenders, assess bids, recommend successful contractor and secure release of funds
7. award contract with committee approval as appropriate
8. appoint consultant to supervise works on site

9. authorize payments to contractor based on interim measurements
10. agree and settle final account for the works; accept the works
11. authorize payment of consultant's fees
12. assess consultant's and contractor's performance; review and modify specifications etc. for next project.

If the purchaser is buying-in a comprehensive project management service, then steps 4 and 6 would be carried out by the consultant and step 8 would be irrelevant. Alternatively, the purchaser role could be more widely interpreted to include the supervision and measurement of the works' contractor, thus replacing step 8 with positive involvement and making step 11 redundant.

While the purchaser can be flexible and — depending on the authority's approach or perhaps the nature of the service, project or programme — perform functions ranging from the minimum necessary to satisfy legal requirements to those which are available from external suppliers, there has to be clear separation from all potential providers. So the purchaser is a role for officers as, at the least, they will be the source of advice to the council on the specification for services, the best providers to supply them and their subsequent performance as a basis for payment.

Providers — or suppliers, or contractors — can take a variety of forms. In-house units may operate under service level agreements (SLAs), setting out standards of performance for general functions (for example, the preparation of technical details, plans, etc. for traffic regulation orders) and specific projects (the design brief for a park and ride scheme, for instance). Internal contracting arms can be set up to work as quasi-commercial units, being commissioned to deliver professional services (the design and supervision of a programme of accident prevention schemes, perhaps, or the drafting of the annual review of car parking charges) or construction works (a bridge strengthening project, for example).

External contractors, drawn from the ranks of the major civil engineering construction companies as well as small local firms have always been involved in public works projects (ranging from major bypasses to fencing, from multi-storey car parks to street lights); they are now beginning to take their part in the provision of routine services (refuse collection, grass cutting, surface dressing, patching, etc.) packaged in term contracts, and even including tasks once considered the exclusive province of direct service organizations (the winter maintenance jobs of gritting, salting and snow clearance, and emergency cover for accident damage, flooding, etc.). Similarly, external professional consultants have provided design and supervision services for public works projects to local authorities, although their involvement has been less widespread than engineering contractors, with some councils using their facilities often and others making a point of carrying out all but the most specialist tasks in-house. As a generalization, their commissions tended to be specialized (large infrastructure schemes such as a major bridge, or projects requiring advanced technology like traffic modelling) or generated by concentrations in workload (for example peak-lopping, as when staff may be seconded or provided on an agency basis to strengthen a site team or prepare a programme of bridge assessments); this picture is also changing with consultants becoming more widely involved in all aspects of service provision through competitive tendering and the voluntary externalization of work and staff resources to private hosts.

So providers are a more varied group than purchasers, comprising council officers of the traditional kind, internal contractors and consultants, commercial firms providing services on a project-by-project basis and external suppliers working in long-term partnerships. Because of these variations it is not accurate to see the purchaser–provider arrangement as being the same as the long-established and well documented employer–contractor combination found on most construction projects, nor the client–consultant relationship which will be considered in the next chapter. It may include these, but it ranges wider and is more flexible in the tasks which can be assigned to each of the participants.

Indeed, it is still possible in small authorities or in specialized functions to envisage the purchaser and the provider role being fulfilled — at different times — by the same people as it is simply not cost-effective to create a real split.

Thus, a programme of bridge assessments and inspection may be drawn up by a team of structural maintenance specialists, who, by defining priorities, timetables and a quality plan, will effectively establish what is to be procured and how its satisfactory delivery can be monitored. The team will then go on to provide that service, inspecting and assessing the bridges within the required schedule and in accordance with the specified procedure.

Practical solutions of this kind must be the exception and not the rule, but when they work for a particular situation there should be no rigid rule to exclude them. Similarly, purchasing need not be tied to the action of buying services (whether by internal transfers of funds or the direct payment to external suppliers), as there are tasks which require the specifying and monitoring of an activity but no transaction — when for instance a voluntary group helps with a project, or a commercial organization provides a facility as a community benefit.

Learning to live with flexible and sometimes inconsistent responses such as these is a new requirement, yet an unavoidable one as the very essence of the enabling concept is that it should accommodate diversity.

Changing roles

The enabling council is, of course, much more than a set of new definitions, repackaging the traditional local government approach and adding consultation and customer care. There has to be a significant adjustment to accommodate the new realities of power, influence and accountability. Whereas most change in public authorities tends to be evolutionary, in this case the pace has been, in relative terms, revolutionary — even earth-shaking.

For members exposed to the regular cycle of appraisal by the voters, adopting a more open, constructive style, recognizing the need to work with local interests both in their wards and divisions and also more widely is a fact of political life. The shifts in the balance of the council, in terms of individual members, the offices they hold and overall political control, which follow from defeats and departures, together with the responsiveness to public opinion (otherwise known as instinct for survival) which most politicians develop, are usually enough to produce organic change in the direction of an enabling culture.

Nevertheless, changes in the council chamber or committee rooms are not always smooth. Working through different political networks, often outside conventional party structures and involving new participants from voluntary organizations, business and grant-aid bodies as varied as departments of state, government agencies and European commission directorates, requires members to have a high degree of adaptability and climb a steep learning curve.

Thus, sharing or devolving power from what was once the centralized main committee to locally-based sections with district, borough, parish or town councillors involved certainly enables communities and their representatives to take an active interest in what happens in their area. It also tends to slow down decision making, undermine consistency, increase pressure on budgets and — often the most critical point — open up debate over a wider range of issues than might have been envisaged in the terms of reference. These are not necessarily disadvantages, but they do require more of members' time and exposure, forcing them to respond to and justify the practical, local implications of those policies and choices which seemed so straightforward when considered at a theoretical and strategic level. Similarly, letting go of functions to other organizations, whether voluntary or commercial, means a loss of direct control and a greater requirement for consultation, cooperation and negotiation — all demanding more time and effort.

The establishment of local highway subcommittees to take delegated responsibility for routine maintenance, traffic management and road safety, and similar arrangements for development or planning is one example of the enabling approach applied to council procedure. Local members from the highway and planning authorities can be joined by representatives from lower tier councils — districts and boroughs, parishes and town councils — whose rights of attendance, and voting, can be set out in the subcommittee's constitution. Representatives from other bodies can also be invited as contributors or observers — they cannot be given a formal vote — so that the views of local business, environment groups, residents, associations, etc. can be heard on matters affecting their interests. As with most meetings of the council and its subsidiary bodies, the press and public can attend, and there may be an opportunity for questions or the presentation of petitions.

Making 'the council' in all its forms less remote and more open to local or external influence involves new structures and new networks for the professionals as well as members.

For local government officers there is nothing comparable to the electoral process to encourage and deliver change, and the new culture of enabling can have quite an impact when it meets the unyielding mass of a large department. Indeed, if change comes from a significant transfer of political power — to newly-elected members or to a different ruling group — or as a result of a major political initiative designed to demonstrate positive action to the public, then the impact is likely to be not only severe, but sudden.

Changing from within, and as far as possible in parallel with changing political objectives, is the preferable option. It means being prepared to work with others, spending time and trouble on finding out what people want, and seeking ways of helping them to get it. Some demands will be impossible, or incompatible with the needs of others, and there will be disappointments: explanation, and the offer of alternatives where possible, form part of the essential ingredients of enabling. In all cases, the aim must be to build good working relationships between the local government organization and the community.

Contact should be proactive rather than reactive, although that is easier written than achieved. Different projects have different interests concerned with them. For instance

- *Cycling:* local cycling action groups; environment groups; schools; police; Royal Society for the Prevention of Accidents
- *Park and ride:* local residents' associations; frontagers and adjoining properties; bus operators; environment and transport pressure groups; chamber of commerce; car park operators
- *Recycling:* environment groups; local waste collection and disposal firms; local businesses, especially major retailers; schools.

These lists are not comprehensive and in any local area there will be other potential partners and participants outside the usual local authority network.

As if learning this role was not enough, officers have to adapt to the purchaser–provider environment. They must either become used to the tasks of specifying, procuring (or perhaps facilitating) and monitoring, without for the most part being involved in the delivery, or concentrate on delivery with the job of deciding what is to be supplied and whether or not it is acceptable handled by others. This division may seem welcome for its clear focus, but in practice, and especially when things do not go according to plan, it can rapidly lose its appeal. It introduces a high degree of accountability, and can be uncomfortable. The linkage between volumes of work and resources, between expectations and performance, and between modern requirements for output and traditional methods of implementation are all exposed to a level of scrutiny that would not have operated a few years ago.

Separating purchaser and provider roles means reviewing organizational structures, job descriptions and resource levels. To be real it means opening up the provider functions to new suppliers. This is nothing to do with compulsory competitive tendering, but reflects the logical extension of the enabling concept to encompass the simple question: who can best provide this service? The answer may be the in-house organization, an external contractor, a voluntary group or a commercial sponsor. The results can have major effects on the way local government is structured, breaking down some of the former power bases which depended upon officers' spans of control, and their capability to arrange private deals that had little or nothing to do with effective service delivery and were actually about exchanging favours.

The consequences of this new approach, and these new participants, bears down hard on existing departments. They have to face up to the human consequences of change, ranging from retraining in different skills and developing new attitudes to what is euphemistically called *right-sizing* or *re-engineering*, and actually means cutting down on the jobs built into the system to free up a more flexible response to demands on resources.

The clear implication is that the providers will include more than works contractors building new projects and consultants covering specialist requirements or peaks in the normal workload. Here is the opportunity to explore varied options for enabling the local community to take part and share control. After all, the most clear-cut relationship is that of the commercial contract for both services and items: if the output is not what you want, you get the supplier to change — or change the supplier.

18. Clients and consultants

While the public sector has always made use of the private sector for professional services, the norm from the 1940s to the beginning of the 1990s was to buy in consultancy on a project-by-project basis. Consultants were commissioned to undertake particular tasks, working to a specific brief; the end of the job marked the end of the commission, and although some consultants and local authorities tended to work together over long periods this was entirely informal — a product of convenience and familiarity, not a true partnership.

Although project commissions remain part of the scene, a new and very different alternative style has been brought about by the operation of four factors

- downward pressure on local government funds, resulting in authorities' seeking to minimize all costs that are not part of front line service
- the acceptance by local authorities of a role focused on representing and enabling, rather than themselves being the providers
- a change in the nature of public works, encouraging consultants to take an interest in fields once left to council organizations
- legislation and regulations aimed at introducing a wide spread of competition into the provision of public authority services.

The initial response to the first two has been the separation of professional staff into client and consultant units. In part this serves to demonstrate cost-effectiveness by concentrating on defined tasks, some of which can be evaluated against comparable services available from private suppliers (market testing); it also reinforces by organizational change the move away from a culture of professional bureaucracy to one centred on delivery of service.

More recently, the second pair of factors have made this division more real. In-house consultants have been established, acting as quasi-commercial units at arm's length, and a number of local authorities and government agencies have introduced long-term contracts for consultancy services, including the transfer of staff as well as work.

This chapter will not attempt to give detailed guidance on the commissioning, controlling and monitoring of consultants for project work, nor on the complex and often delicate task of assembling a viable long-term contract for services and selecting a suitable partner for the workload and the staff — that would take a book in itself. What it summarizes are the key issues that underpin a successful client–consultant relationship, and keep it working.

Job descriptions

The client role in modern public works projects and programmes has to be as clearly defined as that of the consultant. In a standard commission for a single project — a feasibility study, the design of a structure, the supervision of a works contract, etc. — there is a well-established relationship between the client, who prepares the brief, and the consultant, who carries it out. Project management systems (as has been seen in chapter 12) are available in many different forms to provide a framework for the consultant's activities, with facilities to build in reports, progress meetings and specific milestones to enable the client to monitor delivery of the advice or service. The client, as an officer of the council, reviews the advice and, after any necessary adjustments or additional work, feeds it into the council's decision making process. In the case of the implementation of a project, the client, having monitored the consultant on behalf of the council, retains a close involvement to ensure that the authority's interests are covered in both technical areas, such as potential design changes, and non-technical areas, such as consultation and dealing with the public.

This is the conventional separation of tasks envisaged by model conditions of engagement. It is founded on the concept of a professionally-based, in-house organization fulfilling the role of client as one of its continuing functions, with consultants supplying support on an occasional basis. Much less settled is the division of responsibilities involved in those continuous functions — management of the highway network, for instance, or preparation and delivery of road safety programmes — which are no longer the exclusive province of local government departments, but are now coming within the range of services provided under consultancy agreements. Whether the consultant is an in-house unit or a commercial supplier, the operation cannot work effectively unless there is a clear understanding of who does what.

In case this seems self-evident, try a few simple exercises, starting with nothing more than a step-by-step description of a particular service or programme. The steps that ought to be identifiable are those inputs, activities, outputs and decisions which have to be completed to produce the expected deliverable, and which when set in their logical order define the progress of work from start to finish. Getting this done — and it should be done by the people who are involved in the service or programme on the basis of what *actually* happens, not what is *supposed* to happen, nor what people would *like* to happen — concentrates minds wonderfully. It will not be as easy as expected; it will probably reveal gaps between the theories of those managing the organization and the practices of those operating it; it will almost certainly throw up questions of why things are done, which often generate the reply 'because it's always been that way'. The end product will be valuable for these reasons alone.

As a simple example to illustrate the process, take the maintenance of a highway authority's road safety records.

Accident Record Service

Collection and recording of accident data to specified level

Maintenance/revisions to database within specification

Provision of regular monthly and quarterly reports as specified, and respond to irregular requests from specified sources

Despatch to DoT of highway authority returns

Quarterly returns to police authority

Standard member/customer services procedure for enquiries for data

Production of draft annual summary including national/regional comparators (also feeds into road safety plan project)

Consider and process report to committee

Recommendation of any changes to database systems (outside of specification) and to reports generated

Implement amendments to systems and reports specification as agreed

---

The next stage is to assign client or consultant responsibility to each step. Here is where the definition of client becomes important. Local government has, in the recent past, tended to ignore this issue by classifying as consultant the project-related engineering tasks of design, contract preparation and supervision, and letting everything else fall under the client responsibility by default. This is tackling the subject the wrong way round. There is a straightforward definition of the client's role in any client–consultant relationship, namely

- preparation of briefs to define the project/programme and the consultancy service
- selection of the consultant
- managing the consultancy contract (including the provision of inputs or decisions on which progress of the work depends, authorization of changes, and coordination of inputs and activities which the consultant cannot control)
- monitoring progress and standards
- reviewing performance of the consultant and the briefs
- authorizations for finances and fees.

In the case of a local authority, these tasks are supplemented by special responsibilities to

- ensure that all advice on which the council makes decisions has been considered by its own professional officers
- operate statutory powers delegated by the council
- provide sensitive advice which the council, as a body working in a political environment, wishes to receive from its own officers rather than a consultant.

It is these three functions, peculiar to local government, which cause the uncertainty about the scope of the client's role. As far as the first two are concerned, the requirement is for officers to apply their minds to any external advice and satisfy themselves that it is professionally sound; then they can pass it on to the council, or use it as the basis for exercising delegated powers. This does not mean eliminating large areas of work from the consultant's brief, nor going over in great detail work that the consultant has already done. The process might best be labelled *validation*, as its purpose is to ensure that the council is receiving advice which its client officers are prepared to say is valid and adopt as if it was their own. The third function depends very much on the authority's style of operating and the extent of the sensitive areas where it feels that, for political reasons, it has to get (or be seen to be getting) its advice from public servants, with no commercial or external interest involved.

We can now return to the step-by-step analysis of functions, and assign each step to either the client or the consultant. The balance will vary, depending on whether the authority takes a minimalist view of the client role, or a wider interpretation of what is required to validate consultants' advice and cover sensitive topics. In general, however, there will always be more steps for the consultant than the client. Some new steps (two in this case) and explanatory notes will usually be added to give practical effect to the client–consultant working relationship.

Accident Record Service

Collection and recording of accident data to specified level	Consultant
Maintenance/revisions to database within specification	Consultant
Hold current client copy of base data	Client
Provision of regular monthly and quarterly reports as specified and respond to irregular requests from specified sources	Consultant
Despatch to DoT of highway authority returns	Client
Quarterly returns to police authority	Consultant
Standard member/customer services procedure for enquiries for data {	Consultant Client
Production of draft annual summary including national/regional comparators (also feeds into road safety plan project)	Consultant
Consider and process report to committee (consultant to attend for presentations, questions, etc.)	Client
Recommendation of any changes to database systems (outside of specification) and to reports generated	Consultant
Agreement to recommended changes	Client
Implement amendments to systems and reports specification as agreed	Consultant

---

The consultant can be internal or external. The point of this process is not to identify what has to be contracted out, but to clarify roles. Retaining functions in-house is a valid option for any local authority to pursue: but this is best done by ensuring its internal consultancy is clearly defined, operates cost-effectively and works to precise briefs — not by disguising consultancy work as client functions.

Making it work

Getting the responsibilities right and the roles clear is important, but not conclusive. Practical working relationships depend on other, less objective — but potentially more critical — factors.

Understanding each other's function is fundamental. Consultants are there to deliver: 'right first time and no excuses' is the standard which, human nature being what it is, cannot be achieved all day, every day; but, nevertheless, it must remain the goal from which all departures are the exception, not the rule. Clients must know what they want: clear instructions, always in time and properly paid for, comprise the ideal which change and uncertainty will tend to undermine but must never destroy.

From these requirements spring the concepts of the *responsive consultant* and the *intelligent client*.

Responsive consultants are willing to take time to understand what the client wants, not just on the technical aspects of the brief but on the details of presentation, tone and attitude that show a commitment to the client's priorities and interests. Often these features are marginal in terms of the amount of time and effort they involve in comparison with the whole activity, but they are highly visible, very important to those receiving the service and an essential part of the authority's broader objectives.

Thus, double sided printing of all documents on recycled paper will conform with and promote the council's environmental policies and demonstrate that the consultant shares them fully.

Being responsive also means reacting promptly and flexibly to the inevitable changes in any local authority's programme. Looking up the consultancy agreement, or asking for a variation order or an extra, should not be the first step when the client is looking for a 'can do' attitude. This does not mean that changes, particularly those made at short notice, can be accommodated without problems; nor that proper contractual formalities for recording, measuring and, where appropriate, paying are to be ignored. It does mean that a positive response, or a suggested alternative, should be the aim, coupled with a clear agreement on what is to be changed or added and how new or additional work (if any) is to be paid for. Payment may not be necessary if some other, lower priority work or project is deleted and the variation accepted in substitution. A willingness to be reasonable about these swings and roundabouts not only reduces client–consultant bureaucracy: it will be repaid many times over in the client's realistic acceptance of the occasional case of late delivery or a minor lapse in standards.

Increasing demands for action on speed-reduction measures may lead to an accelerated programme for installing enforcement cameras. A positive response would focus on what can be achieved practically. Identifying priority sites where rapid progress is possible and will generate favourable public reaction, with follow-up suggestions on how this work — currently programmed over a much longer period — can be accommodated, within, or as well as, other projects, represents a good outcome for all concerned. Something is seen to be happening; no unreasonable demands nor unfulfillable promises are made; the extra effort is recorded and paid for, or offset by slowing down comparable activity on another road safety or traffic management programme.

Responsive consultants are proactive as well as reactive. New ideas, proposals for more efficient working and the lessons of experience are offered to the client as part of a process of continuous improvement, and not merely in answer to requests, as a by-product of a budget squeeze, or — worst of all — the results of a damage-limitation exercise when something has gone wrong.

The introduction of thermal mapping should come as part of a proposal for a cost-effective system to manage winter maintenance, and not as a reaction to a cut in the budget promoted by unfavourable comparisons with other highway authorities in an audit commission review, or a serious breakdown in salting/gritting operations which left the council handling a stack of insurance claims. New plans for streamlining the handling of correspondence should come as an initiative for enhancing customer care, and not in passive compliance with a new corporate guideline or as a result of criticism; and because of the time saved both in producing replies and minimizing complaints, there would be no question of extra cost ...

The intelligent client is capable of directing the consultancy arrangement through every stage. This requires three key attributes: professional competence, contract management skills and strength. Size does not feature in the list.

Having a sound grasp of the professional areas covered by a consultancy agreement is essential both for the purpose of quality control and the genuine application of the process of validation, touched on earlier. This does not require the client to have either as wide or as deep a coverage of professional expertise as the consultant — that is, after all, what the appointment is supposed to provide — but enough knowledge to define tasks, assess due diligence, challenge excuses and encourage best practice. If the client feels uncertain about detail, a new technical development or a specialist topic, there is nothing to prevent a second opinion being called for.

The consultant's proposed list, in technical priority order, for the next annual programme of footway maintenance schemes did not include two projects that had been the subject of some concern when they just failed to get on the list in the previous year. The client called for the assessment schedules to check their ratings and saw that a fall in traffic flows, particularly goods vehicles, resulting from a major traffic management scheme in the vicinity had reduced the value of these factors in the calculations, and accepted the recommended priorities. However, the client was less impressed with a preliminary design for a new link road which had no features to promote public transport or cycling, and did not accept the consultant's explanation that as the area was predominantly commercial rather than residential such features were not relevant. The design was reworked as a matter of urgency to meet the originally agreed committee date, at the consultant's expense.

Professional capability, and perhaps political awareness too, are required by the client when advising the council on sensitive matters that it does not want handled by a consultant. The client has to be credible in front of members, and while it is acceptable to refer some points of detail or technical specialization back, and to have the consultant present in support for some aspects of a sensitive issue, there must be a sufficient general level of expertise to give advice on what is feasible and, perhaps more importantly, to warn against unwelcome consequences.

The management of consultancy commissions requires a combination of systematic checks — on output measures, response times, content of time sheets, etc. — and the subjective judgement which goes into the preparation of briefs, the assessment of claims for extra fees and the substitution of alternatives for contracted work. A thorough knowledge of the agreement or conditions of engagement is also needed to allow prompt and authoritative decisions on what is explicitly covered or deemed to be included, and what is a variation or new instruction. Consultants generally prefer decisive clients: they make their requirements clear, pay the accepted fees on time and point out what they don't accept and why. For every consultant time is money, and time wasted waiting for instructions, following unclear or incorrect ones, or arguing over what may be covered by the brief is a loss for which someone will have to pay, sometime.

A typical progress meeting on a term contract for professional technical services might cover the following management issues

- confirmation that June monitoring shows performance indicators etc. generally up to standard — but see next item
- satisfactory inspection and response times on carriageways and footways not matched on street lighting — shortfall is relatively small but trend is worsening, consultant to take action to reverse it
- list of queries about time charged for preparation and attendance at public consultations on park and ride — explanations all accepted
- variation issued for park and ride, to cover an additional exhibition venue and public meeting, and to extend consultation period — agreed that extra fees payable, on time charge at standard rates
- revision to brief on town centre pedestrianization feasibility study,

- to clarify coverage of access for disabled people and provision for loading/unloading — no abortive work, and thus no effect on fee
- request from consultant for three weeks' extension to deadline for report on canalside cycle route due to delays in consultation responses — client accepts seven working days' slippage justified; extension of two weeks to last date for despatch of committee papers agreed, provided partial draft, with gaps, available as originally scheduled for preliminary briefing
- new traffic calming scheme at hospital to go ahead in accordance with decision at full council — no increase in traffic management fees can be funded, so agreed to postpone the West Park scheme as an equivalent reduction in programmed work, and client to report to committee
- thanks received from half-marathon organizers for cooperation on signing of diversions and closures — consultant's staff to be congratulated
- confirmation that May fees cleared by client for payment by finance department, subject to retention due to delayed delivery of as-built drawings for Market Way footbridge — consultant promises drawings will be ready by the end of the month
- consultant reports departure of principal engineer from traffic signals and control team (promotion) — c.v. of replacement submitted for approval as required by specification, client sees no problems of acceptability but will confirm in writing.

The provision of a professional overview (with a direct input on sensitive matters) and the application of contract management skills (supported by suitable systems) need not require a large number of staff. A large term-contract for the provision of professional and technical services to a major city or county can be covered by a client unit — remembering the focused definition of client functions set out earlier — of less than 50; and in smaller local authorities a much lower number will suffice, particularly as some contract management functions (e.g. finance) involve skills that can be spread over other activities.

While the client unit does not have to be large it must be strong. This is not just to exercise firm control over the consultant by, for instance, challenging sloppy professional advice, rejecting inadequate technical work or imposing strict performance levels, important as all this is. The real test of strength is not in 'consultant bashing', but in upholding sound professional standards, which will often involve supporting and defending the consultant. The pressures of politics and public opinion can be severe and a consultant needs support when giving unavoidable bad news or having to express an unpopular opinion. That is when the client may have to point out, forcibly if necessary, the difference between wrong advice and unpalatable advice.

The assessment of the traffic impact of major development is always a matter in which technical judgement can become entangled with emotive opinion. This is particularly so when all the possibilities for conclusive land-use arguments have been exhausted and a traffic objection is seen as the last line of defence. When the consultant's modelling and prediction exercise shows that the extra flows generated by the proposal can be accommodated by some improvements, which the applicant is willing to pay for, and do not justify a refusal of permission, this may well be seen as selling out to the developer and worse than useless. The client's job here is not merely to cast an eye over the consultant's work for due diligence and then stand back, but to remind members and the public of the way in which the planning system works and of the risks of pursuing unsubstantiated objections to appeal — to tell them, bluntly, not to shoot the messenger.

A firm stand against pressure to disregard, or even distort, professional advice needs confidence and credibility and is nothing to do with numbers. Similarly, the client will need those qualities and a good reputation with the authority for being firm but fair on monitoring and fees, to handle the inevitable occasions when councillors (or even officers from other departments) take an unreasonable line on contract compliance and payment. Most frequent are the isolated incidents of delay or substandard performance which, although valid and irritating to an individual, do not amount to a significant failure in the context of a large, long-running contract.

A breakdown in office communications resulted in the correspondence from one team being delayed by two weeks, and 50 letters (mostly acknowledgements to councillors and the clerks of parish and town councils about a consultation exercise) were received well outside the contract standard for response times. The client replied to the complaints pointing out that the error was unusual, that it affected a small part of the 900-plus letters handled in a typical month, and that the consultant was achieving slightly better than the contract requirement of 90% of letters in 10 working days, 95% in 15.

Explaining that 100% compliance cannot be a reasonable expectation for every aspect of service delivery is not easy. A single fault may amount to very little when assessed against a total volume, but for an individual customer it is complete failure. A good grasp of the overall picture, and an attitude to the contract standard which recognizes that it must always balance speed, quantity and quality, will enable the client to secure a practical approach to performance monitoring.

Payment for new or extra work can also be a difficulty when funds are in short supply. Members sometimes forget the benefits of a tight contractual regime — payment by results, no charges for resources which are not being used, fixed prices which transfer risk to the provider — when it generates the real cost of specific tasks. Losing the additional cost among large and ill-defined budgets can seem an attractive solution to awkward problems, and consultants may be expected to provide a similar escape route on the grounds of long-term commercial advantage, marketing or good will. The client will have to reinforce the consultant's pleas that such expectations have to be moderated by the realities both of business and effective management.

If new funds are not available, the practical way around this problem is to identify a substitution, so that new or extended projects can be covered by delaying or cancelling similar but lower priority tasks. The adjustment to the planned workload allows money to be reallocated within the overall cash limit subject, of course, to approval by the council. Simple — except that it is a very rare project indeed that can be held up or withdrawn without any reaction. Once again, the client may have to take a strong line and resist the pressure (and the temptation) to fudge the substitution by putting off the selection to some unspecified future date: delay only undermines objective decision making, as projects are committed and the range of choice is narrowed down by time instead of order of priority.

A well-organized campaign for an environmental weight restriction in a village attracted overwhelming political support after a near miss between a lorry and a group of schoolchildren walking in the road. The estimated cost of staff time in preparation, consultation, etc. dismayed the road safety section, which had no uncommitted funds available. The client had to explain firmly that as this was a labour-intensive exercise, involving a number of routes and likely to involve considerable opposition from haulage operators and businesses in the area, the estimate was a reasonable one. A proposal to substitute the project for a similar one in another village was rejected (powerful opposition from the local member, supported by a good road safety case), as was a suggestion to postpone a residents' parking scheme in a housing estate near the University (unbreakable political promise). The client persisted, and eventually secured agreement for the section to cancel a feasibility study into a one-way system (originally programmed as a response to a traders' association petition and now seen as likely to be controversial) and defer to the next financial year the orders for a bus priority lane on one of the town centre roads (in effect a delay of less than six months). The staff resources thus released were redeployed on the lorry ban.

The client function, which is emerging as a key element in the new organizational structures of local government, is not an easy one. The specialism is distinctly different from that of managing works contracts (a role which it resembles only superficially) and much closer to the core tasks of a local authority. In the public service of today and tomorrow client experience and skills are part of the background that will be needed for the highest managerial position. No longer working exclusively through contracts of employment, but also under contracts of service, the people who supply local government with its professional and technical expertise have to adjust to a new environment. Public service cannot be depicted as a job for life in which the thrills (and spills) of the commercial world are foregone in exchange for stability and a certain dullness. Change and variety, uncertainty and insecurity are increasingly part of the scene for politicians, business, local communities and citizens — public servants cannot expect to be immune and if they try to insulate themselves it is hard to see how that can be in the public interest.

Conclusion

A new civic gospel

Twenty-five years ago, towards the end of its period of stability and certainty, the traditional principles of local government service were so widely accepted that their basic justification was taken for granted, and they were generally assumed to have evolved out of some misty and far-off past. Local government had forgotten the origins of its modern form, which are neither dim nor distant. In fact it is possible to pinpoint them very precisely in place and time: Birmingham, in the 1870s and early 1880s.

The heyday of Victorian municipal power is the chief source of the culture of local government, and of the self-image (often unconscious) still promoted by many of its influential participants. For the decisions made in those gas-lit, wood-panelled council chambers laid down not only the basic fabric of our great cities — the roads, sewers, public buildings and parks — but also the foundations on which stand the custom and practice of every local authority. Civic affairs were not just of major local interest in those days, but of great national importance too. The leading personalities in local government were well-known throughout the country: this was a period when the Lord Mayoralty of Birmingham could provide a stepping-stone for both a father and a son — Joseph and Neville Chamberlain — on their way to becoming respectively, a cabinet minister who split two national parties over key policies, and the Prime Minister who led the country through the controversial approach to its greatest war. It has taken almost a century, and a wholly different set of circumstances, to make local authorities once again a viable route to national political prominence for key figures on the front benches of the Government and the Opposition.

Birmingham, fast-growing, confident and proud, stood in the vanguard of Victorian civic enterprise and, more than any other public authority, sought to develop a philosophical basis for its policies and actions. This civic gospel had as its aim the genuine improvement, moral as well as physical, of the lives of the citizens, and its great evangelist was Robert Dale, a powerful preacher whose influence spread far beyond his Carrs Lane Congregational Church into the committee rooms and council chamber of Birmingham Corporation:

> ... see to it that the towns and parishes ... are well drained, well lighted, and well paved; that there are good schools for the population; that there are harmless public amusements; that ... all municipal affairs are conducted honourably and equitably.

It was a vocational approach, and it gave due prominence to public works because of the great need for proper infrastructure in the expanding urban centres, but it was meant to apply to all work in the public service.

What the civic gospel provided was a vision: a theory not of *how* local government should operate, but of *why*.

For 100 years thereafter, the culture of public service was established. As local government grew in the second half of the twentieth century — and it grew particularly fast in the 1960s with expansion in education, social services and major public works programmes — the vision became less clear, obscured perhaps by the vague self-image of public authorities as big business. Furthermore, it was not replaced or supplemented by any clear and practical managerial philosophy: local government was A Good Thing and would always continue to be so. Back in the 1880s Oscar Wilde coined his memorable phrase about knowing the price of everything but the value of nothing — by the mid-1970s the reverse was true of local government.

That was when, for a variety of reasons, central government set out on the path of reform and retrenchment. As a result of this pressure from outside, and a corresponding outbreak of realism within, local government has been transformed. In the same way that fee competition changed the world of professional consultancy and tight margins upset the old order in the construction industry, so the drives for value for money and competitiveness have brought about a fundamental rethink in the public sector. Over this period, local government has often been described as 'under siege', and so it is not surprising that it takes up a defensive posture.

A symptom of that defensiveness is the amount of attention that is given not only to making services effective, efficient and economic, but also to developing management theories and models which prove these qualities to be present in measurable amounts. This effort, laudable as it is, has not always been well-directed, and in many cases has become an end in itself, a growth industry and a distraction.

As we have seen, this introverted debate has been interrupted by the arrival of the enabling council. This concept, expressed in its extreme form, sees local government streamlined to the point where a few — a very few — elected representatives and officials routinely administer contracts for the provision of all services, with occasional sessions of policy making in which the advice on options and new specifications for services is bought in from consultants. (It is often said that this is the American form of local administration, but this is only partly true — in a federation of 50 states, some of which are nation-sized themselves, the public sector takes on a wide variety of shapes and sizes.) The more practical version which was explored in chapter 17 has a small core of central strategists working with the elected council to set the policy aims, and a similarly small group of purchasers specifying the corresponding service requirements and monitoring their delivery through a wide range of providers, that could include both in-house and external organizations.

For those involved in public works, enabling council may be a new name, but it does not represent a brand-new way of working. The separation of the planning and specification of a project from its execution has always been normal practice for construction works; the supervision of a contractor working to a defined level of performance and within a price limit has not been a theory of management, but part of the job; client-side specifiers, consultants and contractors have had well-established roles in public works from the outset. Familiarity, however, should not breed complacency — or worse. The enabling approach does generate tighter control over the provision of services, of all kinds and from all sources. In-house organizations can no longer take for granted their status as monopolies or most favoured suppliers, nor can consultants expect to enjoy the light supervision that sometimes follows from belonging to the same professional club — relationships will be much more contractual. ('And about time too,' will say the contractors of the public works construction kind, who have always reckoned to get a hard time from the staff of both consultants and councils alike!)

The concept of the enabling authority, backed up by the principles of value for money, gives real guidance about the *how* of local government, but not about the *why*. For that we should not be embarrassed to go back to the civic gospel, still valid and not at all incompatible with the requirements of effectiveness, efficiency and economy. It never assumed public works programmes and projects (or any other local services) were good for their own sake or an end in themselves. The goal — serving the community's local needs — did not depend upon the method of delivery, so long as it was sensitive to local needs and based on honest endeavour (not excluding profit-making). This is a good basis for project management, for in today's world of public works no project will survive unless it is seen to be directed at a real need, enjoys support in the community at large and is delivered in a cost-effective manner.

Whatever the future for local government, there will be a large and continuing need for additions, improvements and maintenance to develop and manage the public infrastructure. And local authorities, however changed and streamlined they may become, will retain their public accountability, and probably sharpen it. These requirements are necessitating an approach to procurement in which the range of provision extends beyond the traditional framework of internal suppliers. The establishment of quasi-commercial trading units, the greater involvement of the private sector as contractors and the transfer of local government units to hosts has created a market in which public service standards and skills are valued in a business as well as an ethical sense. Providers who recognize these standards

- value for money: achieved through a balance of quality, speed and cost
- responsiveness to local needs: demonstrated by commitment to the interests of the community as expressed through its representatives
- integrity: delivered professionally, in business dealings and as an employer

will build experience, resources and reputations to match the best traditions of service.

Not everyone involved with public service wants to see beyond the *how* to the *why*, (it would be unrealistic to ignore the large proportion working in-house as well as for external consultants for whom it is just a job), but for those of us who do there is an answer. We may not want to use the same Victorian phrases of Robert Dale to express the purpose of all the effort and commitment, although

Joseph Chamberlain, at about the same time, described local government in strikingly modern terms as 'a cooperative enterprise in which every citizen is a shareholder'. In any case, the underlying theme is the same: public services are provided by the community, equitably and openly, to serve the best interests of all its citizens. Delivered on this basis, public works will add value to people's lives in just the fashion which both the founders of the civil engineering profession and the originators of the civic gospel intended, and in a way that every modern participant can be proud of.